Public schools
and private education

For Juney and Tim

Public schools and private education

THE CLARENDON COMMISSION 1861–64
AND THE PUBLIC SCHOOLS ACTS

COLIN SHROSBREE

Manchester University Press
Manchester and New York

Distributed exclusively in the USA and Canada
by **St. Martin's Press**, New York

Copyright © Colin Shrosbree 1988

Published by Manchester University Press
Oxford Road, Manchester M13 9PL, UK
and distributed exclusively in the USA and Canada
by St. Martin's Press, Inc.
Room 400, 175 Fifth Avenue, New York, NY 10010, USA

British Library cataloguing in publication data
Shrosbree, Colin
    Public Schools and private education: the Clarendon Commission 1861–64
    and the Public Schools Acts.
    1. Great Britain. Public Schools, 1860–1870
    I. title
    373.2'22'9841

Library of Congress cataloging in publication data
Shrosbree, Colin
    Public schools and private education: the Clarendon Commission, 1861–64,
    and the Public Schools acts/Colin Shrosbree.
    p. cm.
    Bibliography: p. 225. Includes index.
    ISBN 0-7190-2580-X: $40.00 (U.S.: est.)
    1. Public schools, Endowed (Great Britain)—Law and legislation—History.
    2. Education and state—Great Britain—History.
    I. Title.
    KD3670.S53 1988
    373.2'22—dc 19

ISBN 0 7190 2580 X *hardback*

Printed in Great Britain
by Anchor Brendon Ltd., Tiptree, Essex
Typesetting by Heather Hems, Tower House, Queen Street, Gillingham, Dorset

Contents

Preface

Like many English children, my education was formed by the public schools before I knew they existed. The grammar school which I attended as a scholarship boy in 1949—with its gowns, its formality, its staff largely from Oxford and Cambridge, its games, its prefects and the classics for the brighter boys—had all the appearance and tone of a very minor public school, without the boarders. To a working-class child, who had arrived there as much by accident as by ability, the school seemed awesome and the lessons largely incomprehensible. The accident of my arrival was the result of an enthusiasm for fire-engines, which featured in the essay subjects for the scholarship examination and about which I must have written quite well. English was a joy and reading an escape into a sunnier, calmer world where children washed in bathrooms, went on holiday and wore pyjamas. But Latin and other, drier intellectual activities did not flourish as well on the kitchen table of our council house and the school tended to assume, in the best public school tradition, that Latin meant ability and ability meant Latin.

But the public school tradition, even in our diluted provincial form, was not intended to encourage working-class children to persevere, develop a love of learning and pass examinations. Middle-class attitudes, middle-class clothes, middle-class accents, early and irrevocable selection by largely middle-class teachers who made little concession to working-class ways or children's circumstances all made of education a barrier, not just to academic success but to a sense of owning a place in our own culture. But as children we did not question these social divisions—school was just a place apart, with different rules and alien ways, that had no place in our personal or family life.

To walk home was to journey through the subtle grades of English social class—from the larger private houses by the school, down private suburban streets of smaller houses, to the terraced council houses and, later when we grew more prosperous, to the modern houses on the new council estate. I did not know then that my walk home was a practical exercise in social mobility and a functional shift in normative cultural values—only that I felt out of place at the beginning of my walk and looked out of place at the end. But my own early journeys through the subtleties of English social class took place only on the edge of the gulf, and it was with shock and disbelief that I once saw boys, visiting us from the King's School in Rochester, wearing straw hats and carrying walking sticks. I thought that such people existed only in public school stories and could neither imagine such a different life nor how such a gulf could be bridged.

The gulf between the public schools and the state schools, together with the social differences between them, has made the public schools places of myth, fantasy and legend (to which public school histories have sometimes contributed). In reality, the origin of the first public schools is very mundane. They were old-established secondary schools, founded by public endowments (hence 'public schools') and privatised by the Public Schools Acts for clearly-stated Conservative political purposes. These schools were lost to public education, and went instead to form the nucleus of a private, fee-paying system. Great national institutions that should have formed the foundation of national, secondary education were given over to the 'higher classes' who could afford to pay: it is as though Buckingham Palace were sold to a hotel chain or the Brigade of Guards sold off to Securicor. The political purpose of the Public Schools Acts makes it impossible to keep politics out of education in England, for the purpose of the Acts was to secure Conservative ascendancy and our present secondary school systems may be traced to these political arrangements in which the common people were unrepresented and from which they gained nothing. It is a sad and savage irony that it is easier today for the son of a South American millionaire or a wealthy African prince to gain admission to an English public school than it is for a poor child of English parents, in spite of the schools' public endowments and the English concerns of the schools' founders and benefactors. But the situation is not irredeemable, and these great national schools may yet be brought back into the service of public education and of more democratic ideals. The purpose of this book is to show how the Clarendon Commission came to be established, and how the Public Schools Acts came to be passed.

My thanks are due to Shropshire Education Committee for granting me a year's secondment to Birmingham University in 1979–80. Without this most generous support, and the initial reading and research that this year made possible, the subsequent doctoral work on which the book is based could not have been done. To the kindness and scholarship of Dr John Hurt, my tutor in the Faculty of Education, I am similarly greatly indebted. Dr W. E. K. Anderson, then Headmaster of Shrewsbury School and now Headmaster of Eton, for some months allowed me free access to the Shrewsbury School Archives. Mr James Lawson BA, the School Librarian and Archivist, gave me much generous help with the documents and kindly agreed to read the chapter on Shrewsbury School, although the views expressed there are, of course, my own. My thanks are due to Shrewsbury School for allowing me to quote from material in the school archives. I am grateful to the present Earl of Clarendon for allowing me to quote from the Clarendon Papers in the Bodleian Library. The quotations from G. M. Young, *Victorian England: Portrait of an Age* (London, 1966) are given by permission of the Oxford University Press. The quotation from John Vincent (ed.), *Disraeli, Derby and the Conservative Party: Journals and Memoirs of Henry Edward, Lord Stanley, 1849–1869* (Hassocks, 1978) is by permission of the Harvester Press Ltd. The quotation from G. Parry, *Political Elites* (London, 1969) is made by permission of George Allen & Unwin Ltd and the quotation from Samuel

H. Beer, *Modern British Politics* (London, 1969) by permission of Faber & Faber Ltd. Duckworth & Co. Ltd kindly allowed me to quote from R. Cobb, *A Sense of Place* (London, 1975) and the Longman Group Ltd to quote from G. W. Roderick and M. D. Stephens, *Education and Industry in the Nineteenth Century* (London, 1978). Macmillan Publishers allowed me to quote from D. Southgate, *The Most English Minister: the Politics and Policies of Palmerston* (London, 1966) and Methuen & Co. Ltd to quote from J. Lawson and H. Silver, *A Social History of Education in England* (London, 1973). Thomas Nelson & Sons Ltd gave permission to quote from T. W. Bamford, *The Rise of the Public Schools: a Study of Boys' Public Boarding Schools in England and Wales from 1837 to the Present Day* (London, 1967). Lawrence & Wishart Ltd allowed me to quote from Brian Simon, *The Politics of Educational Reform, 1920–1940* (London, 1974), and Phillimore & Co. Ltd allowed me to quote from Barrie Trinder, *The Industrial Revolution in Shropshire* (London, 1973). Crown copyright material in the Public Record Office is reproduced by permission of the Controller of Her Majesty's Stationery Office. Finally, I must thank my own family—my wife June and my son Tim. Without their help, patience, encouragement and good humour, nothing would have been possible.

Abbreviations

Bailiff's Bundles   Boxes of documents, known traditionally by this name, in the Shrewsbury School Archives

Cambridge Commission Report   Report of Her Majesty's Commissioners appointed to inquire into the State, Discipline, Studies and Revenues of the University and Colleges of Cambridge, London, 1852

Clarendon Papers   Clarendon Papers in the Bodleian Library as listed in *List of Papers of the Earls of Clarendon deposited by George Herbert Hyde Villiers, 6th Earl of Clarendon in the Bodleian Library, Oxford*, Bodleian Library, Oxford, 1959

Clarendon Report   Report of Her Majesty's Commission Appointed to Inquire into the Revenues and Management of Certain Colleges and Schools, and the Studies Pursued and Instruction Given Therein, London, 1864

Commons Select Committee Report, 1868   Report from the Select Committee on [sic] Public Schools Bill with the Proceedings of the Committee. Ordered by the House of Commons to be Printed, 22nd May 1868

Dict. Nat. Biog.   L. Stephen and S. Lee (eds.), *Dictionary of National Biography*, London, 1928, 22 vols

Hansard   Hansard's Parliamentary Debates, 3rd Series

Lords Select Committee Report, 1865   'Report from the Select Committee of the House of Lords on the Public Schools Bill (H.L.); together with the Proceedings of the Committee, Minutes of Evidence, Appendix and Index. Brought from the H. of L. 4th July 1865 and ordered by the House of Commons to be printed, 5th July 1865', *Reports from Committees 7th February–6th July 1865*, X

Newcastle Report   Report of the Royal Commission on the State of Popular Education in England (and Wales), London, 1861

Oxford Commission Report   *Report of Her Majesty's Commissioners appointed to inquire into the State, Discipline, Studies and Revenues of the University and Colleges of Oxford*, London, 1852

PRO   Public Record Office

Shrewsbury Sch. Arch.   Shrewsbury School Archives

Taunton Report   *Report of the Royal Commission on Schools not comprised within Her Majesty's two recent Commissions on Popular Education and Public Schools*, London, 1868

Trustees' Minutes   *Shrewsbury School Trustees' Minutes, 1798–1882*, Shrewsbury School Archives

Wellesley Index   W. E. Houghton (ed.), *The Wellesley Index to Victorian Periodicals 1824–1900*, London, 1966, 3 vols.

Introduction

The Clarendon Commission of 1861–4 which investigated Eton, Westminster, Winchester, Charterhouse, St Paul's, Merchant Taylors', Harrow, Rugby and Shrewsbury, although frequently referred to in histories of education, is rarely mentioned as more than an interesting but relatively unimportant part of the Newcastle,[1] Clarendon,[2] Taunton[3] trilogy. Much attention is invariably and correctly given to the development of government involvement in primary education, the complexity of the issues and the protracted political bargaining that led to the Education Act of 1870. Much attention is also invariably given to the Taunton Commission's inquiry into endowed schools, the Endowed Schools Act of 1869 and the subsequent development of secondary education. The Clarendon Commission is usually mentioned only in passing, as an interesting but preliminary inquiry into a few great but uncommon schools for the 'upper classes', who were able to safeguard their own interests in Parliament before passing on to consider the interests of the rest of the nation. Often the Public Schools Act of 1868, the direct outcome of the Clarendon Commission, is hardly mentioned, as though the schools of the Commission were by then already separate and of marginal importance to national secondary education.[4]

It is not difficult to suggest why the Clarendon Commission has received so little attention. It had little immediate effect on national education or even on those families who sent their children to any of the schools investigated. A Public Schools Bill, based on the recommendations of the Commissioners, was abandoned in 1865[5] and the Act of 1868, although reforming the government and administration of the schools, did little except encourage reforms in the curriculum, in teaching and in discipline.[6] In the Clarendon schools these reforms came slowly, and the influence of science, modern languages, more modern teaching methods and a more liberal, perhaps vocational approach to the curriculum are more clearly seen in schools that, although subject to the Endowed Schools Act of 1869, were more often clearly boarding schools of the 'public school' type, with national reputations, giving an education of a standard equal to that of Eton, Harrow, or the other Clarendon schools.[7] Thring at Uppingham, for example, considered with some justification, that 'he now had the best school in the country'.[8] The effect of the reforms suggested by the Clarendon Commission perhaps may be seen most clearly in schools not subject to their inquiry.

Another reason for this lack of attention may be that the Clarendon Commission was concerned with such a small number of schools—nine schools with only 2,708 pupils in 1861.[9] The original proposal in Parliament had been that the Royal Commission should investigate all endowed schools, but this was thought to be too much.[10] The Taunton Commission, although only completing a second stage of the work begun by Clarendon, had such an enormous task, investigating nearly 800 schools of differing sizes and educational standards,[11] that it is perhaps natural that its work has received more attention.

The difference in scope between the Clarendon and Taunton Commissions would suggest that the Clarendon schools formed a unique group, clearly divided in some way from the rest, but this was not the case. Since the Commission was the immediate result of critical articles about Eton in the *Cornhill Magazine*[12] and the *Edinburgh Review,*[13] it was understandable that schools similar to Eton should be included, but this distinction proved difficult. 'Most public schools in the middle and late nineteenth century were merely successful and specialized examples of endowed grammar schools'[14] and Shrewsbury, for example, was at first excluded.[15] Evidence suggests that this distinction between the Clarendon schools and other endowed schools was made simply on ill-defined grounds of 'status'[16]—the Clarendon schools were, after all, those from which Members of Parliament, Cabinet Ministers and members of the Commission themselves came[17]—but this distinction, once made, had far-reaching consequences for secondary education in general. It introduced a national classification of schools based on those for whom they were intended, rather than how they were financed or what kind of education they provided. This introduced specific 'class' categorisation into English secondary education where before there had been a certain uniformity.[18] Although, of course, different schools catered for different social groups, and there were obvious differences of size, wealth and prestige, there had previously been no essential legal difference between Eton and many local endowed grammar schools.[19]

Further divisions in secondary education came as a result of the Taunton Commission and the Endowed Schools Act of 1869. The fundamental issue, which had been encountered by the Clarendon Commission, was how secondary education could be financed. The more damaging accusation, for example, in the *Cornhill Magazine*[20] and *Edinburgh Review*[21] articles, was that at Eton there had been misappropriation of endowments.[22] The problems common to all endowed schools, including Eton, were that fees were necessary to maintain and expand the school, that these fees could not be charged to the 'foundation' boys the schools were obliged to accept, and that the original statutes could not easily be changed.[23] The legal recommendations of the Clarendon Commission, which were followed by the Taunton Commission and embodied in the Endowed Schools Act of 1869, established the principle that secondary education should be paid for by the parent.[24] Although the Endowed Schools Act classified schools into grades, the need to attract fees, and to compete for fees from those parents who could afford to pay, meant a tendency for successful schools to raise their fees and attract pupils from a higher social group than was originally intended in schemes for reform approved after the Endowed Schools Act.[25] The division within secondary education, which the Clarendon Commission established between the nine investigated schools and the rest, was followed by further divisions within secondary education suggested by the Taunton Commission, which followed the legal and financial principles of Clarendon (that ancient endowments should be reformed and the schools subsequently financed by fees). The division that came from the Taunton Commission was between those schools which charged high fees, provided a largely classical education for university entrance, catered for the upper middle classes and were, in consequence, successful, and those which did not do these things and were not success-ful.[26] The successful schools all aspired to the status conferred on the original nine by the Clarendon Commission and, in time, joined with them in the Headmasters' Conference. It generally proved financially impossible to sustain the good intentions of the Endowed Schools Act for the provision of schools for the lower middle classes and the maintenance of some educational opportunities for the poor—for whose benefit many endowed schools, including Eton to some extent, had originally been intended.[27] The Clarendon Commission, and the Taunton Commission which followed it,[28] established the principle that secondary education in England was a privilege to be paid for, and in this distinguished sharply the development of secondary from elementary education. Secondary education was developed for established social groups who could afford to pay: elementary education was developed for people who could not bear the whole cost themselves.[29] In secondary education, the nine public schools of the Clarendon Commission provided models of achievement, attitude and organisation that, however unsuitable for public education, had no parallel in the elementary schools.

In secondary education, the example of the public schools was to be both influential and largely unattainable as few schools, private or state, could match the advantages of the great public schools—the long tradition, the educational capital of public endowments and the increasing income from private fees. The schools of the Clarendon Commission and the Public Schools Acts were in secondary education to be like a mirage in the desert—an illusion of what could or ought to be done, for private education flourished on the capital of great public endowments, independence was notional and established on favourable financial terms by the Public Schools Acts, and achievement bought by financial security.

Notes

1 *Newcastle Report*, 1861.
2 *Clarendon Report*, 1864.
3 *Taunton Report*, 1868.
4 See, for example, J. Lawson & H. Silver, *A Social History of Education in England*, London, 1973, pp. 303–4, and T. W. Bamford, *The Rise of the Public Schools: A Study of Boys' Public Boarding Schools in England and Wales from 1837 to the Present Day*, London, 1967, pp. 183, 201.
5 See A. Trollope, 'Public schools', *Fortnightly Review*, 2, October 1865, p. 487.
6 See Lawson & Silver, *Social History of Education*, p. 304 and 'The Public Schools Commission', *Chamber's Journal*, 42, 15 October 1864, pp. 659–63.
7 See Bamford, *Rise of the Public Schools*, pp. 35, 109–11, and Lawson & Silver, *Social History of Education*, pp. 301–3. For contemporary comment on other

boarding schools, see *Clarendon Report*, I, p. 11.

8   Bamford, *Rise of the Public Schools*, p. 182.

9   *Clarendon Report*, I, p. 11.

10 Hansard, CLXXV, 6 May 1864, cols. 126–7.

11 See F. E. Balls, 'The origins of the Endowed Schools Act 1869 and its operation in England from 1869 to 1895', PhD thesis, Cambridge University, 1964, p. 1.

12 M. J. Higgins, 'Paterfamilias to the Editor of the "Cornhill Magazine"', *Cornhill Magazine*, 1, May 1860, pp. 608–15; also 'A second letter to the Editor of the "Cornhill Magazine" from Paterfamilias', *Cornhill Magazine*, 2, December 1860, pp. 641–9 and 'A third letter from Paterfamilias to the Editor of the "Cornhill Magazine" ', *Cornhill Magazine*, 3 March 1861, pp. 257–69.

13 See 'Eton College', *Edinburgh Review*, 113, April 1861, pp. 387–426, attrib, to M. J. Higgins, *Wellesley Index*, I, p. 510.

14 Bamford, *Rise of the Public Schools*, p. 197.

15 *Hansard*, CLXXV, 6 May 1864, col. 125.

16 *Hansard*, CLXXV, 6 May 1864, cols. 125–7.

17 See Bamford, *Rise of the Public Schools*, pp. 229–36 and C. J. Shrosbree, 'The origins and influence of the Clarendon Commission (1861–1864), with special reference to Shrewsbury School', PhD thesis, Birmingham University, 1985, Appendices I, IV and V.

18 The original proposal in the Commons for an inquiry into secondary education, by Grant Duff, asked simply for an inquiry 'into the state of the higher School Education in England and Wales'. *Hansard*, CLXI, 7 February 1861, col. 146.

19 In 1860, for example, a Chancery judgement concerning the Bristol Free Grammar School referred to Eton, Harrow and Rugby as 'free grammar schools'. 'In the matter of Bristol Free Grammar School', *The English Reports*, 54, Rolls Court VII, p. 331, quoted Balls, 'Origins of the Endowed Schools Act', p. 15.

20 See Note 12 above.

21 See Note 13 above.

22 See, for example, 'Eton', *Macmillan's Magazine*, 3, February 1861, pp. 293–9, attrib. H. Sidgwick, *Wellesley Index*, I, p. 561 and the *Clarendon Report*, III, pp. 6–8.

23 See Sidgwick, 'Eton', pp. 293–9 and Balls, 'Origins of the Endowed Schools Act', p. 7.

24 See Balls, 'Origins of the Endowed Schools Act', p. 470.

25 See Balls, 'Origins of the Endowed Schools Act', pp. 451–8.

26 See Balls, 'Origins of the Endowed Schools Act', p. 451.

27 See Balls, 'Origins of the Endowed Schools Act', pp. 454–8.

28 See Balls, 'Origins of the Endowed Schools Act', p. 478.

29 See Balls, 'Origins of the Endowed Schools Act', p. 478.

1 The origins of reform

When Talleyrand visited Eton, he was shown around by an enthusiastic admirer of the school who remarked at the end of the tour, 'Veuillez bien agréer, Monsieur Le Prince, que c'est la plus belle éducation au monde.' 'Certainement', Talleyrand replied grimly, 'et pourtant c'est détestable.'[1]

This praise of the school and Talleyrand's reaction to it illustrated the ambiguity with which Englishmen regarded their public schools.[2] They were extravagantly praised for their formation of English character, but also frequently condemned—not just by radicals, but by moderate politicians, parents and the proprietors of other newer schools—for their conservative, classical curriculum, their out-of-date teaching methods and equipment, the obscurity of their finances, the severity of their headmasters, their primitive living conditions and the ignorance of their pupils.

This ambiguity may be seen in an article by Anthony Trollope, published in the *Fortnightly Review* in October 1865. In this article, which was a contribution to the discussion of the *Clarendon Report*, Trollope described Winchester as he had known the school thirty-four years previously. He was fierce in criticism but concluded, almost reluctantly, that the school had great virtue—so great indeed that the virtue almost justified the evils and in some sense depended upon them, for it was by facing the hardship of school life that boys were made men.

> There [wrote Trollope] we learned to be honest, true and brave. There we were trained to disregard the softness of luxury, and to love the hardihood and dangers of violent exercise. There we became men: and we became men after such a fashion that we are feared or loved, as may be, but always respected—even though it is in spite of our ignorance. Who can define the nobility that has attached itself to Englishmen as the result of their public schools; or can say whence it comes, or of what it consists.[3]

How or why it was that only a small number of English boys

could benefit from this education was not explained. At the time of the Clarendom Commission there were only 2,708 boys in the public schools, while the total school population in England and Wales was something possibly approaching three million.[4] Nor was there any speculation by Trollope, and rarely by anybody else, about how other Englishmen who were unable to benefit from the education of these schools felt, and how it was that they obtained their English character. The theme is, however, a very common one. The quality of the character-training was almost mystical; it could not, of course, be examined, but it did justify what might otherwise have seemed indefensible: the acceptance of pain and the infliction of punishment as educational virtues.[5]

Although public school discipline and corporal punishment had become subjects of controversy by the time of the Clarendon Commission, the practice of the public schools was defended not only on the grounds that it was essential in order to control a large boarding school population, but that it had an inherent moral virtue. In 1853, for example, when Harrow became involved in considerable publicity over a case of severe beating, Dr Vaughan defended the practice in a letter to Palmerston, quoting Dr Arnold and asserting the moral, Christian and political virtues of beating boys. Opponents of corporal punishment, he argued, had attitudes founded in barbarism and Jacobinism.[6]

The irrationality of public school organisation, on the other hand, was defended on the grounds that irrationality was an English characteristic and therefore to be admired. Trollope, writing of Eton, praised the way in which English institutions became complex and irrational; the extent to which Eton had become divorced from much of its original purpose was a matter for patriotic pride and self-congratulation.

> In any other country, a charity school would remain a charity school . . . But at Eton King Henry's poor scholars and the sons of Dukes and Marquises herd together without any difference; and these poor scholars themselves are the sons of the best of our gentry, of fathers who do not deem themselves poor, and of mothers who would be much surprised if they were told that their boys were charity children.[7]

The fact that the rich and poor scholars could be educated together was thus put forward as evidence that the public

schools were indeed irrational, but in a purely English and
beneficial way. In fact, as Trollope admitted, the 'poor scholars'
of Eton or the 'foundation boys' at any of the public schools
were rarely poor, except in comparison with other boys whose
parents were very rich. Nor did boys always 'herd together', as
Trollope suggested. The division between the 'foundation boys'
and those paying fees tended to persist at all the schools. The
Etonian division between Collegers and Oppidans had its
counterpart elsewhere.[8]

The differences between the foundation boys and the fee-
payers were obvious to contemporaries and, as an unsigned
article in *Fraser's Magazine* suggested, probably increased the
greater the number of foundationers there were and the greater
their legal importance.[9] The fact that the rich who were
educated along with the relatively poor were frequently not
those beneficiaries intended in a school's original foundation,
provided further evidence that English institutions, unlike those
of Europe, tended to work in an irrational, obscure, pragmatic
way that suited and expressed the English character. This view
of public school practices, like the contemporary justification
of the pain and discomfort frequently inflicted on boys there,
became more difficult to sustain in the years before the
Clarendon Commission. It was clear, for example, that the
admission of foundation boys did not usually result in an
idyllic school society in which boys from different social
classes associated happily.

The difficulty of overcoming this division was mentioned in
the *Clarendon Report*. The solution proposed, and eventually
adopted, was the gradual elimination of local foundation rights
in favour of scholarships. This not only reduced the number of
foundation boys, limiting their claims on the resources of the
school, but also ensured that future 'foundation boys' were
most unlikely to be poor, since expensive preparation was
required to pass a scholarship examination, particularly an
academic, competitive one. Supporters of the public schools,
even when approving of the admission of 'poor' scholars, often
made it clear by careful qualification that they did not mean
the 'poor', but rather the 'comparatively poor', and even
these were to be carefully selected. Henry Sidgwick, in an
article about Eton for *Macmillan's Magazine* of February
1861, supported reform, particularly of Eton's finances and

government. He too was concerned about the division between the Collegers and the Oppidans within the school, but had no doubt that the school's primary responsibility was towards the fee-paying Oppidans rather than the Collegers. To enable Eton to carry out this responsibility, he was prepared for radical change but hoped that 'no inopportune reverence for obsolete forms, and the letter of the founder's will may prevent the utmost being done to make Eton more fit for the glorious work she has undertaken—that of educating the aristocracy of England'.[10]

This was far indeed from the letter and the intention of Henry VI's original foundation in 1442: the original statutes were designed to exclude precisely those aristocratic land-owners who patronised Eton in the nineteenth century.[11] Sidgwick wished to retain the entrance test in the form of scholarships for which all boys could compete, hoping in this way to encourage a higher standard of learning among the Oppidans. He advocated the complete abolition of the College, since the division between Collegers and Oppidans was marked and formed an unfortunate contrast between 'talent and application on the one hand, and wealth, rank and idleness on the other'.[12] He added ingenuously that this reform would benefit the poor, since they would carry off most of the scholarships—not the real poor, of course, as he was careful to point out, but those comparatively poor from an Eton viewpoint.

> For among the educated classes, the poor are so much more numerous than the rich, and work, on the whole, so much harder that they will always carry off more than nine-tenths of the rewards of talent and application, if impartially given.[13]

The argument eventually presented in the *Clarendon Report* against the preservation of foundation boys' rights was financial—that the foundation boys were being subsidised by the fee-payers, as the original endowments had proved to be inadequate. Moreover, as the *Clarendon Report* pointed out, the boys admitted as foundationers were not always those for whom the benefits were originally intended. Good schools tended to attract strangers into the area, 'sojourners' who came so that their children could enjoy the benefits of the school's endowments. The greater a school's reputation, the fewer opportunities there might be for genuine local children to

benefit from foundation places. The national reputation of
Harrow and Rugby, for example, attracted parents from all
over the country, who bought property in the area of each
school and so further raised local property values. This tendency
was particularly important in Harrow and Rugby, where the
foundation rights at each school were linked with a specific
geographical area so that, by the time of the Clarendon Commission, they had been largely appropriated by parents who
had moved into the area in order to live near the school. In
Shrewsbury, the other school historically and legally most
closely associated with a particular town and with a comparable
obligation to provide education for local children, this
appropriation did not take place because burgess rights, which
included free education at Shrewsbury School, could not be
secured by the purchase of property. Nevertheless, in whatever
way these foundation rights were taken up, they were an
inescapable financial liability on all the schools. The difficulty
of maintaining large schools that had become national
institutions on original endowments that were often inadequate,
restrictive and local was readily apparent. The *Clarendon
Report* clearly indicated the legal anomalies:

> Speaking generally, the foundation boys are, in the eyes of the law,
> the school. The legal position of the Head Master of Eton is that of a
> teacher or 'informator' of seventy poor and indigent boys, received
> and boarded within Eton College: the Head Master of Harrow is legally
> the master of a daily grammar school, established in a country village
> for the benefit primarily of its immediate neighbourhood.[14]

By the time of the Clarendon Commission it was evident that
the public schools no longer educated both rich and poor
together, for the poor no longer attended them, in spite of the
founders' intentions. This contradiction between the ancient
statutes of the schools and the realities of their nineteenth-
century life was reflected in the ambiguity that surrounded the
phrase 'public school'. Before the Public Schools Bills that
followed the *Clarendon Report*, the public schools had no
title that could express their claim to separate consideration
and superior status. Their formal titles, which, like that of
Harrow, often described them as 'free grammar schools',[15]
served only to emphasise implications that the headmasters
generally wished to forget, avoid or dispute—that the schools

had not been provided solely for the wealthy, that there was little legal difference between them and hundreds of other grammar schools throughout the country and that they had some legal, historical obligation to educate local children.[16]

The term 'public school' had been in use from the beginning of the nineteenth century, but in a rather confused way. Sometimes it was used to describe some of the well known schools later investigated by the Clarendon Commission—Eton, Harrow, Rugby, Winchester, Westminster, St Paul's, Merchant Taylors', Shrewsbury and Charterhouse—but with considerable variation. Eton was usually included, unless it was considered as a college of university status,[17] but often some Clarendon schools were omitted and some non-Clarendon schools included. Dr W. Vincent, for example, in *A Defence of Public Education*, published in 1801, included Manchester and Wakefield, but omitted Shrewsbury.[18]

Sometimes the term was used to describe all schools that were similar to the best-known ones. An article from the *Edinburgh Review* of 1810 included in the term '. . . not only Eton, Winchester and Westminster, but the Charter-House, St. Paul's School, Merchant Taylors, Rugby and every school in England, at all conducted upon the plan of the three first'.[19]

The term was also used to describe all schools that were accessible, in some sense, to the general public—either because they were wholly or partly supported by public money or because their endowments had been provided originally for the general public benefit, although, of course, many endowments favoured particular areas or occupations. The public schools also came within this category, although by 1860 most boys paid privately and most of the schools' income came from fees. This ambiguity of description was advantageous to the better-known schools, because it enabled them to claim they were fulfilling a public service, to enjoy financial benefits from the claim that they were providing a 'public' education, to enjoy an income from endowments often given for the express purpose of public education (and often for the education of the poor) while at the same time drawing a considerable income from fees which were often unofficial and unrecorded.

An example of the exploitation of these helpful ambiguities could be seen at Shrewsbury School. In 1853 the Department of Science and Art published a price list of samples and materials for Art and Science teaching in schools for the public. The list, entitled *List of Examples, etc. which may be obtained from the Department by National and other Public Schools at half the prime cost,*[20] and which was clearly intended to help poorer schools to provide basic equipment, was used by Shrewsbury School when contemplating the introduction of Science into the curriculum.[21] In 1855, when this was being considered, the official income of Shrewsbury School was £4,517, which provided a surplus of £1,012. This income excluded fees, which were not included in the School Accounts.[22] Yet this school contemplated using equipment subsidised by public funds at a time when there was increasing Parliamentary criticism of the cost of public education.[23] Shrewsbury School did not have any specific obligation to educate children of the poor, although the word 'free' in its traditional title of 'The Free Grammar School at Shrewsbury' caused much controversy in the years before the Public Schools Act of 1868. The school did have an obligation to educate free the legitimate sons of Shrewsbury burgesses, but even these were few in number in the school in 1855 and declined into insignificance after the Public Schools Act of 1868.[24]

The ambiguity of the phrase 'public school' also enabled headmasters to imply that their schools were synonymous with public education, that provided by the state being unworthy of mention. In September 1864, for example, Dr Kennedy of Shrewsbury gave an address in York to a meeting of the National Association for the Promotion of Social Science. The address was entitled *Notes on Public Education,*[25] but was almost entirely devoted to his comments, mostly critical, on the recently published *Clarendon Report* and to his views on education as it was understood in the public schools. The address was, he said modestly, 'a few stray notes from the experience and reflection of one who, during his lifetime, as child, boy and man, has been brought into contact with the work of Public Education'.[26] Yet Dr Kennedy's experience of both learning and teaching was confined to Harrow and Shrewsbury, apart from a brief period at Cambridge. He had been educated at Shrewsbury under Dr Butler as a boy and had returned there in 1836 as headmaster at the age of thirty-one.[27] In the whole of his address, no reference was made to any educational provision outside the public schools, and it was impossible to tell that any other kind of education existed, although he was speaking at a time of an unprecedented rise in school numbers, in government spending on education and in literacy levels.[28]

These changes were very evident to Dr Kennedy's contemporaries. For example, the 1851 Census Report—in a special section on education written by Horace Mann—concluded that the country had three million children who required education and that, of these, two million were already at school for at least some period of their lives.[29] These figures caused alarm when they were published and it was predicted that state expenditure on education would have to be trebled or quadrupled. The figures that Mann put forward may be questioned today, but were generally accepted at the time. In 1859 the accuracy of these figures was reasserted before the Newcastle Commission[30] so that to Dr Kennedy and his contemporaries it seemed probable that there were about two million children at school in England and Wales and a further million children of school age who were not at school 'without obvious causes'.[31] Yet in the whole of Dr Kennedy's address, these children or their schools are never mentioned, and he refers only to the Clarendon schools (which had only 2,708 pupils in 1861).[32] As the *Clarendon Report* itself observed, this was in itself only a 'small proportion of the whole number of boys . . . whose parents are in sufficiently easy circumstances to afford them a gentleman's education'.[33]

The meaning of the term 'public school' was finally clarified and given legal definition by the *Public Schools Act, 1864* and the further Public Schools Acts of the following years. The Clarendon Commission, by its investigation of only nine schools, formally recognised those schools' claims to a superior, distinct status, and the Public Schools Acts gave them a separate legal title, endorsing and maintaining a hierarchical structure of secondary education that had already become divided on class lines by 1860. The adoption of the title 'public school' in the subsequent Acts was a formal recognition that the assumption implied in the appointment of the Clarendon Commission—that secondary education was to be graded and categorised according to the class it was provided for—had become the assumption behind government policy concerning secondary education in general. This same assumption was to underlie the *Taunton*

Report and, indeed, has underlined the development of secondary education ever since—along with the assumption that secondary education can rely on the commercial principle for finance.[34] The public schools were pre-eminently capable of doing this. They had been forced to adopt the commercial principle of charging the customer for education because, by and large, the original 'public' provision of money through endowments and bequests of various kinds had proved inadequate. The Clarendon Commission accepted this commercial principle and so, in turn, did the *Taunton Report*.[35] The commercial principle implied that the value of secondary education could be measured by its cost. Genuine 'public schools', which provided free secondary education at public expense, therefore provided an education of little value once education was assessed by cost or, rather, by the social class of the people who obtained it. The Clarendon Commission and the subsequent Public Schools Acts not only gave a precise new legal status to the public schools and regularised the commercial principle on which they already operated, but gave them the misleading although helpful title of 'public' schools. The Public Schools Acts enabled the public schools to retain the ambiguity of title which had proved so helpful before the Clarendon Commission while resolving the financial and legal ambiguities which had previously hindered the schools in their attempts to improve facilities so that the degree of income from fee-paying boys could be further increased.

In spite of the ambiguities of their financial and legal position before 1868, the schools had made attempts to change and survive. They had done this successfully to the extent that they had become well-known schools when many other endowed grammar schools of similar foundation had remained mere local institutions or lapsed into complete oblivion. The reasons for the relative success of these schools are complex and obscure. Personable headmasters, fashion, royal patronage, proximity to London and the Court, famous pupils, favourable or royal endowments, the successful encouragement of fee-paying boarders as a supplementary source of income, close legal, financial or personal links with Oxford or Cambridge colleges and even a convenient railway station were all contributing factors.[36] In the years before 1860, however, there was an increasing public interest in what actually went on in the public schools, and much public criticism in newspapers and periodicals. This was partly the result of a growing public interest in education generally, which was coupled with the growing public awareness, apparent throughout Europe, of the importance of education for the political and economic life of a country.[37] Partly, it was a reflection of the growing demand for fee-paying secondary education and the growth of newer 'proprietary' or 'private' schools, as these newer schools, offering a similar education, provided a standard by which the public schools could be judged.[38] The barbarous or negligent treatment of boys that was commonplace in the earlier years of the nineteenth century became more difficult to conceal and harder to justify as the century progressed. As a result, the schools themselves generally attempted to improve living conditions and avoid scandal, being urged to do so by their own supporters.

Anthony Trollope, writing about his own school, Winchester, found the main reforms in thirty years to be that the boys were given 'tea and tubs' and the meat given out at mealtimes was 'cut for them into slices'.[39] At Eton, the food was as bad as the accommodation and given out without supervision, so that the bigger boys took more. All that was usually provided was mutton, bread and beer, and any food not eaten at dinner was then given to the Collegers for supper.[40] The furniture in the schoolrooms of Eton, 'of the meanest character originally', was 'worn and hacked about and broken almost to ruin'. The masters' desks were 'mean, coarse, deal boxes, such as one would scarcely expect to see in the humblest rural police-office'.[41] In 1865 an Old Carthusian writing anonymously to *The Times* found conditions at Charterhouse little changed during the preceding thirty years. The boys were 'buried in the very midst of the slums of London . . . a more dreary prison-house than the school cannot be imagined' where gentlemen and clergymen 'demean themselves to make out their incomes by charging the highest prices for the worst board and lodgings'.[42] At Westminster a committee of 'Old Westminsters' was appointed to confer with the Dean and Chapter about improving the school's facilities. The Committee's comments, reported in *The Times* in 1860, found fault with 'the want of repair, comfort and convenience of almost every part of the premises' which reflected 'little credit upon those who are responsible for them'.[43] As late as 1866, a report in *The Times* described with astonishment the situation at St Paul's, where boys played 'behind a grill under the gloomy portico . . . in a cage, without light or air'.[44]

A serious problem for some schools, particularly in London, was that their sites were too restricted to allow much improvement in their facilities. Schools like Rugby and Eton were fortunate in having room for expansion, but others, like Charterhouse and Shrewsbury, were eventually forced to move to improve standards of accommodation, which were already rising before the Clarendon Commission was appointed. Another difficulty arose not just from the opposition of traditionalists, although this in itself could be formidable, as at Charterhouse and Shrewsbury, but from the legal difficulties of adapting the schools' endowments for this purpose, particularly when the governing bodies were often unwilling to implement reforms suggested by headmasters, former pupils or the newspapers. Sometimes the governors represented local interests, as at Shrewsbury, and feared that the removal of the school to other premises, or the improvement of existing accommodation, would put the school further beyond the reach of local children— either geographically or financially. Sometimes, as at Westminster, it was because the governing bodies had other financial responsibilities. Sometimes, as at Eton, it was because members of the governing body were also beneficiaries of school endowments, and so diversion of more money into school improvements meant a reduction in their own income. Before the Public Schools Act of 1868 headmasters generally wished to improve accommodation but received little support from their governing bodies, who tended to entrench themselves in a strictly legalistic interpretation of their schools' constitutions and endowments, just as headmasters in turn tended to entrench themselves behind similar legalistic interpretations in their defence of the classical curriculum.

The *Clarendon Report* made clear that the reform of school accommodation, although so desperately needed in many cases, could not take place until legislation had removed from the schools the restraints of their original endowments and replaced the existing governors with new governing bodies more willing to promote and finance the drastic changes needed. The reform of the curriculum required, in turn, new headmasters more willing to provide and establish new subjects, but subsequent legislation left this to the new governing bodies which, however willing they were to improve the schools' accommodation, were generally unwilling to reform the classical education provided there. In this, the new governing bodies were frequently more conservative than the unreformed governing bodies they had replaced; their predecessors frequently expressed local support for a more modern, more vocational curriculum but the new governing bodies—which were largely composed, unofficially but no doubt intentionally, of a school's former pupils—tended to perpetuate the Classical tradition. The Public Schools Acts, in reforming the government and finance of the schools, removed legal and local obstacles to the reforms, which the headmasters themselves generally wished to make. The Acts did not, however, implement changes in the curriculum—the introduction of science and of modern languages, for example—which had seemed so urgent and expedient to public opinion before the Clarendon Commission.

Before the Clarendon Commission, the headmasters had made considerable and acknowledged progress in improving the conduct of their boys and maintaining school discipline. This progress is usually associated with the work at Rugby of Dr Arnold, who dramatically improved the general conduct of the school by placing great trust in his monitors, or praeposters, and giving them greater responsibilities—supporting them by Christian exhortation and giving them a regularised, recognised power to beat more junior boys. The casual, un-supervised, sometimes brutal nature of school life in the early years of the nineteenth century gave way, under Dr Arnold's influence, to a more formalised pattern of conduct. Exceptional unruliness, violence or severity could still bring a school national notoriety, but such incidents, if more publicised, became rarer. The growing importance of the national press made such scandals more difficult to cover up and headmasters became more circumspect, perhaps as a result. The consequences of a scandal at Shrewsbury in 1874, when the headmaster gave a boy eighty-eight strokes of the birch for having beer in his study, were considerable. There were verses in *Punch* and questions in Parliament; one of the newly-appointed governors resigned and, although a public inquiry cleared the headmaster of excessive severity, he was dogged by the scandal for the rest of his life.[45]

The general improvements in conduct and discipline had perhaps come about more easily because they involved none of the legal difficulties that bedevilled attempts to reform accommodation or the curriculum, and because the increasing size of the schools made personal control by the headmaster and his staff more difficult and more expensive, particularly as boys were now usually living in houses belonging to the school rather than to a master. Dr Arnold's monitorial system, which placed on senior boys the delegated authority of the headmaster, greatly influenced all the public schools—not least perhaps because the monitorial system was cheap and reduced staffing costs, enabling the schools to expand as private, commercial enterprises without the need to change school statutes or to hire teaching staff beyond the minimum funded by the schools' public endowments. Educational conviction followed upon practical necessity; the monitorial system provided good order and better conduct, and was a way to control large numbers of boys which also offered a heady combination of cost-effectiveness, Christian morality, corporal punishment and conservative ideals of hierarchy and order. The attractions of the monitorial system were so compelling that the school prefect and the whole concept of 'boy government' became symbolic of the special character of the public schools and the unique advantages of public school education.[46]

By 1860 the general tone and conduct of the public schools had been greatly improved, which must have been very evident to contemporaries. In the early years of the century even the severest headmasters could face great difficulties in maintaining order. Dr Keate at Eton, for example, was pelted with rotten eggs while publicly birching about eighty boys in 1810.[47] In 1818 boys rioted when he brought the hour of lock-up forward from six o'clock to five o'clock in an attempt to curtail hunting, shooting and tandem-driving.[48] A few days later he was shouted down in Upper Hall, had more eggs thrown at him and subsequently found his desk smashed.[49] The frequency of similar incidents elsewhere demonstrated the precarious nature of a headmaster's authority. At Shrewsbury under Dr Butler, two boys went to the races and returned to the school drunk. They then ran away, were chased by the headmaster and his servant, and attacked the servant with a knife when caught.[50] A particularly bad year was 1818, when most of the schools were affected by unrest of some kind. There were particularly bad disturbances at Eton, Winchester and Charterhouse; at Shrewsbury, among other events, some boys sent out the local Town Crier to denounce the appointment of a praeposter of whom they disapproved.[51]

As the century progressed, incidents of this kind became much less common. Headmasters became less directly involved in discipline. By the time of the Clarendon Commission, public comment was not so much about general unruliness but rather about whether the monitors themselves were properly guided and supervised, or whether punishment, administered either by boys or headmasters, was too severe. Severe and unreasonable punishment did not cease to be administered after Dr Arnold or after the Clarendon Commission, as was made clear by the flogging at Shrewsbury in 1874. What did happen was that the general context of school conduct and discipline, in which such punishment occurred, was radically changed in the period between Dr Arnold's appointement at Rugby in 1828 and the appointment of the Clarendon Commission in 1861. Two cases in particular illustrate the extent of the changes in school discipline in the years before 1861: the killing of Ashley-Cooper at Eton in 1825 and the beating of Randolph Stewart at Harrow in 1853.

Ashley-Cooper, who was killed in a savage and protracted fight against an older boy, was kept fighting for sixty rounds and for more than two hours. On the several occasions that he was knocked unconscious, his supporters revived him with brandy and pushed him back into the fight. When he finally collapsed, he was taken to his tutor's house, but the tutor was out and nobody fetched a doctor. When a doctor eventually came, six hours later, the boy was in a fatal coma. At the inquest, it was alleged that his supporters, who included his two elder brothers, had given him half a pint of brandy during the fight. Dr Keate and the other masters blamed the older boys for not stopping the fight, but seemed little concerned about the school's failure to maintain good order and reasonable conduct.[52]

The incident, although it led to an unusually tragic outcome, well illustrates the position of boys, particularly boarders, at the public schools in the earlier years of the century and shows what could happen when boys were left unsupervised for long periods. Masters took a limited view of their responsibilities outside the classroom. Older or stronger boys were left to establish their own dominance, but were given little formal authority. Differences were commonly settled by fighting, sometimes with some brutality. Intoxicating spirits were freely available. The responsibilities of supervision were diffused and uncertain, as at Eton: Ashley-Cooper's tutor, when absent, left no one to assume responsibility for the boys in his care; the older boys certainly assumed no responsibility. The other masters, including Keate himself, assumed no responsibility for the affair and Keate continued unaffected as headmaster until 1834.

The beating of Randolph Stewart took place at Harrow in 1853 and was administered by Platt, the son of Baron Platt.[53] The incident, which led to some correspondence between the fathers of the boys and Dr Vaughan, and eventually between Dr Vaughan and Palmerston, illustrated the extent to which a close, formal, almost ritualised hierarchy of authority and responsibility had become established in the schools—extending even to the now-organised games field. Stewart became involved in an argument with Platt during a game of football. Although Platt was a monitor, Stewart refused to accept the judgement that he was off-side and accused Platt of not knowing the rules. Platt later tried to beat Stewart for disobedience but he refused to allow this. Both boys went to see Dr Vaughan, the headmaster, who supported Platt. When Platt subsequently punished Stewart, he beat him thirty-two times about the shoulders with a thick cane, causing him such physical injury that he required immediate medical attention and remained under medical supervision for some days. In the subsequent correspondence between Stewart's father and Dr Vaughan, it was clear that Platt himself had not followed the school's code of discipline— he had acted on his own, from malice; he had not consulted the other monitors; he had not given Stewart an opportunity to defend himself before the other monitors and he had used an unusually heavy cane.[54]

The changed circumstances, although at different schools, show how greatly the management, discipline and conduct of public schools had been changed by Dr Arnold's ideas. The boys at Harrow in 1853 were under the formal authority of senior boys, appointed by and responsible to the headmaster. Their authority went beyond regulations and encompassed what Dr Vaughan called 'the good order, the honourable conduct, the gentlemanlike tone, of the Houses and of the School'.[55] There was the possibility of appeal to the headmaster and the authority itself was exercised by the monitors acting as a body, by which the offender had normally the right to be heard. The emphasis on proper gentlemanly conduct is evident throughout, and nothing could be further from the unsupervised, bloody brawl that led to Ashley-Cooper's death at Eton. Clearly there was a need for even the monitors to be supervised if excesses were not to occur, and subsequently some headmasters issued instructions defining monitors' powers, although no doubt these were usually already defined by tradition and school custom. At Shrewsbury, for example, such instructions were issued by Alington in 1913. This appears rather late, but Shrewsbury had been later than other schools in giving corporal punishment powers to monitors, which had been introduced only after 1866, during the headmastership of Moss.[56] At Harrow medical attention was immediately available and the whole Randolph Stewart affair, although open to much criticism on other grounds, was conducted soberly. The game of football that led to the incident was one of those organised on a regular basis and under the supervision of the monitors, whose authority extended even to the conduct of players on the field.

By the time of the Clarendon Commission, criticisms of public school discipline had changed from general, concerning unruliness, lack of supervision and violence, to specific, concerning the occasional excesses of a monitorial system that was generally accepted throughout the public schools and, indeed, had become regarded as an essential part of their structure and character. In 1853, when defending the Harrow system in a letter to Palmerston, Dr Vaughan could describe it as 'the universal rule of Public Schools:—[which was] until lately, when the experience of its salutory effects has led to a wider extension of it, was the one distinguishing feature of a Public as contrasted with a Private school'.[57]

There were, of course, some people—although they were rarely in the public schools—who wished to abolish corporal punishment altogether. Dr Arnold had found that his insistence on giving boys at Rugby the right to beat other boys was 'a point on which the spirit of the age set strongly and increasingly against him'.[58] Clarendon himself was opposed to corporal punishment, and the need for corporal punishment in other areas of national life was questioned increasingly in the years immediately before and after 1861. Nevertheless, there was no general outcry against public school discipline at the time of the Clarendon Commission. The tradition of flogging and beating was well established in these schools, besides which the House of Commons was predominantly composed of public school men who were inclined to defend the traditions of their own schools. Flogging and beating, it was alleged, were only the most severe sanctions, in theory used only when more minor penalties had failed.

Two factors, however, must have weighed heavily with contemporaries when they saw Dr Arnold's system, with its insistence on corporal punishment, as a reform. Firstly, the monitorial system—with all its potential evils and occasional excesses—must have seemed infintely preferable to the near-anarchy that had so often prevailed in the schools before Dr Arnold's reforms were widely adopted. Secondly, the practice of public schools must have seemed rather more humane than the practices elsewhere in Victorian society, where criminals were commonly flogged with a whip and when executions still took place in public. It is against this background that the seemingly bizarre defence of the birch as a comparatively harmless instrument must be seen. In March 1862, in a Commons debate on the whipping of criminals in prison it was argued that 'the instrument to be used was only a birch rod', which was 'rather a harmless instrument'.[59] In 1863, when an attempt was made to introduce a Bill into the Commons to protect children from excessive punishment, the use of the birch was advocated as a reform to prevent use of more serious methods, to end 'irregular and cruel treatment' and to stop 'severe and permanent injuries' being inflicted by schoolmasters, particularly in national schools.[60] The Bill was eventually withdrawn, being described by Sir George Grey, the Home Secretary, as 'unnecessary and almost of a ridiculous character'.[61]

Many examples could be given to illustrate the cruelty with which Victorians frequently treated children in the home, at school and at work, but it is perhaps sufficient to refer to just two Parliamentary debates which took place in the year of the *Clarendon Report*, to illustrate the context in which the monitorial system at the public schools could be seen as a humane and Christian reform. In February 1864 Mr Hibbert—the Member for Oldham—moved an 'Address for Papers' in the Commons on public executions. He referred to a recent public execution in London, on 22 February 1864, at which five pirates had been hanged. He graphically described the scene and the unpleasant nature of the occasion which seemed, he said, to bring out the worst feelings of the crowd. The motion was eventually withdrawn. Sir George Grey, the Home Secretary, argued that public executions had a salutory effect on others and that the large, unruly crowd was merely the result of infrequent executions.[62] In June 1864 the Lords considered and approved a Bill by Lord Shaftesbury to protect small boys used as chimney sweeps. The House heard of appalling cruelties inflicted on these children, sometimes less than five years old, not just by their masters but by the fashionable families who employed them.[63] By the time of the Clarendon Commission, the public schools must have seemed a haven of well-regulated order when compared with the violence, squalor, cruelty and poverty so often evident in nineteenth-century England.

The curriculum of the public school was not, however, likely to encourage boys to study contemporary society. The slow but noticeable attempts to improve buildings and accommodation and the great changes in school conduct and discipline had not been matched by reform in this area. The schools themselves were generally in favour of improving school buildings and reforming school discipline; they were not, in particular the headmasters, in favour of reforming the curriculum. It was this unwillingness on the part of the schools to abandon their overwhelming concentration on the classics, or to admit that their teaching of the classics could be improved, which particularly attracted public criticism. There were two variations of this criticism: the first was that the classics were being badly taught; the second was that the classics were taught too exclusively and that other subjects such as science, modern history, modern geography and modern languages, that were arguably of equal importance, were neglected.

The prominence of the classics in the public schools was the result of two historical circumstances. The first was that most of the public schools were, in origin and in foundation, endowed grammar schools. That is, the schools had been founded by gifts of money or land—sometimes from public funds, sometimes from private benefactors—to teach 'grammar'. The nature of a 'grammar' school was defined legally by Lord Eldon in 1805 as 'a school founded for teaching grammatically the learned languages'.[64] The learned languages were Latin and Greek. This definition determined and limited the curriculum of all grammar schools until the time when the Clarendon and Taunton Commissions led to legislation for all grammar schools, for 'Eton, Winchester, Harrow, Rugby and the rest . . . were only the most prominent examples of a host of other endowed schools designed to give a "grammar" school education'.[65] The courts upheld this strict definition of a 'grammar' school, following Lord Eldon who, in 1805, had refused to allow the revenues of Leeds Grammar School to be used for anything other than the teaching of Latin and Greek and legalised a definition of a 'grammar' school from Dr Johnson.[66] This was a most conservative and restrictive interpretation, because Lord Eldon was a man of extreme and rigid Conservative views. It was said of him that the only reform he ever supported was the abolition of trial by combat for convicted criminals.[67]

This legal view put the grammar schools into a difficult situation. They were compelled to teach Latin and Greek, almost exclusively, to boys who often had neither use for, nor interest in, these subjects. At the same time, the insufficiency of their endowments, and their usual obligation to provide some cheap or free education under the terms of these, compelled them to attract boys who would pay fees. The difficulty of reconciling the needs of local, foundation boys, who might be entitled to free education, with those of the fee-paying boys, who were often necessary for a school's survival, led to frequent conflict over the importance of the classics between headmasters and locally appointed governors. For if a school was to attract fee-paying boys or boarders (who would also provide an income), it had to maintain a reputation for scholarship and for getting boys into the universities. University scholarship almost invariably meant classical scholarship, as places, scholarships or prizes in other subjects were few in number and not held in high regard. The parents of local children often did not want their offspring to receive the classical education which grammar schools were compelled to provide but which a school that was dependent on endowments and educating some children free might not be able to afford. Maintaining a high standard of classical scholarship was expensive because it meant employing well-qualified staff, who could usually only be paid for by the admission of fee-paying boys or boarders. Poor facilities or the presence within the school of local children receiving free education could reduce the ability of a school to attract fee-paying boys. The difficulty was that the admission of boarders or the charging of fees often contravened the terms of a school's foundation. The only remedy, apart from making unofficial arrangements, was usually to make an application to the Court of Chancery, asking for a revision of a school's statutes. Between Lord Eldon's ruling in 1805 and the appointment of the Clarendon Commission in 1861, there was a succession of applications to the Court of Chancery from grammar schools throughout the country.[68]

An early case was Bingley Grammar School, decided in 1820. Three local inhabitants complained that the Trustees and headmaster had departed from the school's traditional statutes by charging for the teaching of English, writing and arithmetic, and by admitting boarders. The headmaster was accused of neglecting the free scholars, of behaving with particular severity towards them and of giving too much attention to the boarders. There was also complaint about an entrance test, imposed in 1814, and other regulations imposed by the Trustees, which included the banning of clogs in school. In defence, the Trustees and headmaster argued that the Founder had intended to found a *grammar* school, and therefore their concentration on Latin and Greek and the entrance test were justified. They objected to the introduction of a general, rather than a classical, education and defended the admission of fee-paying boys on the grounds that they had been obliged to employ an extra teacher. In his judgement, Lord Eldon supported the Trustees and the headmaster. He found that there was no obligation on the school to provide a free, general education and the entrance restrictions were supported. Boarders were to be allowed, provided that the free scholars were not neglected. Lord Eldon's comments indicated that the dilemma of Bingley Grammar School was a common one, for he observed that if he prohibited boarders, legal proceedings would begin against the trustees of half the grammar schools of England. He recognised that Bingley Grammar School had ceased to be of much use to local children, but he could provide no remedy. The school was a grammar school by foundation and the revenues could not be used to provide a general education.[69]

The public schools, in their concentration on the classics, were no different from most other grammar schools. The difference lay simply in that, for a variety of reasons, they had managed to attract boarders on a national basis and to achieve such a national reputation that they claimed separate consideration. Some—like Eton, Westminster and Winchester—had associations with the Court and the aristocracy. Some—like Harrow, Rugby and Shrewsbury—had flourished under great headmasters. The great day-schools were either well-endowed—like St Paul's, which educated all 153 boys free on the foundation—or were able to attract enough fee-paying day-boys in London to flourish without boarders—like Merchant Taylors'. Sometimes there were variations in a school's original statutes which enabled it to accept boarders or charge fees more easily. At Eton, for example, the original statutes provided for not more than twenty *commensales*, 'the sons of noblemen and special friends of the College',[70] who would pay for their own board. At the Free Grammar School of Harrow, the statutes of 1571 provided for boarders, or *foreigners*, 'in addition to the boys of the district who receive free education'.[71] At Shrewsbury, masters were legally allowed to take boys into their own houses as boarders after the 1853 Chancery Scheme for the school, although the headmaster argued that the practice was based on ancient custom.[72]

The obligation to teach the classics, and associated subjects like ancient history, was an obligation that rested on all grammar schools. The public schools had, however, been more successful than most grammar schools in maintaining numbers and in supplementing their public income from endowments with a potentially more lucrative private income derived from fees and boarding charges. The public schools had no financial incentive to provide what was called a 'commercial education' for local people. When local people pressed for this more vocational education, the pressure was usually strongly resisted—

not just because it may have been contrary to a school's statutes, but also because the study of the classics was traditionally the education of a gentleman. For some, the attempt to teach *anything* well, even the classics, lowered the tone of the school, for it meant that the aristocracy were judged by what they could do rather than by who they were.[73] Shrewsbury, arguably the public school with the best record of any school for classical scholarship in the nineteenth century, was on the borderline between the public schools of the Clarendon Commission and the other grammar schools; Eton, the school with the most fashionable Court connections, had arguably the worst record of classical scholarship.[74]

This somewhat casual aristocratic attitude to scholarship was more difficult to sustain in the years immediately before the Clarendon Commission. Even Eton could not ignore the political changes since 1832 or the growth of wealth and influence among the commercial and industrial middle classes, particularly when other public schools could demonstrate superior scholarship. The Reform Act of 1832, although not concerned with the public schools, had direct consequences for the future of these schools because the Parliamentary forum within which their future was discussed and decided became more open to the comments and criticisms of a new middle-class electorate. In the event, the public schools were sheltered from the more radical middle-class demands for curricular reform, government control or the extension of free education by an adept use of Parliamentary procedure which kept the Public Schools Bills almost exclusively in the House of Lords. After 1832, however, the public schools—in particular Eton—could no longer depend upon the uncritical loyalty of public school men in Parliament or among the electorate to minimise scandal, refute criticisms or prevent legislation. The most damaging general criticisms were irrefutable—that endowments were often improperly used and that the classics were often taught very badly. Both these general criticisms applied particularly to Eton. A successful manufacturer who sent his son to Eton might not be concerned about the curriculum as it was, after all, that most suitable for gentlemen. Although in the second or third generation of a successful enterprising family, commercial or technical education might in any case be disregarded, bad teaching suggested negligence and contrasted unfavourably with the school's vast wealth and pre-eminent social esteem. University results proved that other schools offered an education superior to that of Eton.[75]

Appeals to the foundation statutes and attitudes of social or scholarly contempt for other subjects were still no defence against the criticism that the classics themselves were badly taught. With the notable exception of Shrewsbury, this criticism was commonly levelled at all the public schools in the years before 1861. The importance of this criticism was increased firstly by the increase in competitive examinations for entry into the professions and government service, and secondly by the growth of private or proprietary schools which, though frequently modelled on the older public schools and like them concentrating on the classics, were less bound by traditional public school methods. Sometimes, as at Uppingham under Thring, the newer schools set out to deliberately challenge the methods and attitudes of the older schools.[76] Shrewsbury, although small in numbers, had built up a formidable reputation for classical scholarship under Dr Butler and Dr Kennedy and therefore probably had less to fear from the competition of these newer schools.[77] Yet even at Shrewsbury, there was concern at this growing competition and it was hinted that it was not entirely fair, for the public obligations of the public schools put them at a disadvantage in the private market. A pamphlet published by the school in 1851 lamented the growth of competition and the decline in its own numbers:

> Proprietary companies . . . are enabled to under-sell the Public Grammar Schools,—fettered as these latter are by their constitution; and it is the notorious tendency of the age to buy education, like food and clothing, in the cheapest markets . . . Against such unequal competition it is evident that the Masters of Public Grammar Schools in this country cannot successfuly strive; they can only express their hope that the revolution thus wrought in the government of English education may issue in greater good than at present they see reason to anticipate.[78]

Then as now, the most evident measure of a school's efficiency for parents was that provided by examination results and the pamphlet concluded with an impressive list of the school's academic successes since 1840, including sixteen first class degrees in classics at Oxford and Cambridge and eighty-four university college scholarships. Shrewsbury was, however, the public school regarded as most progressive in its teaching methods and was a school to which other public schools sometimes looked for ideas. Most public schools had reason to fear a comparison of their methods with those of the newer schools and this awareness, that even within their own chosen subject areas the public schools were not generally teaching competently, goes a long way to explaining why even the schools' supporters in Parliament raised no objection to the appointment of the Clarendon Commission.

At Winchester, for example, the curriculum was wholly classical but the classics were not taught except by the older boys. No attempt was made to understand grammar or the cultural value of classical scholarship. The aim of education at Winchester was to learn as many lines of Latin and Greek as possible and this was 'the great literary feat of the school'.[79] Harrow was worse than Winchester, for although at Winchester it was the older boys who taught, at least the necessity of teaching was recognised. At Harrow, the school's organisation made it impossible for any proper teaching to take place since the whole duty of both headmaster and staff was to hear boys construe. Some boys did eventually master Thucydides and Juvenal, but the headmaster did not teach them and did not think it was his responsibility.[80] Poor or non-existent teaching at most public schools was partly the result of poor accommodation, which made it necessary to collect large numbers of boys together for classes. When better accommodation was provided at Westminster in 1860–1, the change in teaching methods was a matter for national comment.[81] The reorganisation of existing accommodation could sometimes lead to improved teaching—not just because there was more privacy for the class but because younger teachers could experiment away from the eye of authority. At Eton the reforms of Hawtrey in the organisation of the classes using the Upper School, and the fact that Hawtrey himself ceased to teach there, enabled younger masters to surreptitiously introduce newer teaching methods. Although Hawtrey himself did not wish to change the traditional method of teaching at Eton, which was 'the ceaseless inculcation of "rules for the formation of tenses" ',[82] his absence from Upper School enabled the assistant masters to experiment.[83]

Many of the younger masters 'had learnt at the University

the more modern and intelligent methods of teaching which had been introduced by Kennedy of Shrewsbury and others',[84] but teaching methods at Eton, as elsewhere, were very much influenced by class size. At Eton, for example, Hawtrey's class of thirty-two boys was unusually small[85] and schools were generally reluctant to engage more staff than the minimum required by statute or tradition. Although many schools, particularly Eton, Harrow and Rugby,[86] were wealthy, the money was rarely used to provide more staff. Sometimes this was partly because much of the school's income went else-where—at Eton, to support seven Fellows and a Provost. Some-times it was because the existing masters did not wish to see their own incomes—both official and unofficial—diminished by newcomers. The difficulty of employing more staff is perhaps the only reason why the teaching of the classics would not have continued to improve had the Clarendon Commission not been appointed. The pressure of competition between schools and the growing importance of public examinations would eventually have compelled the older public schools to reform. The funda-mental problem, however, was that adequate reform—of either teaching or accommodation—often depended first on a reform of a school's finances and government. This was particularly so at Eton, where the Fellows had for generations enriched themselves—often illegally—at the expense of the school.[87] The reform of the public schools' finances and government could not, however, be achieved by the schools themselves without legislation and this explains why conservative supporters of the schools were prepared to accept a Royal Commission, particularly after the finances of Eton had received wide publicity in a series of articles in the *Cornhill Magazine* in May 1860, December 1860 and March 1861. These revealed that misappropriation of school funds had reached scandalous and, indeed, almost criminal proportions.[88]

The second major criticism of the public schools was that the curriculum was too exclusively classical, even when the un-obtrusive introduction of new subjects was legally and financially possible. This was not such a damaging criticism, as before 1861 only the more radical critics suggested that any other studies should form the basis of a scholarly education. In the debate that followed the presentation of the *Clarendon Report* in the Commons in 1864, none of the speakers—including Grant Duff who had proposed the appointment of the Commission[89] — argued against the continuence of classical education, only that it was badly taught and that other subjects, especially science and modern languages, were neglected. Duff himself, who had travelled widely in Europe and was sympathetic to the need for scientific and other modern studies, firmly believed in the value of a primarily classical education for general cultural reasons—he thought there was no substitute for the study of the classics and he dismissed the idea that the classics were worthwhile simply because they were difficult.[90] In *A Plea for Rational Education*, published in 1871, he drew up suggested courses of Greek and Latin 'suitable for the brevity of human life'[91] which were far more exhaustive than anything taught in the schools. He advocated teaching the classics as Kennedy at Shrewsbury attempted to do, as though they were modern languages that could provide an insight into contemporary problems—indeed, events in Greece and Italy were frequently in the forefront of European politics.

Subjects such as science, modern languages and even mathematics, which the reformers wished to see included had already gained a place in public school education but, even when formally part of the curriculum, like mathematics at Eton and Shrewsbury, were little regarded. Little time was spent on them and the marks gained were frequently not included in the total that determined a boy's place in the school. Modern languages and science were rarely established in a formal sense, but were more usually available, in some form, through private tuition. For these subjects to be established in a formal sense there had to be a combination of favourable circumstances— a competent teacher, a favourable headmaster and governors, available money and not too much hostility from the other masters and boys. Such subjects thus became available in only a haphazard and precarious way, having no assured place in the timetable and dependent on the enthusiasm of one teacher or the tolerance of the headmaster. Sometimes, these innovations achieved permanence. The introduction of mathematics at Eton was a good example of how, given favourable circumstances, an innovation could achieve permanence and a measure of respectability.

'Before the year 1836,' runs the Report of the Public Schools Commission, 'there appears to have been no mathematical teaching of any kind at Eton.' The Master, Mr Hexter, after that date gave some instruction in arithmetic, but he was not competent to teach any other branch of mathematics, and, in his old age at any rate, not even competent to teach that. One of the masters, Stephen Hawtrey—a cousin of the Headmaster— . . . received permission to give some 'extra' mathematical classes outside regular school hours to those boys whose parents wished them to receive it, but his activities were very circumscribed 'in order not to tread on the interests of Mr Hexter'. Then in about 1839 it was found possible to pension off Hexter with £200 a year and Stephen Hawtrey was left with a free hand.[92]

His status as an assistant master was, however, inferior to the classics masters and equal only to the drawing master or fencing master. The school did eventually build a big, new Mathematical School and when Hawtrey started teaching there in 1851 he was given full assistant master status. Every boy had to do three mathematical lessons a week and Hawtrey was able to hire several assistants. These assistants remained in an inferior position, however; they could not wear academic dress and had no right of access to the headmaster.[93]

The preponderance of time spent on the classics meant, however, that even in schools where these subjects were available, the opportunities for studying them must have been very limited. Of the usual timetable of twenty-six to thirty hours a week, the classics and associated subjects occupied anything from eighteen or nineteen hours at Harrow to twenty-one hours at Rugby. 'At least three-quarters and in some cases four-fifths, of the time was spent in class on Latin and Greek.'[94] This situation, which had prevailed in the schools from the time of their foundation, was not just acknowledged but indeed defended by the headmasters on a number of grounds, apart from the legal requirements of their foundation. Dr Kennedy of Shrewsbury, who perhaps of all the headmasters could most claim to have taught the classics successfully and to have attempted innovation, put these arguments in his address to the National Association for the Promotion of Social Science in September 1864. The arguments were that, although other subjects could be taught, they could not in practice be given equal importance; that other subjects were available although they might not appear formally on the curriculum; and that modern languages could not in any case be taught effectively at public schools because they had to be learnt in early childhood.[95] These arguments must, however, have been difficult to sustain in the years before 1864. Although restricted by old statutes, many schools were wealthy. Shrewsbury, for example, had in the main School Account in 1864 a surplus of £1,820 which did not include income from fees.[96] Other schools—notably Eton, Harrow and Rugby—were wealthier, even allowing for misappropriation. Of course much of a school's income usually went directly to the staff as fees, without appearing in the school accounts. The emphasis on the classics meant that boys wishing to study other subjects seriously must have wasted much time and suffered much discouragement. The argument that some subjects could not be successfully taught in the schools or that their inclusion was impracticable was weakened by the establishment of many schools which did teach these other subjects to a high standard, often also maintaining a high standard of classical scholarship.

Yet this concentration on the classics and the relative neglect of other subjects had typified the public schools since their foundation and, if anything, the position of other subjects was more favourable in 1861 than at any time previously—just as conduct and discipline were better and accommodation was generally, if slowly, improving. The schools had greatly changed since the attempts to include them in Brougham's Bill in 1820.[97] At that time, attempts to include six of the schools in the Bill[98] met with determined resistance, both from the schools and within Parliament. In 1861 Grant Duff's proposal of a Royal Commission met with no objection whatever in Parliament, even though Duff himself observed that 'there is no subject on which the rank and file of the Conservative Party are so unreasonable'.[99] The schools themselves, consulted beforehand by the government, did not object and were 'disposed to give information to a Royal Commission'.[100] The lack of opposition to the appointment of the Clarendon Commission, at a time when most schools could show some evidence of reform, indicated that circumstances had changed since 1820 and that this had left the schools more exposed to and conscious of criticism.

Public school life in the late 1850s was rigorous but organised. The casual supervision and occasional incidental brutalities of earlier times had disappeared following Dr Arnold's example and influence. Some reform of the curriculum, of teaching and of general living conditions had been attempted, but only where this could be done with little expense and within the legal constraints of ancient foundations. These legal constraints could be widened through the Court of Chancery, but only when headmaster and governors were prepared to pursue this long and costly process which might, as at Shrewsbury, change little. By 1861 the public schools had reached the limits of the reforms that could be legally accomplished without legislation. It is true that this early movement towards reform was obscured by argument about the place of the classics in the curriculum, about the precise charitable intentions of the original benefactors or about the educational value of hardship, but the public schools had nevertheless made significant reforms in the years before 1861—most notably in organisation and discipline, but also in their teaching and in curricular innovation. These reforms, however, although creditable, seemed meagre when measured against the educational requirements of an industrial economy, against educational reforms in Europe or against the achievements of the newly-established proprietary schools. The reform of the public schools became a public issue because, in these circumstances, the reform of all endowed grammar schools became a public issue, the public schools being just the most well-known examples. It was at Eton, the most celebrated endowed grammar school, that the need to reform the school's government and finance was seen to be most urgent, and the impossibility of doing this without legislation was seen most clearly, as the governors were closely associated with financial misappropriation and the example of Eton was one of extravagance, incompetence and the private pursuit of financial advantage, which paid little heed to public responsibility or educational principle.

Notes

1 Lord Edmond Fitzmaurice, *The Life of Granville, George Leveson Gower, Second Earl Granville KG 1815–1891*, London, 1906, I, p. 15.
2 Generally throughout, the term 'public school' refers to the nine schools investigated by the Clarendon Commission: Eton, Westminster, Winchester, Charterhouse, St Paul's, Merchant Taylors', Harrow, Rugby and Shrewsbury.
3 A. Trollope, 'Public schools', *Fortnightly Review*, 2, October 1865, pp. 476–87. See also G. M. Young's comment that 'public opinion did not want knowledge. It wanted the sort of man of whom Wellington had said that he could go straight from school with two NCOs. and fifteen privates and get a shipload of convicts to Australia without trouble'. (G. M. Young, *Victorian England: Portrait of an Age*, London, 1966, p. 98.)

4 *Clarendon Report*, I, p. 11. For the rise in school numbers, the number of children at school and the statistical problems involved, see E. G. West, *Education and the Industrial Revolution*, London, 1975, pp. 9–24 and G. Sutherland, *Elementary Education in the Nineteenth Century*, London, 1971, p. 11.
5 See, for example, R. H. Cheney, 'Public school education', *Quarterly Review*, 108, October 1860, pp. 413–14.
6 C. J. Vaughan, *A Letter to the Viscount Palmerston M.P. Etc.*, p. 7. (A bound collection of Vaughan's correspondence of 1853–4, concerning Harrow School, in Birmingham University Library). Charles John Vaughan (1816–97) was headmaster at Harrow 1844–59.
7 Trollope, 'Public schools', p. 481.
8 See T. W. Bamford, *The Rise of the Public Schools: A Study of Boys' Public Boarding Schools in England and Wales from 1837 to the Present Day*, London, 1967, p. 196.
9 'Public schools—report of the Commission', *Fraser's Magazine*, June 1864, pp. 659–60.
10 'Eton', *Macmillan's Magazine*, 3, February 1861, p. 299, attrib. H. Sidgwick, *Wellesley Index*, I, p. 561.
11 See C. Hollis, *Eton*, London, 1960, pp. 1–13.
12 Sidgwick, 'Eton', p. 299.
13 Sidgwick, 'Eton', p. 300.
14 *Clarendon Report*, I, p. 8.
15 See J. F. Williams, *Harrow*, London, 1901, pp. 13, 16. Shrewsbury, for example, was described as 'Shrewsbury Free Grammar School' in the statute establishing the new governing body under the Public Schools Acts. See 'A statute for determining and establishing the constitution of the new governing body of Shrewsbury Free Grammar School made by the Public Schools Commissioners', *Copy of Statutes, Schemes and Regulations made under the Public Schools Acts by the Public Schools Commissioners, September 1874. Ordered by the House of Commons to be printed, 10th March 1876*.
16 For the schools' obligations to educate the poor or the children of a particular locality, see the *Clarendon Report*, I, pp. 9–10. For the legal similarities of all endowed grammar schools, see Note 69 below. Kennedy of Shrewsbury admitted that Edward VI had founded 25 similar schools in 16 counties. See B. H. Kennedy, *Shrewsbury School: A Letter to His Grace the Archbishop of York on the Public Character of Shrewsbury School, as affected by the Public Schools Bill*, Cambridge, 1865, p. 8.
17 For Eton as a university college, see Sidgwick, 'Eton', pp. 292–300. For Winchester, see Sir William Heathcote, *Hansard*, CLXII, 23 April 1861, col. 984.
18 W. Vincent, *A Defence of Public Education*, London, 1801, quoted in Bamford, *The Rise of the Public Schools*, p. ix.
19 'Public schools of England', *Edinburgh Review*, 16, August 1810, p. 330, attrib. Sidney Smith in Bamford, *The Rise of the Public Schools*, p. x.
20 *List of Examples, Etc. which may be obtained from the Department by National and other Public Schools at half the prime cost*, Department of Science and Art, Marlborough House, Pall Mall, London, List No. 30, May 1853 in Bailiff's Bundles No. 111.
21 See Chapter 5, pp. 143–4.
22 *Shrewsbury School Accounts, 1855*, Bailiff's Bundles No. 122.
23 See J. S. Hurt, *Education in Evolution*, London, 1971, pp. 186–90.
24 The definition of a burgess was a wide one:

> The constitution of a burgess is this: any person born in the town is entitled to become a burgess upon being sworn and paying a small fee; and his sons in perpetual descent are entitled to burgess rights . . . The way in which persons could acquire the burgess rights, except by birth and parentage, was by servitude under an apprenticeship in one of the incorporated trades of the town.

> (J. R. Kenyon QC, *Lords Select Committee Report, 1865*, 29 May 1865, p. 269.)

The provision of completely free education for the sons of burgesses dated from the Act of 1798, which transferred control of the school from the head-master and Corporation to Trustees who were men of standing in Shropshire. The meaning of 'free' in the school's name was much disputed, Kennedy arguing that the word meant not 'gratuitous' but 'free from ecclesiastical control'. See J. B. Oldham, *A History of Shrewsbury School 1552–1952*, Oxford, 1952, pp. 70–1, 111. See also Kennedy, *A Letter to His Grace the Archbishop of York*, pp. 6–14. For sons of burgesses at Shrewsbury School, see C. J. Shrosbree, 'The origins and influence of the Clarendon Commission (1961–1864), with special reference to Shrewsbury School', PhD thesis, Birmingham University, 1985, Appendix X. See also Chapter 5, Note 3.

25 B. H. Kennedy, *Notes on Public Education: A Paper read, by the Rev. Dr. Kennedy, at the Meeting of the National Association for the Promotion of Social Science, York, September, 1864*, Bailiff's Bundles No. 122.

26 Kennedy, *Notes on Public Education*, p. 1.

27 Benjamin Hall Kennedy (1805–89) was headmaster 1836–66. For his early life and teaching experience, see the chapter on Kennedy in F. D. How, *Six Great Schoolmasters*, London, 1904 and Oldham, *A History of Shrewsbury School*, pp. 104–6.

28 For school numbers, See Note 4 above. For government spending, see Hurt, *Education in Evolution*, pp. 186–90. For literacy rates, see West, *Education and the Industrial Revolution*, pp. 38–43 and R. D. Altick, *The English Common Reader*, Chicago, 1957, p. 171. Also, *Minutes of the Committee of the Council on Education, 1840–1841*, Appendix III, p. 138.

29 West, *Education and the Industrial Revolution*, pp. 23–5.

30 *Newcastle Report*, Minutes of evidence taken on 6 December 1859; an answer to Question 849 by Horace Mann, quoted West, *Education and the Industrial Revolution*, p. 24.

31 *Newcastle Report*, Minutes of evidence taken on 6 December 1859; an answer to Question 849 by Horace Mann, quoted West, *Education and the Industrial Revolution*, p. 24.

32 Numbers in December 1861; *Clarendon Report*, I, p. 11.

33 *Clarendon Report*, I, p. 11.

34 See F. E. Balls, 'The origins of the Endowed Schools Act 1869 and its operation in England from 1869 to 1895', PhD thesis, Cambridge University, 1964, pp. 475–8.

35 The *Clarendon Report*'s view was that foundation boys were benefiting unfairly from the money provided by fee-paying parents; see *Clarendon Report*, I, p. 10. On the other hand, there was some contemporary chagrin that the poor benefited too much from wealthy endowments. Anthony Trollope, for example, commented on Winchester where the scholars, intended by William of Wykeham to be poor, benefited from the school's wealth. 'The funds have so increased in value, that these charity children are the inheritors of such an education as is fit only for the children of the upper classes.' Trollope, 'Public Schools', p. 486. The *Clarendon Report*'s view was that the poor should be educated provided they paid for it themselves; see *Clarendon Report*, I, p. 11.

The advantage of this approach was that it enabled both the public schools and the other grammar schools of the Taunton Commission to expand without any additional expenditure. The disadvantage was that the endowments mainly benefited classes that could afford the fees. Although the Endowed Schools Commissioners, and the Charity Commissioners after 1874, attempted to provide schools for the poorer classes, the working of the Endowed Schools Act inexorably aided the transfer of grammar schools from public to private education and from the poor to the wealthy. For a discussion of this process and the consequences of private funding, see Balls, 'Origins of the Endowed Schools Act 1869', pp. 448–78.

36 See T. W. Bamford, 'The prosperity of public schools, 1801–1850', *Durham Research Review*, III, No. 12, September 1961, pp. 85–96.

37 See Chapter 2, pp. 63–5.

38 Trollope, for example, compared the public schools with St Andrew's College in Bradfield. 'I expect to see that our old institutions will at last be driven to

the truth by the examples which these new institutions have set and by the successes which they achieve.' Trollope, 'Public schools', pp. 484-5. To the public schools, this competition could seem unfair for the new schools had greater freedom and were less governed by considerations of gentlemanly conduct—they did, for example, advertise. See *Shrewsbury School 1800-1851*, a leaflet published in 1851 by the school, in *Paget's Scrap Book*, Shrewsbury Sch. Arch.

39 Trollope, 'Public schools', p. 479.

40 C. Hollis, *Eton*, London, 1960, p. 234.

41 'The Public Schools Commission', *Chamber's Journal*, Fourth Series, 42, 15 October 1864, pp. 662-3.

42 *The Times*, 15 April 1865, p. 9.

43 *The Times*, 13 August 1860, p. 9.

44 *The Times*, 26 October 1866, p. 7.

45 The headmaster was Henry Whitehead Moss (1841-1917), headmaster at Shrewsbury 1866-1908. See 'Salopienses flagellati', *Punch*, 8 August 1874, p. 62 and *Hansard*, CCXXI, 31 July 1874, cols. 1036-7. For the public inquiry, see *Shrewsbury Chronicle*, 31 July 1874. For the relevance of this incident to the school in 1874, see Chapter 5, pp. 162-4.

46 See P. Gwyn, 'The "tunding row": George Ridding and the belief in "boy government" ', in R. Custance (ed.), *Winchester College: Sixth-Centenary Essays*, Oxford, 1982, pp. 431-77.

47 Hollis, *Eton*, pp. 201-2. John Keate (1773-1852) was headmaster of Eton 1809-34.

48 Hollis, *Eton*, p. 203.

49 Hollis, *Eton*, p. 203.

50 Oldham, *A History of Shrewsbury School*, p. 78. Samuel Butler (1774-1839) was headmaster at Shrewsbury 1798-1836.

51 Oldham, *A History of Shrewsbury School*, pp. 80-1.

52 Hollis, *Eton*, p. 222. Anthony Francis Ashley-Cooper (1810-25) was the fifth son of the 6th Earl of Shaftesbury.

53 Randolph Henry Stewart (1836-1920) was the second son of the 9th Earl of Galloway and later succeeded as the 11th Earl. Herbert Edwin Platt (1834-1913) was the son of Sir Thomas Joshua Platt QC, a baron of the Court of Exchequer. He left Harrow in 1853 and later became a clergyman in the Church of England.

54 Vaughan, *A Letter to the Viscount Palmerston*, pp. 5-8.

55 Vaughan, *A Letter to the Viscount Palmerston*, p. 13.

56 See Oldham, *A History of Shrewsbury School*, p. 169.

57 Vaughan, *A Letter to the Viscount Palmerston*, p. 4.

58 A. P. Stanley, *The Life and Correspondence of Thomas Arnold D.D.*, London, 1844, I, p. 105, quoted Vaughan, *A Letter to Viscount Palmerston*, p. 5.

59 Adam Black, amendment to the *Whipping (No. 2) Bill* in *Hansard*, CLXVI, 26 March 1862, cols. 123-4. Adam Black (1784-1874) was Liberal MP for Edinburgh 1856-65.

60 Viscount Raynham, *Hansard*, CLXXI, 30 June 1863, col. 1842. Viscount Raynham (1831-99) was Liberal MP for Tamworth 1856-63.

61 Sir George Grey, *Hansard*, CLXXI, 30 June 1863, col. 1842. Sir George Grey (1799-1882) was Liberal MP for Devonport 1832-47, for Northumberland North 1847-52 and for Morpeth 1853-74. He was Home Secretary 1846-52, 1855-8 and 1861-6.

62 *Hansard*, CLXXIII, 23 February 1864, cols. 941-55. J. T. Hibbert (1824-1908) was Liberal MP for Oldham 1862-74 and 1877-86.

63 *Hansard*, CLXXV, 3 June 1864, cols. 1123-34. Anthony Ashley-Cooper (1801-85) was the 7th Earl of Shaftesbury. As Lord Ashley, he was Conservative MP for Woodstock 1826-30, for Dorchester 1830-1, for Dorset 1831-46 and for Bath 1847-51. An active and compassionate philanthropist, he was concerned with many social reforms, including working conditions in factories and mines, the condition of chimney sweeps, children in ragged schools and housing for the poor.

64 Lord Eldon, *The English Reports*, 32, Chancery XII, p. 1080, Attorney General

v. Whiteley, quoted Balls, 'Origins of the Endowed Schools Act', pp. 1, 9. Lord Eldon (1751–1838) was Lord Chief Justice 1799–1806 and Lord Chancellor 1807–27.

65 Bamford, *Rise of the Public Schools*, p. 168.

66 Balls, 'Origins of the Endowed Schools Act', p. 7.

67 See Jasper Ridley, *Lord Palmerston*, London, 1970, p. 84.

68 Some notable examples were at Bingley in 1820, Nottingham in 1833, Bury St Edmunds in 1839, Berkhamstead in 1841 and 1864, Bristol in 1842 and 1860, Leeds in 1847, Wolverhampton and Norwich in 1858 and Manchester in 1867. See Balls, 'Origins of the Endowed Schools Act', pp. 7–43.

69 The 'information' was filed against the Trustees and headmaster, the Rev. Dr. Hartley, of Bingley Grammar School, by three local inhabitants. See *The English Reports*, 37, Chancery XVII, Attorney General *v.* Hartley, pp. 666–7, quoted Balls, 'Origins of the Endowed Schools Act', pp. 9–10. The case was significant because the Master of the Rolls, Sir John Romilly, accepted the legal uniformity of the endowed grammar schools, including the schools later considered by the Clarendon Commission, although he thought that the grammar schools with no boarding facilities catered for the 'lower class' and those with boarding facilities catered for the 'higher classes'. Sir John Romilly, Master of the Rolls, *The English Reports*, 54, Rolls Court VII, pp. 330–1, quoted Balls, 'Origins of the Endowed Schools Act', pp. 14–15.

70 Hollis, *Eton*, p. 8.

71 A. Fox, *Harrow*, London, 1911, p. 3.

72 Oldham, *A History of Shrewsbury School*, pp. 112–13.

73 Hollis, *Eton*, p. 223.

74 For Shrewsbury scholarship, see Chapter 5, pp. 149–51. For critical comments on Eton's scholarship, see M. J. Higgins, 'Eton College', *Edinburgh Review*, 113, April 1861, p. 419 and 'Public schools—report of the Commission', p. 657.

75 Hollis, *Eton*, p. 223.

76 Edward Thring (1821–87) was headmaster of Uppingham 1853–87. When he arrived at the school there were only 25 boys there, but he 'rescued the school from obscurity and transformed it into one of the most progressive of public schools'. G. W. Roderick & M. D. Stephens, *Education and Industry in the Nineteenth Century*, London, 1978, p. 36. See also G. R. Parkin, *Edward Thring*, London, 1898, W. F. Rawnsley, *Edward Thring, Maker of Uppingham School*, London, 1926 and G. Hoyland, *The Man who Made a School: Thring of Uppingham*, London, 1946.

77 For numbers at Shrewsbury, see Shrosbree, 'Origins and influence of the Clarendon Commission', Appendix VIII. At Eton in 1834, the year of Keate's resignation, numbers fell from 627 to 486 and no new boys entered the school. See Hollis, *Eton*, pp. 222–3.

78 *Shrewsbury School 1800–1851* in *Paget's Scrap Book*.

79 Trollope, 'Public schools', p. 479.

80 Trollope, 'Public schools', pp. 482–3.

81 *The Times*, 16 February 1861, p. 9.

82 Hollis, *Eton*, p. 224. Edward Craven Hawtrey (1789–1862) was headmaster of Eton 1834–52.

83 Hollis, *Eton*, p. 224.

84 Hollis, *Eton*, p. 224.

85 Hollis, *Eton*, p. 224.

86 See Bamford, *The Rise of the Public Schools*, pp. 127–9 and Hollis, *Eton*, p. 274.

87 The *Clarendon Report* gave Eton's annual income from endowments as £20,000 of which one third was distributed amongst the Provost and Fellows. The income of Harrow from endowments, by comparison, was £1,500. *Clarendon Report*, I, pp. 4–5. See also Higgins, 'Eton College', pp. 415–17; Sidgwick, 'Eton', pp. 293–6; M. J. Higgins, 'A second letter to the Editor of the "Cornhill Magazine" from Paterfamilias', *Cornhill Magazine*, 2, December 1860, p. 646.

88 See Introduction, Note 12.

89 See Chapter 3, p. 86.

90 Rt Hon. M. E. G. Duff, 'First rectorial address at Aberdeen, 1867', *Some Brief Comments on Passing Events made between February 4th 1858 and October*

5th 1881, Madras, 1884, p. 235.
91 Grant Duff, 'A plea for rational education, 1871', *Some Brief Comments on Passing Events*, pp. 256–8.
92 Hollis, *Eton*, pp. 249–50.
93 Hollis, *Eton*, p. 250.
94 Bamford, *The Rise of the Public Schools*, p. 62.
95 Kennedy, *Notes on Public Education*, p. 2.
96 See *Shrewsbury School Accounts, 1864*, Bailiff's Bundles No. 122.
97 See J. Lawson & H. Silver, *A Social History of Education in England*, London, 1973, pp. 249–50.
98 Westminster, Eton, Winchester, Charterhouse, Harrow and Rugby. See Bamford, *The Rise of the Public Schools*, p. x.
99 Grant Duff at Elgin on 27 October 1864, in *The Times*, 29 October 1864, p. 6.
100 Sir George Lewis, *Hansard*, CLXIII, 4 June 1861, col. 546.

2 The public schools as a public issue

The criticisms of Eton that appeared in the periodicals in 1860–1 were, in some ways, no different from the common criticisms of the public schools in the years before the Clarendon Commission. What made these criticisms so damaging was that they were concerned with money and appeared in national periodicals of great influence. The extravagance and irresponsibility of Eton contrasted starkly with the social and educational needs of the poor and the assertive financial acumen of the middle classes, who were concerned with their own educational needs. An awareness of educational and technological change in Europe, fostered by these same national periodicals, made the preoccupation with the classics, at Eton and all public schools, seem anachronistic and silly. The indifference to change, in particular the neglect of English and science, seemed almost perverse when Europe provided both an example and a challenge. In its extravagance and its wealth, its poorly taught classics and its lordly indifference to change, Eton appeared to be almost a caricature of the public schools and a startling example of where success might lead an endowed grammar school and public charity.

By long-established custom the public schools had financed their activities by charging fees not sanctioned in their statutes— by admitting and charging non-foundation boys, by charging tuition fees, by charging for extra subjects or by admitting boarders. Usually, the money went directly to the headmaster or masters, often not appearing in any school accounts. By 1861 every public school had an unofficial income, a 'black economy' of unofficial fees and payments, which sometimes—as at Eton particularly—far outweighed the official income from endowments and which was regulated only by the traditions of the school or the wishes of the headmaster. At Eton, for example, a master received £45 per annum for his regular work for the school: this was the only fixed part of his income.

Unofficially, however, he received much more from private payments. This amounted to £600–£900 per annum for a master without a boarding house, and £1,000–£2,000 per annum for a master with a boarding house. His formal work for the school might produce only about one-twelfth of his income, although it might take up most of his time.[1] This was an extreme case, as masters at Eton were paid rather less by the school than masters elsewhere, whose normal annual payment was about £150–£200 a year. The masters' official income from endowments could vary greatly from school to school, a fact which was later to attract criticism in the *Clarendon Report*. Some of the highest salaries were at Rugby, where in 1862 the thirteen classics masters received an average of just over £1,000 each, the highest payment being £1,617.[2]

The unofficial financial arrangements had often existed for decades. Over the centuries the original endowments sometimes proved insufficient for the proper maintenance of the school; private bequests were by their nature not renewable and governments did not augment royal or state-funded endowments to keep pace with inflation. The rising demand for education, and the large number of parents who could pay fees, made potential private finance available to fund the schools' growth beyond the original endowments and the founders' intentions. If the extra money obtained unofficially had been used for the benefit of the schools or the pupils, there would have been less comment, although there were obvious dangers in and disadvantages to such a system. Private funding could so change and dominate a school that the purpose of the original endowment could be lost. The interests of foundation boys could become marginal and little-regarded. Private funding might pay little regard to public interest or the pious intentions of a school's founder. Masters paid from the foundation could become dependent on unofficial private incomes from the pupils and a large, or major, part of a school's income might not pass through the accounts. This unofficial system was ruthlessly exposed to public criticism by the publication of articles about Eton which contained detailed accounts of its affairs, particularly of its finances, which showed that the unofficial, private enterprise system had been used not to promote education but to enrich individuals and that the rising value of public endowments had been used for private profit.

The first of these articles by Matthew Higgins appeared in the *Cornhill Magazine* in May 1860, December 1860 and March 1861, under the pen-name of 'Paterfamilias'.[3] Another article, by Henry Sidgwick, appeared in *Macmillan's Magazine* for February 1861[4] and yet another article appeared in the *Edinburgh Review* for April 1861.[5] These articles aroused some public indignation and made it impossible for the government to ignore the urgent need to reform public school finances. After the publication of these articles, some form of inquiry was inevitable, for the articles accused the masters and Fellows of Eton of misappropriating money that should have been used for the benefit of the school, and on a considerable scale. Sidgwick, for example, estimated the total income of a Fellow to be about £1,000 'for doing a minimum of work; and it may be doubted whether this minimum might not most advantageously be dispensed with'.[6]

The *Edinburgh Review* went further.

> That the statutes of such a foundation as Eton College should be carried out to the letter in the present day is, we admit, neither possible nor desirable; but it is both possible and desirable that the enormous revenues willed by an English king for the promotion of education . . . should not be illegally diverted from their original destination into the pockets of a small number of individuals who are not entitled to them.[7]

These articles were the immediate cause of the Clarendon Commission. Not only did they accuse the staff at public schools of financial greed and misappropriation, but by concentrating upon Eton—where the abuse was greatest—they made it impossible for Old Etonians in Parliament, who formed by far the greatest number of public school men there, to object to an inquiry without appearing to condone financial impropriety.[8] The concentration of the criticism on financial irregularities made political objections impossible and partly explains why the Public Schools Bills met with such determined attempts at obstruction or defeat, while the Clarendon Commission was appointed without opposition.

The periodicals were also at the height of their influence. The relationship between the periodicals and leading politicians was close and, in the absence of newspapers with mass circulations, which were only to come later in the century, provided an important channel of communication between the government, leading politicians and the growing middle-class electorate. The Reform Act of 1832, while not creating a mass electorate, had begun the process of extending legitimate political involvement beyond the traditional circles of the great aristocratic families and their followers. Throughout the 1850s and 1860s, the further reform of the franchise was a major political issue and the literacy rate in England, already high by European standards at the beginning of the nineteenth century, continued to rise.[9] One consequence of this high literacy rate was the creation of a large new market for reading material, including a demand for serious news and comment on current affairs.

This demand had been evident earlier in the century in the rapid growth of serious provincial newspapers, which trebled in number between 1780 and 1830, from about fifty to over a hundred and fifty.[10] The national press, however, apart from the traditional newspapers such as *The Times*, the *Morning Post* and the *Morning Chronicle*, was dominated by the great periodicals such as the *Quarterly Review*, the *Edinburgh Review* and *Blackwood's Magazine*, whose influence on both politicians and public opinion was 'greater than all the provincial and national middle-class papers put together'.[11] To these could be added the newer periodicals like the *Cornhill Magazine* and *Macmillan's Magazine* which, although containing serious comment, added a more varied, literary, and entertaining style. The periodicals were the place where the 'great debate' took place and where the 'mind and imagination' of the nation were nourished.[12] What made these periodicals so influential at this time was that for a comparatively brief period they stood between two journalistic functions, benefitting temporarily from both. Traditionally, they were the house-magazines of the great established political parties, the family magazines of the literary, the influential and the great—particularly in London society. They were the magazines in which, for example, ministers could write defending their policies, knowing that their articles would be read by all those with national influence. The leading politicians wrote articles for these magazines, advised them, sometimes acted as editors and took care to present their own cases. Sir George Lewis, for example, who was Secretary for the Home Office in 1861 and who subsequently became Secretary of State for War in August 1861, was previously Editor of the *Edinburgh Review*. He resigned in 1855 when he succeeded Gladstone as Chancellor of the Exchequer, but renewed his connection with this periodical as a contributor when out of office again in 1858. Clarendon himself had close links with the periodicals and the press, particularly with the *Edinburgh Review*, which was regarded as the periodical of the Liberal Party.[13] The articles about the public schools, and in particular about Eton, which appeared in 1860 and 1861 were in periodicals with which the influential people in government and the most famous literary figures were intimately connected. Dickens, for example, edited *All the Year Round*, which first appeared in April 1859 and which had achieved a circulation of about 120,000 copies by its fifth weekly edition.[14]

It was this second function, that of mass communication, which gave the periodicals their particular influence at this time. Traditionally, the periodicals had been read by the kind of people by whom they were written—the great and influential in national and, particularly, in London society. The growth in circulation, particularly of the newer, more topical periodicals, meant that the discussion of current issues was carried to a far wider public than ever before—in the first instance to middle-class readers who read the periodicals themselves, and subsequently to the rest of the population by means of further discussion and reporting in the provincial press. Never before had the informative and detailed discussion of current events, of political and of educational issues, been brought to the whole of the electorate with such immediacy.

Aristocratic disquiet with the public schools was widespread but rarely expressed in print—perhaps because the school most criticised, Eton, inspired the most loyalty from those most influential. Disquiet was, however, common in letters, diaries and conversation. For example, Lord Stanley recorded in his diary the comments he heard during the winter of 1861–2 about the public schools and about Eton in particular. He recorded much disquiet about indecent practices, extravagance, drinking and gambling. One parent 'was warned against Eton, as the worst of all . . . but finds Harrow not much better'.[15] An awareness in aristocratic circles of these grave faults made outright opposition to any reform difficult. From an aristocratic point of view, it was politic to accept some measure of educational and administrative reform—tactfully, plausibly and skilfully arranged in the House of Lords—before the more

scandalous failings of the public schools became public knowledge through the periodicals and popular press. Perhaps it was
an unwritten aristocratic code of class loyalty, fostered in
the schools themselves, which prevented public expression of
this disquiet in the *Clarendon Report*, the Parliamentary debates
or the press, when it was so commonly expressed in private and
about such serious matters. The rather idealised discussions
which preceded legislation, the protracted and tedious proceedings in the Lords and this tacit reluctance of the aristocracy to
admit in public to the schools' faults all helped to prevent
public school reform from becoming a major matter of public
controversy, and so the implications of such arbitrary and
divisive legislation were never adequately discussed in the
periodicals or in the popular press.

The influence of the periodicals meant that reform was
inevitable, but the potential influence of the periodicals on the
middle-class electorate meant that reform was managed quietly,
to allay criticism, rather than opposed outright. Middle-class
criticism of the public schools extended to most endowed
grammar schools and the provision of education in general for
the middle classes. In 1861, reform of the public schools was
presented in Parliament as an essential prelude to the reform
of the other endowed grammar schools, and this met with
little comment. Not until after the Public Schools Acts did their
divisive consequences become apparent or the association of the
public schools with privilege become complete. The Radicals,
too, had little to say about public school reform—for similar,
but different political reasons. They realised that reform of
education for the poor could not take place without first
making provision for the middle classes upon whom their
political survival depended.[16] The drama and immediacy of
contemporary events—the turmoil in Europe, conflict and
civil war in America, the long struggle for political reform at
home—dominated men's minds and diverted the electorate
from serious consideration of the issues raised by public school
reform. Reform of Eton alone would have provoked damaging
criticisms of aristocratic privilege at any time, but the
importance of Eton to the privileged reformers in the Lords
and the national consequences of such separate legal consideration for the school were alike obscured from the electorate by
the camouflage provided by other, less important grammar

schools. The price of separate consideration for Eton was the creation of a separate, arbitrary category within which Eton could be included. The periodicals—like the middle classes and the Radicals, and perhaps for similar reasons—gave little thought to the consequences of such an arbitrary division between the public schools of the Clarendon Commission and the rest. It is arguable that, had the periodicals not raised the issue of public school reform when they did, and had Grant Duff not raised the issue in Parliament, that such separate consideration would have become immeasurably more difficult after the Reform Act of 1867 and that a later Parliament might have reformed all the endowed grammar schools together. The influence of the periodicals was perhaps sufficient to get the issue raised in Parliament, but not sufficient to prevent the management of reform in the interests of privilege.

The supremacy of the periodicals in the discussion of national issues was not to last and declined rapidly after the Reform Act of 1867 and the Education Acts of 1870 and 1902. New, national, large-circulation newspapers quickly became more important and after 1867 the electorate was no longer largely middle class. For a brief period between 1850 and 1870, however, the periodicals enabled the governing and influential few to communicate directly with the electorate, and the spread of literacy enabled those still outside the franchise to follow the debate. The influence of the periodicals at this time, in politics and in education, was the projection of London controversy, informed and influential, before a new national audience.

Clarendon himself had a long involvement with the press and the periodicals, in particular with the *Edinburgh Review*. In January 1855, for example, an article by Sir George Lewis appeared defending the government against much public criticism, including some from *The Times*, over the government's handling of the Crimean War. Sir George Lewis, who was editor of the *Edinburgh Review* at that time, was Clarendon's brother-in-law, a close political colleague and a trusted personal friend. Before publishing the article, he submitted it to Clarendon, who wrote for him a long commentary.[17] In November 1858, Lady Theresa Lewis wrote to Clarendon urging him to use his influence with the press after some critical articles had appeared in the *Saturday Review* about his recent visit to Compiègne.[18] Many such articles were written under pseudonyms or left unattributed, so that political leaders were often suspected of writing anonymously or of encouraging articles to be written on their behalf. Such suspicions were often well-founded when there were such close links as between the Liberal Party and the *Edinburgh Review* and between the *Quarterly Review* and the Conservative Party, and when leading politicians were, or had been, editors and contributors.[19] Clarendon's close association with the *Edinburgh Review*, particularly in its presentation of articles favourable to the unity of the Liberal Party, was important during the Derby–Disraeli administration of 1858-9 because the government was known to be considering a measure of Parliamentary reform which was a major policy issue within the Liberal Party, dividing the more traditional Whigs, like Palmerston, from the Radicals, like John Bright and Milner Gibson.[20] Clarendon was the man who, above all, handled the negotiations between the Liberal Party and the *Edinburgh Review* in its presentation of articles favourable to Liberal Party policy and party unity. The article about Eton in the *Edinburgh Review* of April 1861 must have been written with Clarendon's knowledge and approval, so that Clarendon himself helped to initiate the criticisms of Eton that led to the Royal Commission. For the Liberals, the reform of the public schools was a good issue to pursue: it did not threaten party unity, it was supported by public opinion, and it attacked, on irrefutable financial grounds, an institution associated with Conservative tradition and Tory politics. In its financial dealings, Eton could not be defended without appearing to condone greed and mismanagement; here was an issue where the Liberals could not lose and the Conservatives could not win.

The political circumstances of the time and the prominence of education in the discussion of national affairs made the disclosures about Eton a particular embarrassment for the school's supporters. Here was a school, patronised by the most wealthy and most influential in the land, which made a vast profit, squandered public money and produced only meagre academic results, while government money was being used with increasing care and economy in the provision of state aid for elementary schools. By 1860 the Education Department—although nominally under the control of the Privy Council—

was one of the largest government departments with a staff of 127 and a total budget of over £893,000.[21] This growth in government expenditure came under much Parliamentary and public criticism—partly because of philosophical or religious objections, but particularly for financial reasons in the search for government economies in the period after the Crimean War. This criticism, in turn, led to the introduction of the *Revised Code* in 1861, by which the size of a school's grant was made dependent mainly on its pupils' performance in three basic subjects.[22] Eton's wealth was immense and its academic record unremarkable, even in terms of its own narrow definitions of education and scholarship.

Along with the controversy over growing public expenditure on education, there was increasing concern amongst the middle classes that the government was subsidising a better education for the working classes than they themselves could afford or find—dependent as they were on fee-paying schools of various kinds or on the older-established endowed grammar schools, which were unevenly distributed and which often provided no more than an elementary education. In 1860 it was the education of the middle classes, especially secondary education, that seemed neglected and in need of reform. In Parliament, there were frequent attempts by politicians and petitioners to bring about some educational provision for the middle classes who 'complained that their children were being displaced by those who were getting, at the expense of the state, a better education than they could provide for their own children'.[23] The agitation for the better provision of schools for the middle classes continued until 1861, when it was given increased urgency by the report of the Newcastle Commission.[24] In July 1861, during discussion of the *Newcastle Report*, Lord Brougham argued that 'the middle-class was the class most neglected of all in respect to the means of a good education' and suggested that there were about 120,000 middle-class children whose education was not given sufficient consideration. On previous occasions, he had presented 120 petitions, signed by 40,000 people, asking for better middle-class schools and a system of government inspection.[25] No doubt these middle-class protests would have led to an eventual inquiry into all the endowed schools, whether there had been previous criticism of the public schools or not. The increasing importance of educational qualifications for entry into the professions and government service made such an inquiry, and subsequent reform, inevitable.[26] Such an inquiry was an enormous task, however, fraught with religious and political pitfalls for any government that attempted it.[27] The articles about Eton and other public schools by the nature of the allegations demanded an urgent response, but it was less onerous and politically less dangerous to begin an inquiry into Eton and the schools associated with it, than to attempt an inquiry into all the endowed grammar schools, although this was to follow soon after with the Taunton Commission. Although the government thus eased its political difficulties by selecting only some endowed grammar schools for the Clarendon Commission, it did this by accepting and emphasising social divisions within the endowed schools— schools which *together* provided the basis of a secondary school system and which had a common legal identity. The public schools, no doubt, would have attempted to gain exemption from any general inquiry and any government control, but this would have been difficult. Grant Duff himself originally asked for an inquiry into all endowed schools, and claims for exemption on grounds of superior scholarship would have been difficult to sustain, except perhaps for Shrewsbury which, of all the public schools, probably remained closest, in size and social background, to its origins as a 'free grammar school'.[28]

What did require urgent inquiry and reform was the public schools' curriculum which, in its almost exclusive concentration on classical scholarship and its studied neglect of English language, English literature and science, appeared increasingly contrary to the 'spirit of the age'[29] and became increasingly difficult to defend at a time of rich creativity in literature and rapid innovation in science and technology, not just in Britain but throughout Europe. The schools blamed Oxford and Cambridge for not encouraging scientific studies and the Universities blamed the schools for giving only limited and elementary instruction in science. While it is true that both the public schools and the Universities faced some practical legal and financial difficulties in introducing science, the most fundamental difficulty in both schools and Universities was that the men in authority shared a common classical culture and the attitudes that usually accompanied it—a conservative love for classical education, a gentlemanly mistrust of studies associated with trade and engineering, a fixed and sometimes theological disdain for the scientific and a studied disregard of European progress. In the public schools, the practical difficulties came from the terms of their ancient foundations and the narrow legal definition of a grammar school curriculum, but these legal restrictions proved a barrier to scientific education only because Classicists in the schools exploited them to obstruct and delay the introduction of new subjects of all kinds, including science. At Eton, as elsewhere, the strict letter of the law was waived for private profit and could have been waived, more commendably, for educational reform. Nor was there any shortage of Science teachers or of scientific books. There may have been a national shortage of science teachers, but it is difficult to believe that such a small number of such well-known schools would have had any difficulty in recruiting suitable staff. University College, London after 1826 and King's College, London after 1828 provided advanced courses in science and engineering and many Englishmen followed advanced courses in Europe, particularly in Germany.[30] After 1845 the Davy College of Practical Chemistry provided advanced courses which were modelled on those of Europe, under a Professor of Chemistry brought from Bonn and with the active support of the Prince Consort.[31] In 1851, the Museum of Economic Geography, originally founded in 1839, became the School of Mines and of Science Applied to the Arts and provided a wide range of science subjects applicable to mining. By 1851 there were four colleges in London offering advanced courses in science and, after 1851, Owens College in Manchester began to provide courses in the north of England.[32] In the twenty years before the Clarendon Commission, there must have been an abundance of science teachers had the public schools chosen to employ them. The science teachers who were rare were those who had been educated at public schools or at the Universities of Oxford and Cambridge.[33]

There were many Science books available, too, had the schools chosen to use them. The text-books written by Classical scholars like Dr Kennedy of Shrewsbury[34] are better known today because they did not date and were used in grammar schools throughout the country for many years, but science text-books, although now outdated and forgotten, were then freely available. The humblest working man in the remotest part of England had easy access to scientific text-books and the Department of Science and Art itself provided financial help for science teaching after 1852.[35] It was not the shortage of teachers or of text-books that prevented the development of science education in the public schools, but the reluctance of Classical scholars to consider Science worthy of serious scholarship. Some well-known schools did teach Science seriously and had no difficulty in finding staff and text-books. Such schools managed to achieve high academic standards in both Classics and Science. The Devonshire Commission later commended a number of schools for their Science teaching[36] and three schools—Cheltenham, Marlborough and the City of London School—were included in the *Clarendon Report* on the initiative of the Commissioners because they were successful schools where modern subjects, including Science, were seriously taught and given an important place in the school curriculum. The purpose of the Commissioners in persuading these schools to take part in their inquiries was clearly to show what could be done.[37] The City of London School, in particular, was arguably one of the most progressive schools in the country and taught Science through lectures, experiments and an organised system of work-books.[38]

The Universities of Oxford and Cambridge provided only limited opportunities for academic advancement in science and, to that extent, did not encourage the study of science in schools. The number of science subjects taught was small, the facilities limited and the Colleges reluctant to support science teaching.[39] The great expension of science teaching and research at the two older Universities did not come until after the Devonshire Commission—between 1872 and the end of the century—but there were opportunities for the study of science at Oxford and Cambridge before 1860.[40] The lecturers and professors were not numerous but their classes were small. The facilities and resources provided were small compared to those provided for the study of classics,[41] but what was provided was under-used so that schools would have had no difficulty in finding places at Oxford or Cambridge for science students. For students willing to travel to London or Scotland, there was available a university education in science that was comparable to the best in Europe.[42] The public schools chose not to use the opportunities that were there for science education, even when English society around them was transformed by scientific and technological change. At Shrewsbury, when the school's classical reputation was being established by Dr Butler and Dr Kennedy, the school was only fifteen miles away from a major European area of scientific and technological innovation centred around Ironbridge in the Shropshire coalfield.[43] By the 1770s, the leading local ironmasters were 'deeply concerned with scientific investigation for its own sake'[44] and a number of them had their own laboratories in which they conducted experiments in physics, industrial chemistry and metallurgy.[45] Little hint of these scientific activities, so apparent in Shropshire and so important for both local and national prosperity, may be found in the school curriculum of the time.[46] The importance in Shropshire of scientific, technological and commercial innovation and the school's determined preoccupation with the classics posed a contradiction to which the school's headmasters seemed oblivious, even though the school governors included local men with commercial and industrial experience.[47] These men disappeared from the governing body after the Public Schools Acts, to be replaced largely by men of distinguished classical scholarship, including Kennedy himself.[48]

The classics had achieved their pre-eminence in the English grammar schools by an accidental combination of legal and historical circumstances. Often founded by, or as a replacement for, ecclesiastical institutions and at a time when the education provided by the Church was the traditional education for government service, it was not surprising that their original statutes should have placed such importance on Latin and Greek and that this emphasis should have continued throughout the eighteenth century. Latin was still the language of international scholarship long after it ceased to be the language of government and administration, and the classical inspiration of eighteenth-century culture made classics arguably a necessary part of any scholarly education. The French Revolution of 1789 perhaps marked a symbolic point at which classics ceased to be a uniform and underlying basis of European culture. Philosophical, literary and political development, before and after 1789, was expressed in national languages and it is inconceivable that the work of Chaucer, Shakespeare, Thomas Paine, Edmund Burke, Blake or Wordsworth could have been written in Latin. Even Dr Johnson, the conservative epitome of the classical literary tradition, had a dictionary of English as one of his most memorable and lasting achievements. In Europe, the political events of the French Revolution and of the Napoleonic Wars, the settlements of 1815, and the revolutions of 1830 and 1848 had all intensified the importance of national languages as an expression of patriotism. In the German states, the Italian states, in Hungary and in Poland, the national language was the basis of claims for national sovereignty and the test of territorial integrity.[49] In Europe, the study of the Classics survived in 1860 as a scholarly pursuit rather than, as in England, the basis of public education. Moreover, it was clear in Europe that a knowledge of the classics was not a prerequisite for scholarly distinction or intellectual advance. In no European country was the importance of the national language greater than in Germany, and no country enjoyed such an international reputation for scholarship.[50]

The neglect of English language and literature at the public schools in the 1850s was indeed astonishing, even within an English context, both in its totality and its obstinacy. The attitude was characterised by the famous answer given by Edward Balston, the headmaster of Eton, to the Clarendon Commission's question about what measures were taken to 'keep up' English (and French) at Eton. 'There are none at present,' said Balston, 'except through the ancient languages'.[51] The public school headmasters could argue, of course, that the translation of Latin and Greek required a knowledge of English grammar, but it was impossible to defend in this way the almost total neglect of English literature. At Shrewsbury, for example, which was generally regarded as one of the more progressive public schools and which taught some French and German, some modern history and some modern geography throughout the 1850s, no English literature appeared formally until 1872; Shakespeare did not appear until 1880 and then it was *Hamlet* for the sixth form only.[52] This general neglect of English literature was the more obvious in that it included the whole of English literature, not just contemporary works, and that contemporary English literature was itself going through an astonishing period of creativity in the years before the Clarendon Commission. In 1859 alone, for example, Dickens re-issued *A Tale of Two Cities* in book form after its successful serialisation in his own periodical *All the Year Round. The Virginians* by

Thackeray was completed in serial form, George Eliot completed *Adam Bede*, Tennyson completed the first four *Idylls of the King* and the first edition of Fitzgerald's translation of *The Rubaiyat of Omar Khayyam* was published. John Stuart Mill's *Essay on Liberty* was published, as was *On the Origins of Species by means of Natural Selection or the Preservation of Favoured Races in the Struggle for Life* by Charles Darwin.[53]

This neglect was partly the result of the contemporary view that the novel, in retrospect so important in Victorian literature, was a trivial art-form meant primarily for entertainment. Not all Victorian novels seemed trivial, even to the Victorians, however, and this argument does not explain the almost complete absence of any contemporary English literature from the public school curriculum—even when it was written by authors like Anthony Trollope, with some pretence to literary merit and from a conservative viewpoint. Some Victorian novelists, Dickens for example, would have inevitably been unwelcome in a conservative public school curriculum—his concern for and his love of common humanity would have appeared both vulgar and radical. His exposure of the cruelty of public institutions must have seemed profoundly revolutionary in such circles. Yet up until the Clarendon Commission, and for many years after, English literature—even of a traditional kind or of a conservative viewpoint—was almost totally absent from the English public schools. Their cultural isolation from English language and literature, later intensified by the development of a distinctive pronunciation and vocabulary, was equalled only by their increasing geographical isolation. This cultural isolation from the national language and literature is so remarkable and was so long sustained that it cannot be entirely explained by the legal constraints of school statutes or by contemporary arguments about the cultural value of the classics. Partly, no doubt, it was sustained by class pride in the gentlemanly attributes of an education completely useless for anything but cultural or scholarly purposes and which, if pursued only to the common mediocre level, was useless even for that. Yet even this can hardly explain the almost total absence of English language and literature from the public school curriculum.

There are perhaps two political explanations—one which would have been apparent to contemporaries and one which would have not. For educated men of the time, it was apparent that in Europe the study of the national language was linked with nationalism and liberalism. The liberty that was claimed in the revolutions of 1848, for nations and for individuals, was based on a new linguistic definition of nationality for, 'the politically minded cannot feel truly free except in a state which they acknowledge as their own: that is, in their own national state: and the nationalisms which in 1848 entered the political arena, and held it during the next one hundred years were primarily linguistic'.[54] The force of this new nationalism, asserting both national liberty and democracy within newly-created national boundaries, was to sweep away both arbitrary boundaries and established ruling classes, continuing the European revolution which had begun in France in 1789. From the 'year of revolutions' in 1848 until 1870, when the unification of Germany and Italy was complete, the force of linguistic nationalism seemed to threaten the basis of traditional, conservative, hierarchical, territorial society throughout Europe, just as the French Revolution had done sixty years earlier.[55]

In Europe, the new nationalism was chiefly concerned with pressing the claims of one modern language against another, but the link between the classics (particularly Latin) and an older, more conservative European society was everywhere evident. In Hungary, for example, 'the language of State and Parliament was Latin, and so remained till the nineteenth century, when a growing Magyar linguistic nationalism transformed the nature of the Hungarian state'.[56] The attachment to the classics was an instinctive conservative response to a changing and tumultuous Europe, the assertion of old certainties from the 'Age of Reason'. England had no revolution but there were obvious similarities between political events in England and those in Europe during the 1850s and 1860s—particularly the demand for more democratic institutions—and the study of national languages in Europe was everywhere associated with individual liberty and revolution. The classics were the languages of reason, order and hierarchy, while English was the voice of the common man, whose liberty Dr Arnold dismissed as 'neither reasonable nor Christian but essentially barbarian'.[57] The contrast between this view and that of Mazzini, that 'liberty is sacred, as the individual is sacred',[58] illustrates the political conflict between English Conservatism and European radicalism.

In Europe, national languages were associated with revolution, nationalism and democracy; the classics were associated with tradition, conservatism and rule by a landed gentry, often of foreign origin. Antipathy towards the classics was characteristic of Italian nationalism, even in Rome itself, during the struggle for unification and independence.[59]

In England, where the struggles of a nation against a foreign landed aristocracy were a matter of remote history, a sense of nationality was too established and assured to need any further assertion through the English language. The English landed gentry were so assuredly English that they could afford to cultivate the distinctive classical culture of the English gentleman that was, with its nuances and overtones, impenetrable by the outsider. The need for such a distinctive culture was greater in England than in Europe because there were no other barriers, except wealth, between them and other classes, and even their wealth could be equalled in London or the great manufacturing towns. Nor had the English landed gentry any distinctive capabilities within English society. Their political supremacy was threatened in 1832, undermined in 1835 in local affairs and challenged directly by the subsequent struggle for political reform in the 1860s. Except for a few gifted and eccentric men like Tennyson, they made little contribution to the artistic and cultural life of the country, their literary aspirations being expressed in a classical obscurity of which Lord Derby's translation of Homer affords an example.[60] They took little part in trade or industry, although they might invest in order to buy more land. The army, into which many of them went, was an institution on the fringes of English society and was not the nation in arms, as in France, or the embodiment of the state, as in Prussia. The difficulties of the Crimean War must have had a significant effect on public opinion for the landed gentry had long associated the public schools with Britain's military success. The story of Dr Keate, headmaster of Eton, dining in Paris with Guards officers after the battle of Waterloo and congratulating them on their discipline, which they had learned at Eton, is well known. The public schools' supporters claimed credit for the Duke of Wellington's successes in much the same way that Hoby, the Duke's bootmaker, attributed British victories to the Duke's comfortable boots.[61] The Crimean War, which brought credit to English courage, brought discredit upon those responsible for directing and managing the war so that even in their one chosen profession, in which the qualities and character of the English gentleman were most sought and admired, the landed gentry retained little claim to superior knowledge or greater merit. The greatest and only unchallenged function of the landed gentry was to provide the ideal of the English gentleman. Much of the country aspired to this ideal through the acquisition of wealth, or land or of the appropriate education in the classics. Later in the century, when the public schools' emphasis on the classics became unfashionable and impossible to maintain, the schools' emphasis on accent, manner and slang provided an alternative hallmark of an exclusive, gentleman's education.[62] The demands for the reform of the public schools' classical curriculum corresponded with the agitation for political reform that ended the rule of the landed gentry and led to the Reform Act of 1867. The passage of the Public Schools Bills between 1865 and 1868 was delayed and endangered by the political conflict and confusion that accompanied the Reform Act, so the circumstances of political and educational reform were inseparable.

The political importance of the classics, the gentleman's education and the neglect of English may be further explained by modern political sociology. Men from the public schools, and particularly from Eton, formed a political élite at the time of the Clarendon Commission—an élite that was not dependent on knowledge, or ability, or democratic approval, but was buttressed and kept in place by a restrictive educational system, in which any equality of opportunity was stifled by the classical requirements of the public school system. It is only infrequently and accidentally that a sociological model conforms closely to historical reality, but the public school political élite of 1861 conformed closely to the 'sponsored mobility' élite of Ralph Turner.[63] In terms of this model, the classics—and thus public school education—had the important function of providing both governing and restricting qualifications for élite membership.

The 'sponsored mobility' model for élite education is one in which

> the criteria for élite membership are only fully understood by those who are already members. The aim of the system is not so much the creation of a larger, well-educated élite with a wide range of skills as the filling of limited vacancies in the established élite. The élite

'sponsors' new members by determining the qualifications for membership—ability at classical languages, mastering legal precedents or Chinese
calligraphy. The authorities in the art assess the performance of the
aspirants. Training for élite positions is highly specialized and involves
the selection and segregation of the potential leaders at an early age.
Those not believed capable of attaining the qualifications laid down
are hived off to schools where opportunities for education in the
requisite skills are few, and instead training is given in the less influential
and prestigious functions.[64]

A knowledge of the classics was an ideal qualification for
élite membership because it was virtually impossible to obtain
this knowledge outside an institution dominated by élite
members and élitist ideas. A good classical education took a
long time to acquire and was available, in general, only to
members of a leisured class that had risen above the necessity
of work. A classical education was of no obvious practical value
and the investment such an education represented in time and
money bought little that was helpful to the individual, in
occupational terms, or of use to the country, in economic terms.
What a good classical education did was to confer or confirm
the status of a man as an English gentleman. The requirement
for a classical qualification made it virtually impossible for a
poor but able man to achieve entry to this élite by natural
ability and through private study. The success of so many such
people in science and engineering affords a striking illustration
of the restrictive nature of classical education.[65] The 'less
influential and prestigious functions' of Turner's model are an
apt description of the 'modern' or 'commercial' subjects that
some public schools, like Shrewsbury, made half-hearted
attempts to provide,[66] and which flourished in less influential
and less prestigious schools. The irrelevance of the classics to
'the spirit of the times' or to scientific and economic progress
was an advantage to a public school élite; a knowledge of
science or success in business could be gained by natural ability
and life's experience, but a knowledge of the classics remained
the characteristic of a gentleman's expensive education. The
classics fulfilled the same sociological function in Victorian
England as calligraphy in ancient China—a device to regulate
and limit entry into a governing élite.

The description of public school education as an élitist
activity is not necessarily critical. Traditional Tory philosophy,

with its view of society as a hierarchy, naturally implied an élitist view of government in which 'the wiser, the more expert, and the more opulent conduct, and by conducting enlighten and protect the weaker, the less knowing and the less provided with the goods of fortune'.[67] In Tory philosophy the governing élite did not have any innate superior abilities but was formed by being brought up from childhood in 'favourable circumstances'.[68] This 'Old Whig' philosophy of the eighteenth century formed Tory views in the nineteenth,[69] and Burke's description of how the governing élite should be formed was strikingly reminiscent of the common defence of the public schools—that the merit of the public schools lay not in their examination results but in the character of those who came from them, who were 'bred in a place of estimation to see nothing low and sordid', who were 'habituated in the pursuit of honour and duty' and who formed 'a *natural* aristocracy, without which there is no nation'.[70] Even the geographical move from the crowded towns to the neighbouring countryside, which many public schools attempted, thus had its justification in Tory political philosophy.

Such a '*natural* aristocracy', which the public schools claimed to produce and which was, in any case, the product of most unnatural circumstances and a highly specialised education, was increasingly difficult to justify in the 1850s as public education spread and the extension of the franchise continued to be a national political issue. Even the Conservative Party had to base its claim to govern on public, though not yet popular, support and the classics had to be defended on educational grounds. This became increasingly difficult as the importance of more modern subjects, like science and engineering, became apparent, particularly in the light of educational developments in the rest of Europe.

In Italy, for example, the Vice-President of the Council of Public Instruction, Signor Matteucci, presented a report to the Italian government in 1864 which covered 'the whole field of education, higher, secondary and elementary' and suggested improvements 'in all directions'.[71] In Holland, the primary schools, which had been established by law in 1806 under the Grand Pensionary Schimmelpenninck, were re-established in 1857 on an unsectarian basis and secondary education was established in 1863.[72] The attempts at educational reform in

England were part of a European movement, for many English reformers attempted to bring into England what they thought was best in European developments. Matthew Arnold, for example, who was from 1851 an Inspector of Schools for the Committee of the Privy Council, in 1861 produced reports on education in France, Holland and Switzerland.[73] In 1863 and 1864, *Macmillan's Magazine* published a long three-part article by Matthew Arnold, entitled 'A French Eton', about education in France.[74]

The comparison with Europe continued to provoke discussion throughout the period between the publication of the *Clarendon Report* and the Public Schools Acts, particularly in view of European progress in science and engineering and the political events in Europe which led to the defeat of Austria in 1866, of France in 1970 and eventually to German unification.[75] The reform of the public schools, and of education in general, was advocated from a European point of view and within the context of comparisons with Europe which rarely showed English schools, of any kind, in a favourable light. Many of the men associated with the Clarendon Commission were either closely involved with European affairs or had been educated in Europe. Both Granville and Clarendon himself had gained much of their informal education in Europe, and both were closely involved in foreign affairs.[76] Grant Duff, who proposed the motion in the Commons for the appointment of the Commission in 1861, had travelled extensively in Europe, wrote books and articles on European affairs and had many European friends who were eminent in education.[77] Even Henry Reeve, editor of the *Edinburgh Review* in 1861 when the critical and crucial article about Eton was published, had been educated in Geneva from the age of fifteen and had associated, as a young man, with prominent French intellectuals in Paris.[78] Although the appointment of the Clarendon Commission was inspired by European experience, the implementation of the *Clarendon Report* was not, being, as it was, left to MPs and peers who came overwhelmingly from public schools and who represented the schools' traditional interests. This was particularly so in the House of Lords and the Lords' committees, where the Public Schools Bills were most exhaustively discussed and delayed. In the long progress of the Public Schools Bills through Parliament between 1864 and 1872, the European inspiration for curricular reform was obscured by traditional respect for the autonomy of the public schools and the authority of their headmasters. The European inspiration, which stressed a modern curriculum of service to the country and a secondary school system organised rationally for national needs, was finally lost in the interminable wrangling, between the schools and the Public School Commissioners, about the details of school statutes. From the European point of view, the school curriculum was too important to be left to headmasters, since national progress depended on a willingness to accept new areas of study. In England, the schools' reluctance to change and the headmasters' unwillingness to question the place of the classics in public school education continued for many years after the Clarendon Commission.

The public schools' neglect of science was almost impossible to defend on educational grounds. There was no substitute for science in the curriculum, as the classics were supposed to be a substitute for English, and it was evident that scientific education was a matter of great national importance. In many other schools, science was already well established; it had a growing academic respectability but was almost totally 'excluded from the education of the higher classes' in the public schools at the time of the Clarendon Commission.[79] At most schools, some science teaching was sometimes available, but in a casual, irregular and optional manner. Often, as at Eton, Harrow and Rugby in the early nineteenth century, science teaching took the form of optional, occasional lectures by visiting scientists.[80] At Eton and Rugby, these lectures became more regular in the 1850s, and the first compulsory science lectures at Winchester began in 1857 as a result of the *Oxford Commission Report* of 1852. At Rugby, where science had perhaps made most progress as a result of the arrival of William Sharp in 1849, and subsequently through the work of his successors, there was still little encouragement for this subject and in 1861 'only the most modest start on a science curriculum had been made'.[81] No room could be found at the school for the work and experiments were carried out in the cloakroom of the Town Hall down the road, with the apparatus locked up in two cases at night.[82] The subject was taught by J. M. Wilson who, although an eminent scientist, was employed as a Mathematics master and taught science for only four hours a week.[83]

Attempts had been made before the Clarendon Commission to call attention to the lack of science teaching in the public schools, but the ten years before 1861 had seen events that made both science, and other applied engineering subjects, matters of public concern. The Great Exhibition of 1851 began this process by demonstrating that other countries, notably Germany and the USA, had engineering skills and an industrial capacity at least equal to those of Britain. The years after 1851 saw increasing imports of mass-produced goods, particularly from Germany and the USA, and competition from other countries in world markets. Three examples of products from the USA which were imported into British markets were the sewing machine, the revolver and the mechanical reaper. In 1852 the American firm of Colt established a factory in England to make revolvers, using American machinery, which much impressed British engineers. Sir John Anderson, who visited the factory, commented that it was 'impossible to go through that works without coming out a better engineer'.[84] In 1853 George Wallis, an official of the Department of Art and Science, and Joseph Whitworth, a prominent engineer and industrialist, went to the New York Industrial Exhibition, visited American factories and were impressed by the machine tool industry. In their report, they drew attention to the practical nature of education in America which was 'fundamental to its industrial growth'.[85] The need for both elementary education and technical training for the working classes was evident and became increasingly important as the century progressed. The *Report of the Select Committee on Scientific Education*[86] which resulted from the Paris Exhibition of 1867 at which British goods 'were beaten in everything',[87] was influential in securing support for Forster's Education Bill of 1870 which was, as Forster argued, a necessary preliminary to better technical education.[88] The campaign for science education by men like T. H. Huxley throughout the 1850s, the publication of Darwin's *Origin of Species* in 1859 and the appearance of Herbert Spencer's *Education* in 1861 all promoted public discussion about science education.[89] The neglect of science in the public schools was seen as important not because they were required to produce scientists—although they might—but because public school men controlled national policy and because the public schools 'set the standards of education generally'.[90] The public schools' traditional assertions that they were both 'public' and 'national' made these responsibilities difficult to evade.

Public criticism of their curriculum received Royal support after the Great Exhibition of 1851, when the Prince Consort publicly and enthusiastically associated himself with the cause of science education, following a Royal tradition that extended back at least as far as Charles II and the foundation of the Royal Society. He knew about German education, the importance of science for national economic development and the need to establish science education on a firm and respected basis. Yet his reforms at Cambridge University met with protracted opposition and, by the time of his death in 1861, little had been done at either Oxford or Cambridge to improve science teaching, although an Honours school in Natural Sciences had been introduced at Oxford in 1850 and at Cambridge in 1851. His interest in science achieved as little in the public schools as it had in the Universities. This was particularly true at Eton, where he was a frequent visitor and which had a close association with the Royal Family. Science was introduced as a regular subject of study, for the fifth form only, in 1869, and for the Remove in 1875. Even in 1869, it was compulsory for only part of the fifth form and was part of a general programme of reform which included the introduction of French, German, Italian and 'political economy'.[91] The public school headmasters showed little awareness of the national economic implications of science teaching and their reluctance to offer science seemed to have no effect on their recruitment. Eton, for example, was rapidly expanding at the time of the Clarendon Commission, even though its science teaching was non-existent and it sent to the Universities 'the idlest and most ignorant men'.[92] What made the issue so important, even to the public schools' supporters, was that the Newcastle Commission and the continuing pressure for the reform of 'middle-class' schools seemed likely to leave the public schools less able to prepare boys for public and professional life than other schools. Although their popularity was as yet unaffected, the growth of scientific education amongst other classes would inevitably weaken the influence of the classes the public schools educated and for whom they had come to exist. Although the schools were not yet directly threatened, the sudden and dramatic growth of scientific knowledge had created an important area of national life, an important intellectual culture, from which their boys might find themselves debarred through ignorance. The upper classes were quicker to perceive the danger than the schools themselves. The imminent reform of working-class and middle-class education provoked class jealousy—the feeling that the upper classes ought to learn as much about science as anybody else. This feeling, and the uneasiness felt by the aristocracy towards science and scientists, was graphically expressed by Clarendon in a letter to the Duchess of Manchester in November 1862, during the Clarendon Commission's investigations.

> The spirit moves me to ask how you are before I set out for the metropolis, where I have been and must go every day this week for the Schools Commission, which, as far as travelling goes, is a great bore, but as respects the business had been most interesting. We have had before us all the biggest swells in science—Dr. Carpenter, Sir Charles Lyell, Farraday [sic], Hooker, Owen and Max Müller. I don't know when I have been so interested as in hearing the opinions of these eminent men, each from his own point of view, upon the deplorable neglect of physical science and natural history in our system of public education, and the national loss that is sustained . . . The chief task of examining these giants fell upon me as President, and I never felt more shy, as of course I did not want to expose my own ignorance more than was necessary . . . Can't you fancy all this being very interesting, when you consider the immense national importance of the education of the upper classes in these days of active and general competition, and the stick-in-the-mud system of our great public schools, which places the upper classes in a state of inferiority to the middle and lower? Heaven knows whether we shall be able to effect any good; but the existing state of things calls loudly for enquiry and reform.[93]

Grant Duff put the argument to parents more brutally in 1877 when he criticised the continuing delay in the reform of the public school curriculum. 'You console yourselves, perhaps, with the reflection that your sons are gentlemen, and that is something . . . but it will not enable your sons to keep their place in society in these pushing democratic days.'[94]

Notes

1 'Eton', *Macmillan's Magazine*, 3, February 1861, pp. 293–4, attrib. H. Sidgwick, *Wellesley Index*, I, p. 561. Henry Sidgwick (1838–1900), Fellow of Trinity College, Cambridge, was a philosopher and educational reformer, concerned

also with the universities and women's education.

2   See T. W. Bamford, *The Rise of the Public Schools: A Study of Boys' Public Boarding Schools in England and Wales from 1837 to the Present Day*, London, 1967, pp. 127–32 and the *Clarendon Report*, I, pp. 48, 263.

3   See Introduction, Note 12. Matthew James Higgins (1810–68) was educated at Eton. He became a friend of Thackeray and one of the chief writers for the *Morning Chronicle*.

4   See Note 1 above.

5   'Eton College', *Edinburgh Review*, 113, April 1861, pp. 387–426, attrib. M. J. Higgins, *Wellesley Index*, I, p. 510. See also Note 3 above.

6   Sidgwick, 'Eton', p. 294.

7   Higgins, 'Eton College', p. 425.

8   There were 105 Eton men in the Commons, including the Speaker and the Chancellor of the Exchequer. See *The Times*, 16 February 1861, p. 9.

9   See E. G. West, *Education and the Industrial Revolution*, London, 1975, pp. 38–43.

10   H. Perkin, *The Origins of Modern English Society 1780–1880*, London, 1974, p. 302.

11   Perkin, *The Origins of Modern English Society*, p. 302.

12   Michael Wolff, 'Victorian reviewers and cultural responsibility', in P. Appelman, W. A. Hadden & M. Wolff (eds.), *1859: Entering an Age of Crisis*, Indiana, 1959, p. 269.

13   Sir George Lewis (1806–63) was editor of the *Edinburgh Review* from January 1853 to April 1855. He was afterwards Chancellor of the Exchequer 1855–8, Secretary for the Home Office 1859–61 and Secretary of State for War 1861–3. He was also Clarendon's brother-in-law, having married in 1844 Mrs Theresa Lister, who was Clarendon's sister. See George Villiers, *A Vanished Victorian, Being the Life of George Villiers, Fourth Earl of Clarendon 1800–1870*, London, 1938, pp. 150–1. For Clarendon's letters to Sir George Lewis, see Clarendon Papers, MSS Clar. Dep. c. 544. For his letters to Clarendon, see Clarendon Papers, MSS Clar. Dep. c. 531. For the connection between Clarendon, Sir George Lewis and the *Edinburgh Review*, see Rt Hon. Sir Herbert Maxwell, *The Life and Letters of George William Frederick, Fourth Earl of Calrendon*, London, 1913, II, pp. 51–2, 169–72, 189–92, 277–8. For the Whigs and the *Edinburgh Review*, see *Wellesley Index*, I, pp. 417–21.

14   R. D. Altick, 'The literature of an imminent democracy', in Appleman, *Entering an Age of Crisis*, pp. 219–20.

15   J. Vincent (ed.), *Disraeli, Derby and the Conservative Party: Journals and Memoirs of Edward Henry, Lord Stanley 1848–1869*, Sussex, 1978, 10 June 1868, p. 334. See also pp. 177, 179, 182.

16   See Keith Robbins, *John Bright*, London, 1979, pp. 150, 153.

17   See Sir George Lewis, 'Parliamentary opposition', *Edinburgh Review*, 101, January 1855, pp. 1–22. Also, Maxwell, *Fourth Earl of Clarendon*, II, p. 171.

18   Lady Theresa Lewis to Clarendon, 24 November 1858, quoted Maxwell, *Fourth Earl of Clarendon*, II, p. 168. Palmerston and Clarendon had just returned from a much-criticised visit to Napoleon III. See Jasper Ridley, *Lord Palmerston*, London, 1958, pp. 484–5.

19   See, for example, Lady Theresa Lewis to Clarendon, 1 December 1858, quoted Maxwell, *Fourth Earl of Clarendon*, II, pp. 169–70.

20   For a detailed analysis of party politics 1858–9, see J. B. Conacher, 'Party politics in the age of Palmerston', in Appleman, *Entering an Age of Crisis*, pp. 163–80. The terms used here follow the conventional practice of calling the party of Derby and Disraeli the 'Conservative Party' and the party of Palmerston and Gladstone the 'Liberal Party'. For a more detailed discussion of contemporary political terms, see G. Watson, *The English Ideology: Studies in the Language of Victorian Politics*, London, 1973, esp. Chapter 6. For party history before the period of the Clarendon Commission, see J. B. Conacher, *The Peelites and the Party System 1846–1852*, Newton Abbot, 1972. Clarendon's own career illustrated the uncertainty of party definitions; in early life he had 'strong Whig and Free Trade principles', in 1865 he was 'a very Conservative Whig' and joined Gladstone's Liberal government as Foreign Secretary 1868–70. See

Maxwell, *Fourth Earl of Clarendon*, I, p. 12 and G. Saintsbury, *The Earl of Derby*, London, 1906, p. 167.

21 See J. S. Hurt, *Education in Evolution*, London, 1972, pp. 186–96.
22 See Hurt, *Education in Evolution*, p. 201.
23 Lord Harrowby, *Hansard*, CXII, 2 July 1850, col. 821, quoted E. E. Rich, *The Education Act, 1870: A Study of Public Opinion*, London, 1970, p. 72. Lord Harrowby (1798–1882) was MP for Tiverton 1819–31 and for Liverpool 1831–47, Chancellor of the Duchy of Lancaster in 1855 and Lord Privy Seal 1855–7.
24 The Newcastle Commission, set up by Derby's government in 1858 to inquire into 'the state of popular education in England (and Wales)', produced a six-volume report in 1861.
25 Lord Brougham, *Hansard*, CLXIV, 8 July 1861, cols. 491–2. Lord Brougham (1795–1886) was a barrister and Master in Chancery 1835–52. He sat as MP for Southwark 1831–5. For a statistical summary of middle class incomes for 1854 and 1863 based on Inland Revenue statistics, see F. E.. Balls, 'The origins of the Endowed Schools Act 1869 and its operation in England from 1869 to 1895', PhD thesis, Cambridge University, 1964, Appendix 3, p. 485. His statistics show, for example, that the largest middle class income-group, those earning £100 to £200 a year, grew from 149,398 persons to 162,841 persons. For a discussion of the problems of class analysis and definition, see R. J. Morris, *Class and Class Consciousness in the Industrial Revolution*, London, 1979.
26 See Balls, 'Origins of the Endowed Schools Act', pp. 128–33.
27 For the political difficulties that had come from the *Newcastle Report* and the Revised Code, see Lord Edmond Fitzmaurice, *The Life of Granville, George Leveson Gower, Second Earl of Granville K.G., 1815–1891*, London, 1906, I, pp. 421–32.
28 See C. J. Shrosbree, 'The origins and influence of the Clarendon Commission (1861–1864), with special reference to Shrewsbury School', PhD thesis, Birmingham University, 1985, Appendices IX, X, XI, XII, XIII.
29 Sometimes also 'the enlightened opinions of the age' or 'the requirements of the age'. For examples, see the Petition to Clarendon from Eton of 17 May 1865, in *The Times*, 18 May 1865, p. 7 and M. J. Higgins, 'Paterfamilias to the Editor of the "Cornhill Magazine"', *Cornhill Magazine*, 1, May 1960, p. 612.
30 See G. W. Roderick & M. D. Stephens, *Education and Industry in the Nineteenth Century*, London, 1978, pp. 84–5.
31 Roderick & Stephens, *Education and Industry*, p. 85.
32 Roderick & Stephens, *Education and Industry*, pp. 85–6.
33 The scientists who gave evidence to the Clarendon Commission had almost no connection with the Universities of Oxford and Cambridge. The only one was Max Müller who came to Oxford in middle age, after a distinguished career at the University of Leipzig and in Paris. Most had associations with academic institutions in London, some were self-taught and some came from Scotland. See Note 93 below.
34 B. H. Kennedy, *Public Schools Latin Grammar*, London, 1871. The book was used widely as a standard Latin text-book in public schools and grammar schools for many years.
35 See Roderick & Stephens, *Education and Industry*, p. 5, 61–3.
36 See Roderick & Stephens, *Education and Industry*, p. 42.
37 See the letters from the Clerk of the Clarendon Commission to the headmaster of Marlborough on 22 August 1862, 29 August 1862 and 13 October 1862, HO73/58/11/1, PRO. See also letters to the headmaster of Cheltenham on 22 August 1862 and 29 August 1862, HO73/58/11/1, PRO. Also, letter to the headmaster of the City of London School on 15 October 1862 and his replies on 15 October and 23 October 1862, HO73/58/10, PRO.
38 Letter from the headmaster of the City of London School to the Clerk of the Clarendon Commission, 23 October 1862, HO73/58/10, PRO.
39 See Roderick & Stephens, *Education and Industry*, pp. 89, 91.
40 See Roderick & Stephens, *Education and Industry*, p. 89.
41 See Roderick & Stephens, *Education and Industry*, p. 89.
42 Glasgow University, for example, founded the first chair of Civil Engineering

in 1840. See Roderick & Stephens, *Education and Industry*, p. 135.
43 When Butler became headmaster in 1798, the Ironbridge area was already famous. 'Visitors to the district included many of the most distinguished engineers and innovators' including Thomas Telford, Matthew Boulton, James Watt, John McAdam and Richard Trevithick. See Barrie Trinder, *The Industrial Revolution in Shropshire*, London, 1973, pp. 181–3. In 1797, the Ironbridge area made about 27 per cent of the iron produced in Great Britain and in 1800 had more than 200 steam engines in use. See Trinder, *The Industrial Revolution in Shropshire*, pp. 55–6, 158–9.
44 Trinder, *The Industrial Revolution in Shropshire*, p. 199.
45 Trinder, *The Industrial Revolution in Shropshire*, pp. 199–200. The ironmasters encouraged the study of science among their men. A Literary and Scientific Institution was founded in Coalbrookdale, for example, with the help of the Coalbrookdale Company in 1853. See Arthur Raistrick, *Dynasty of Iron Founders: The Darbys and Coalbrookdale*, Newton Abbot, 1970, pp. 263–4.
46 As late as 1853, in the Chancery Scheme, the only science subject stipulated was mathematics. See *The Free Grammar School of King Edward the Sixth at Shrewsbury. Order, Report and Scheme as made and settled by the Court of Chancery in 1853*, Shrewsbury, undated, p. 22.
47 In the years before the Public Schools Acts, the Shrewsbury governors included merchants and tradespeople, brewers, a lead manufacturer, a large-scale dealer in coal and the manager of a local textile mill. See Shrosbree, 'Origins of the Clarendon Commission', Appendix XIII. See also Chapter 5, Note 42.
48 The governors appointed after the Public Schools Acts included, for example, two professors of Greek. See Shrosbree, 'Origins of the Clarendon Commission', Appendix XIV. See also Chapter 5, Note 129.
49 See Sir Lewis Namier, 'Nationality and Liberty', in *Vanished Supremacies: Essays on European History 1812–1918*, London, 1962, pp. 46–72.
50 The importance of the German language was summed up in the contemporary phrase, 'Was deutsch spricht, soll deutsch werden', quoted Namier, *Vanished Supremacies*, p. 64. The reputation of German scholarship was high in classical, theological, literary, historical and scientific studies. See George Haines IV, 'Technology and liberal education', in Appleman, *Entering an Age of Crisis*, p. 109 and Noel Annan, 'Science, religion and the critical mind', in Appleman, *Entering an Age of Crisis*, p. 34. According to G. M. Young, English theologians could hardly understand, still less equal, the work of German Biblical scholars. See G. M. Young, *Victorian England: Portrait of an Age*, London, 1966, p. 74.
51 Edward Balston, *Clarendon Report*, I, p. 85. Edward Balston (1817–91) was headmaster of Eton 1862–8. See also C. Hollis, *Eton*, London, 1960, pp. 271–2 and A. Clutton-Brock, *Eton*, London, 1900, p. 243.
52 What appeared was part of Tennyson's *In Memoriam* for the sixth form and *The Talisman* by Sir Walter Scott for the Lower School. See the annual prize lists in Bailiff's Bundles No. 122.
53 See H. M. Jones, '1859 and the idea of crisis: general introduction', in Appleman, *Entering an Age of Crisis*, pp. 13–22.
54 Namier, *Vanished Supremacies*, p. 46.
55 Lord Acton, 'Nationality', *Home and Foreign Review*, July 1862, quoted Namier, *Vanished Supremacies*, p. 51.
56 Namier, *Vanished Supremacies*, p. 70.
57 Dr Arnold, quoted in C. J. Vaughan, *A Letter to the Viscount Palmerston M.P., Etc.*, p. 7. (A bound collection of Vaughan's correspondence of 1853–4 and other pamphlets concerning Harrow School in Birmingham University Library.)
58 Mazzini, quoted Namier, *Vanished Supremacies*, p. 55. Giuseppe Mazzini (1805–72), Italian patriot, statesman and propagandist, played a prominent part in the events leading to the unification of Italy.
59 See Rt Hon. Sir Mountstuart E. Grant Duff, *Notes from a Diary 1851–1872*, London, 1897, II, p. 56.
60 See Saintsbury, *The Earl of Derby*, pp. 148–64. For an early example of contemporary criticism of the public schools for their concentration on the Classics, their neglect of English literature and their meagre contribution to

English culture, see the review of R. L. Edgeworth, *Essays on Professional Education*, London, 1809, in the *Edinburgh Review*, 15, October 1809, pp. 40–53.

61 See D. C. Coleman, 'Gentlemen and players', *Economic History Review*, Second Series, XXVI, February 1973, pp. 96–101. For an example of the schools' view, see *The Book of Rugby School: Its History and Daily Life*, Rugby, 1856, p. 206. For Dr Keate's dinner in Paris, see Captain Gronow, *Captain Gronow's Recollections and Anecdotes of the Camp, the Court and the Clubs at the Close of the Last War with France*, London, 1864, pp. 208–10, 272. For Hoby's claims, see Gronow, *Recollections*, p. 272.

62 See T. H. Pear, 'Psychological aspects of English social stratification', *Bulletin of the John Rylands Library*, XXVI, No. 2, May–June 1942, quoted D. W. Brogan, *The English People: Impressions and Observations*, London, 1945, p. 50.

63 Ralph Turner, 'Sponsored and contest mobility and the school system', *American Sociological Review*, XXV (1960), No. 5, pp. 855–67. See also Ralph Turner, 'Modes of social ascent through education: sponsored and contest mobility', in A. H. Halsey, J. Floud & C. Anderson (eds.), *Education, Economy and Society: A Reader in the Sociology of Education*, New York, 1965, pp. 121–39. The term 'élite' is used in this chapter to describe 'a minority group who take major decisions in society'. For a fuller discussion of élite theory, see G. Parry, *Political Elites*, London, 1969; T. Bottomore, *Elites and Society*, London, 1964; W. G. Runciman, *Social Science and Political Theory*, Cambridge, 1963, esp. Chapter IV, 'Elites and oligarchies'. For modern élitist views of the public schools, see the following: A. Sampson, *Anatomy of Britain Today*, London, 1965; T. J. H. Bishop & R. Wilkinson, *Winchester and the Public School Elite: A Statistical Analysis*, London, 1967; Ian Weinberg, *The English Public Schools: The Sociology of Elite Education*, New York, 1967.

64 Parry, *Political Elites*, p. 84.

65 Eminent men of science or engineering were usually brilliant amateurs, except for a few trained in Europe or in Scotland. For the English dependence on the amateur, the dominance of the classics and the comparison with Europe, see Haines, 'Technology and liberal education', pp. 97–112. For the public school influence on scientific and technical training, see Correlli Barnett, 'Further education and the development of an industrial society', *The Development of F. E.*, VI, Study Conferences 75/39 and 75/39B, FE Staff College, Coombe Lodge, 1975. Also, Roderick & Stephens, *Education and Industry*, esp. Chapter 3.

66 See Chapter 5, pp. 142–5.

67 S. H. Beer, *Modern British Politics*, London, 1969, p. 12.

68 Beer, *British Politics*, pp. 9–13.

69 Beer, *British Politics*, p. 12.

70 Edmund Burke, 'Appeal from the new to the old Whigs', *The Writings and Speeches of Edmund Burke*, Boston, 1901, IV, p. 174, quoted Beer, *British Politics*, p. 12. See also, Ronald King, *The Sociology of School Organization*, London, 1983, pp. 80–3.

71 Rt Hon. Sir Mountstuart E. Grant Duff, 'Italy in 1867', an article first written for the *North British Review* and reprinted in extracts in Duff, *Notes from a Diary*, II, p. 98. Carlo Matteucci (1811–68) was a Florentine physicist, chemist and politician. Formerly at the University of Pisa, he was Minister of Public Instruction for most of 1862 and later became Vice-President of the Council of Public Instruction. See Matthew Arnold, *Schools and Universities on the Continent*, London, 1868, Chapter X, reprinted in R. H. Super (ed.), *The Complete Prose Works of Matthew Arnold*, Michigan, 1964, IV, pp. 150–61. For extracts from Matteucci's Report, see Carlo Matteucci, *Raccolta di Scritti varii intorno all'istruzione publica*, Prato, 1867, I, cited Super, *Works of Matthew Arnold*, IV, p. 367.

72 See Mountstuart E. Grant Duff, *Studies in European Politics*, Edinburgh, 1866, pp. 322, 323, 326. Rutger Jan Schimmelpenninck (1765–1825) was Batavian Ambassador to Paris 1798–1802 and to London in 1802. He was briefly Grand Pensionary 1805–6, being forced to make way for Napoleon's younger brother. See G. Newton, *The Netherlands: An Historical and Cultural Survey 1795–*

1977, London, 1978, p. 47.

73 Matthew Arnold, *The Popular Education of France, with notices of that of Holland and Switzerland*, London, 1861. See also, Sir Mountstuart E. Grant Duff, *Out of the Past: Some Biographical Essays*, London, 1903, II, pp. 74–5.

74 Matthew Arnold, 'A French Eton', Part I, *Macmillan's Magazine*, 8, September 1863, pp. 353–62; 'A French Eton', Part II, *Macmillan's Magazine*, 9, February 1864, pp. 343–55; 'A French Eton', Part III, *Macmillan's Magazine*, 10, May 1864, pp. 83–96. See also, D. Masson, *Macmillan's Magazine*, 10, May 1864, pp. 175–6.

75 See, for example, Oscar Browning, 'Mr Matthew Arnold's "Report on French Education" ', *Quarterly Review*, 125, October 1868, pp. 473–90; J. B. Mozley, 'The education of the people', *Quarterly Review*, 128, April 1870, pp. 473–506; John Scott Russell, 'Technical education a national want', *Macmillan's Magazine*, 17, April 1868, pp. 447–59. Clarendon, for example, pointed out the dangers of foreign competition in a speech at Coventry on 21 October 1867 at the opening of an Industrial Exhibition. See *The Times*, 23 October 1867, p. 4. See also Grant Duff's speech to the electors of Elgin, 10 October 1866, in *The Times*, 12 October 1866, pp. 8–9.

76 See Chapter 3, pp. 74–7.

77 In Holland in 1862, for example, he met Groen van Prinsterer, 'the head of the High Orthodox and Conservative party' and they 'talked much of education here and in England'. Duff, *Notes from a Diary*, I, 7 December 1862, p. 214. With many influential contacts in both Europe and England, he had a wide and personal knowledge of European developments; he knew also two members of the Clarendon Commission (Edward Twisleton and Halford Vaughan) and the headmasters of Harrow and Rugby. See Shrosbree, 'Origins of the Clarendon Commission', pp. 114–15.

78 See Duff, *Out of the Past*, pp. 146–7. Henry Reeve (1813–95) was editor of the *Edinburgh Review* 1855–95 and had previously been a political leader-writer for *The Times*. The French intellectuals included Alfred de Vigny, Victor Cousin, Pierre-Simon Ballanche, Montalembert, Jean-Baptiste Lacordaire, Tocqueville, Charles Sainte-Beuve and André-Marie Ampère. See Shrosbree, 'Origins of the Clarendon Commission', p. 115.

79 Grant Duff, *Hansard*, CLXXV, 6 May 1864, col. 115, quoting the *Clarendon Report*, I, p. 32.

80 See Bamford, *Rise of the Public Schools*, p. 87.

81 Bamford, *Rise of the Public Schools*, p. 88. William Sharp was appointed Reader in Natural Philosophy at Rugby in August 1849 but resigned in December 1850.

82 Bamford, *Rise of the Public Schools*, p. 88.

83 See Bamford, *Rise of the Public Schools*, p. 88 and Roderick & Stephens, *Education and Industry*, pp. 37–9. Wilson was an energetic advocate of science education in schools. See J. M. Wilson, 'On teaching natural science in schools', in F. W. Farrar (ed.), *Essays on a Liberal Education*, London, 1867. Also, J. M. Wilson, *A Letter to the Master and Seniors of St. John's College, Cambridge, on the subject of the natural and physical sciences, in relation to school and College*, London, 1867.

84 Sir John Anderson, quoted in D. L. Burn, 'The genesis of American engineering competition 1850–1870', *Economic History*, II, 1930–33, p. 296, quoted Haines, 'Technology and liberal education', p. 102. Sir John Anderson (1814–86) was an engineer at Woolwich and lecturer at the Royal Military Academy 1842–50. He planned the small-arms factory at Enfield in 1855 and was Assistant Superintendent at the Royal Gun Factory 1859–66. He was Superintendent of Machinery to the War Department 1866–74.

85 'Special reports of Mr. George Wallis and Mr. Joseph Whitworth', *Parliamentary Papers, 1854*, XXXVI, quoted Haines, 'Technology and liberal education', p. 102. George Wallis (1811–91) organised the first industrial design exhibition in Manchester in 1845 and was asked by Clarendon, then President of the Board of Trade, to draw up a scheme for art and design in industry, which led to the formation of the Science and Art Department. He was Head of the Birmingham School of Design 1851–8. Sir Joseph Whitworth (1803–87) was an engineer

who first established a common pitch of thread for screws. The two men went to the New York Industrial Exhibition of 1853 and later wrote a book about their experiences. See George Wallis & Joseph Whitworth, *The Industry of the United States in Machinery Manufactures, and Useful and Ornamental Arts*, London, 1854.

86   *Report from the Select Committee on Scientific Instruction, together with the Proceedings of the Committee, Minutes of Evidence and Appendix. Ordered by the House of Commons to be Printed, 15 July 1868*, cited as *Report of the Select Committee on Scientific Education* in Haines, 'Technology and liberal education', p. 104. See also 'Fifth report of the Commissioners for the Exhibition of 1851', Appendix O, *Parliamentary Papers, 1867*, XXIII, pp. 117–43, cited Haines, 'Technology and liberal education', p. 104.

87   W. T. Thornton, 'Technical education in England', *Cornhill Magazine*, 24, September 1871, pp. 324–41, quoted Haines, 'Technology and liberal education', p. 104.

88   W. E. Forster, *Hansard*, CXCIX, 17 February 1870, cols. 465–6.

89   See Haines, 'Technology and liberal education', p. 105.

90   Eton's petition to Clarendon, 17 May 1865, in *The Times*, 18 May 1865, p. 7. The claim was made particularly for Eton.

91   See the *Eton College Chronicle*, 21 May 1868, quoted in *The Times*, 23 May 1868, p. 9. Also H. C. M. Lyte, *A History of Eton College 1440–1910*, London, 1911, p. 529. For the Prince Consort's interest in science education, see Sir Theodore Martin KCB, *The Life of His Royal Highness the Prince Consort*, London, 1875–90, esp. Vol. II. For attempted reforms at Cambridge, see Haines, 'Technology and liberal education', pp. 103–4 and D. A. Winstanely, *Early Victorian Cambridge*, London, 1940, pp. 197–213. For science at Oxford and Cambridge, see the 'Oxford University Commission report', *Parliamentary Papers, 1852*, XXII, pp. 256–60 and the 'Cambridge University Commission report', *Parliamentary Papers, 1852-1853*, cited Haines, 'Technology and liberal education', p. 107.

92   'Public schools—report of the Commission', *Fraser's Magazine*, June 1864, p. 657.

93   Clarendon to the Duchess of Manchester, 20 November 1862, in Maxwell, *Fourth Earl of Clarendon*, II, pp. 269–70. William Benjamin Carpenter (1813–85) was Fullerian Professor of Physiology at the Royal Institution, London 1844–9. He was Professor of Forensic Medicine at University College, London 1849–59 and Registrar of London University 1856–79. Sir Charles Lyell (1797–1875) was a geologist whose book *Principles of Geology*, London, 1830–3, established the modern classification of geological time. He was President of the Geological Society in 1835, 1836, 1849, and 1853, and was knighted in 1848. He was President of the British Association in 1864. Michael Faraday (1791–1867), chemist and physicist, was Professor of Chemistry at the Royal Institution, London 1833–65. Sir William Jackson Hooker (1785–1865) was Regius Professor of Botany at Glasgow University 1820–41 and Director of the Royal Gardens, Kew 1841–65. Sir Richard Owen (1804–92) studied at Edinburgh University and St Bartholomew's Hospital, London. He was Hunterian Professor of Comparative Anatomy and Physiology at the Royal College of Surgeons, London 1836–56 and Superintendent of the Natural History Department of the British Museum 1856–83. Frederich Max Müller (1823–1900), orientalist and philologist, studied at the University of Leipzig and settled in England in 1848. He was Taylorian Professor of Modern European Languages at Oxford University 1854–68 and Curator of the Bodleian Library 1856–63.

94   Rt Hon Mountstuart E. Grant Duff, *Some Brief Comments on Passing Events made between February 4th 1858 and October 5th 1881*, Madras, 1884, pp. 260–1.

3 The Clarendon Commission

The Palmerston administration which took office in June 1859 did not, at first sight, seem favourable to educational reform. Palmerston, although interested in his old school of Harrow, was not a reformer in domestic affairs and his main interest lay with foreign policy.[1] Lord John Russell, who became Foreign Secretary after a famous reconciliation with Palmerston at Willis' Rooms in 1859, had earlier supported popular education, and was to introduce a mild measure of Parliamentary reform in 1860 but, in general, agreed with Palmerston that reform at home had gone far enough.[2] Gladstone, although regarded by many as radical, was not much interested in educational reform and, at this time particularly, was far more concerned with matters of finance and foreign affairs.[3] A few radicals were offered posts in the new administration, but even fewer accepted. Cobden refused the post of President of the Board of Trade and Bright, after much discussion and some apologies, was not offered a post at all.[4] Palmerston's Cabinet of 1859–65 was the oldest on record, with an average age of over sixty at his death.[5]

The circumstances in which the administration took office made the predominance of foreign affairs inevitable. Indeed, the emergence once more of Palmerston as Prime Minister instead of Lord John Russell or Lord Granville was largely the result of personal disagreements over foreign policy between the Liberal leaders and the Queen. These disagreements, and the negotiations that accompanied the fall of Derby's ministry, were to have far-reaching consequences for education; the two men who disagreed with Palmerston and Russell over foreign policy were both excluded from the Foreign Office and became involved in educational reform—Lord Granville as Lord President of the Council and Lord Clarendon as Chairman of the Clarendon Commission.[6] The importance of foreign affairs, which at first seemed unhelpful to domestic reform, thus had the effect of directing into education men who already had national reputations and who had already occupied high political office. These men, together with Grant Duff who proposed the Commission in the Commons in 1861, were men with a wide experience of Europe and a desire to see European reforms established in England.

Lord Granville entered Parliament in 1836[7] and had been Foreign Secretary for a brief period from December 1851 to February 1852. Even then, Palmerston's suspicion of Clarendon's ambitions at the Foreign Office[8] had led Russell to offer the post to Granville although he was then 'a comparatively new and untried man'.[9] Although not Foreign Secretary again, he remained active in foreign affairs—in 1856, for example, leading a special mission to Russia for the coronation of the Czar.[10] His reputation and influence were at their height in 1859. The Queen had asked him to form an administration on the fall of Derby's government[11] and, although his attempts failed, he came to education in 1859 as a national figure, a potential Prime Minister and the political equal of Palmerston and Russell.

His own education had been unconventional. Although he had entered Eton in 1829, at the age of fourteen,[12] he had an early knowledge of European affairs through his father Lord Granville Leveson-Gower, later Viscount Granville,[13] who had been a diplomat before the age of twenty and who was appointed Ambassador to Russia in 1804, Ambassador to Holland in 1823 and Ambassador to France in 1824.[14] Granville, who was eight years old when his father was appointed to Holland, visited the Hague and Paris, rode through France with his father and elder sister and took lessons in circus riding from the Auriols, the famous French clowns with the circus in the Champs Elysées.[15] He then went to a fashionable private school at Beaconsfield, where he remained for five years. He described it later as 'a very bad school, and I remember no merit in the master; but it was very fashionable and called . . the little House of Lords'.[16] He passed uneventfully through Eton, but his knowledge of a wider European culture, his ability to speak French and his political views made him conspicuous.[17] After Eton, he studied under a private tutor for entry into university having previously, as his mother observed, spent more time learning those things which enabled him 'to take a proud position in Paris among the young men who were able to *soutenir les bals* than to shine in writing bad Latin verses in imitation of Ovid, which was then the main idea of education as then conducted at Eton'.[18] On leaving Oxford in 1829, he was given the nominal post of attaché to his father's Embassy in Paris and completed his education by enjoying 'the best of what was to be found in Paris or in London, in a period when society, and especially political society, was exceptionally brilliant'.[19] He knew Talleyrand, attended the receptions, went to balls at the Tuileries, visited the English aristocracy living in Paris and enjoyed 'the *entrée* of the *vie intime* of the entire diplomatic circle of Europe'.[20]

By the standards of the day, Granville became in education an active, radical reformer. In 1853 he attempted to introduce an Education Bill, but was unable to secure its passage through Parliament. This Bill, which was introduced into the Commons by Russell on behalf of the government, would have enabled boroughs with a population of more than 5,000 to give aid from the rates to local elementary schools, but had to be abandoned under the pressure of events that led to the Crimean War.[21] Granville had still hoped for some more modest aid to education from taxation, but failed to overcome opposition from Gladstone who, believing that private funding could be adequate, was reluctant to use public money.[22] Gladstone's opposition, the events of the Crimean War and the opposition of both the Church of England and the Nonconformists brought Granville's plans to nothing. He then went on to take up suggestions about science education which had been made by the Prince Consort.[23] These suggestions were for the extension of Science and Art teaching, which had begun in 1837 with a Parliamentary grant to the National School of Design.[24] But Granville was unable to succeed even in this, and the only legislation affecting education passed by Aberdeen's government was the extension of the Factory Acts of 1833 and 1846, limiting the hours of work for children to between six o'clock in the morning and six o'clock in the evening.[25] He left the Privy Council in 1853 and became Chancellor of the Duchy of Lancaster, but returned in 1855. Once more he took up the cause of educational reform and obtained the consent of the Cabinet, which no longer included Gladstone, 'to propose a very liberal Education Bill' and to increase the Privy Council vote in order to extend the capitation grants from the rural districts to the towns, so that town councils could build or assist schools without any restrictive conditions. The Bill was, however, delayed until the following year, when it was defeated in the Commons.[26] Once again, Granville turned to less controversial reforms in education. An Act was passed for the permanent appointment of a Vice-President of the Council on Education and for the transfer to that department of more responsibility for education. It had now to supervise Civil Service examinations and to provide advice on educational matters to the Charity Commissioners.[27] He returned to the question of science education once more, continuing an association with the Prince Consort that had begun with work for the Great Exhibition of 1851.[28] The Prince, who was trying to raise the standard of science and art teaching, wanted to use surplus funds from the Exhibition for this purpose and, as a result of his support, the Science and Art Department was at last formed in 1857.[29] In 1858, in the last days of Palmerston's first administration, Granville persuaded the government to appoint a Royal Commission to inquire into public elementary schools. The Chairmanship was offered first to Russell and then to the Duke of Newcastle, who accepted.[30] This Commission was still sitting when Palmerston took office again in 1859.

Granville thus went to the Privy Council Office in 1859 not just as a statesman of national reputation, but as the man chiefly responsible for earlier attempts at educational reform. He was identified with the more progressive ideas of the time—especially the extension of state provision and the encouragement of science education—and had formed a close and cordial relationship with the Prince Consort. He also advocated the reform of the public schools and agreed with Clarendon over the direction such reform should take.

> Lord Clarendon had identified himself with the reform of the great public schools, a task which he had taken in hand with the support of the Government, and the special goodwill of Lord Granville, who like Lord Clarendon, desired to see modern languages, history and science, occupying some proportion of the time too exclusively devoted, especially at Eton, to the practice of writing Latin verses.[31]

Clarendon's previous career had been concerned chiefly with foreign affairs. He had not been involved in any aspect of the

political struggles for educational reform, and had not himself
been educated at a public school.[32] He took a keen interest in
his eldest son's progress at Harrow, however, and it was from
this that his wider interest in the public schools developed.[33]
His previous career was distinguished. At the age of twenty, in
1820, he had been appointed as an attaché at St Petersburg
and was subsequently Commissioner of Customs from 1823 to
1832.[34] In 1831 he went as an envoy to Paris to sign a commercial treaty, and was then Ambassador to Spain from 1833
to 1838.[35] He owed this last appointment to Palmerston, who
was Foreign Secretary at the time, and although he sometimes
disagreed with Palmerston over foreign policy in later years—
including over Palmerston's views on Italy in 1859—he was
always conscious of this debt of gratitude. Palmerston's later
suspicion about Clarendon's ambition, although present in
1859, did not extend to home affairs and Clarendon's support
for the reform of the public schools must have gained weight
from his long personal association with the Prime Minister.

Clarendon's career after he returned from Madrid was
distinguished both by the offices he held and the offices he
declined. He declined the Governor-Generalship of Canada in
March 1839 and Mastership of the Mint in August 1839, but
accepted office as Lord Privy Seal in October 1839.[36] He
became, briefly, Chancellor of the Duchy of Lancaster in
1840, during Melbourne's administration, and President of the
Board of Trade in 1846, during Russell's administration.[37] He
was appointed Lord-Lieutenant of Ireland in 1847 and made a
Knight of the Garter in 1851, after an initial attempt to decline
the honour on the grounds that he could not afford the fees.[38]
He remained Lord-Lieutenant until the fall of Russell's
administration in 1852.[39] He declined the post of Foreign
Secretary under Russell in 1851, but accepted the post under
Aberdeen in 1853. In 1855, in the confusion surrounding the
fall of Aberdeen's administration, his name was put to the
Queen by Lord Lansdowne as a possible Prime Minister, but she
did not take this advice. The advice had been given without
Clarendon's knowledge and, when he heard of it, he declined to
allow his name to be resubmitted.[40] He became Foreign
Secretary again in 1855 during Palmerston's first administration,
having first declined a similar offer from Russell.[41] He declined
to go to Vienna for a preliminary peace conference, but

suggested instead that Lord John Russell be sent to 'keep him out of mischief in the House of Commons', an arrangement with which both the Queen and Palmerston agreed.[42] Clarendon did, however, accompany the Queen to Paris in August 1855, and attended the peace conference at Paris in 1856.[43] He declined the Grand Cross of the Legion of Honour in April 1856 and a marquisate shortly afterwards.[44] He was Foreign Secretary throughout the period of the Indian Mutiny and until the end of Palmerston's administration in January 1858.[45] When Palmerston formed his second ministry in June 1859, Clarendon had no position in the government—not having been offered the Foreign Office and having declined the Colonial Office.[46]

In 1859, Clarendon was thus a man who, although sympathising with the general policies of Palmerston's government, held no government post; he had not been offered the Foreign Office and had declined to accept anything else. He was, like Granville, a man with a national reputation who might have been Prime Minister and who might well be Prime Minister in the future. He was therefore available as an obvious choice to lead an important Royal Commission, particularly because of his friendship with Granville and his interest in the reform of the public schools. His influence with the Queen was perhaps another reason for his appointment. His relationship with her had always been good, but at this time she looked on him with particular favour because she saw in him a counterweight to Palmerston's views on foreign policy, with which both the Queen and Clarendon disagreed.

The Queen's personal relationship with Clarendon and his wife had been close since 1849, when the Queen had made her only visit to Ireland. Clarendon, as Lord-Lieutenant, had been responsible for her reception and the visit had been a great success.[47] He went with the Queen to Paris in 1855 and to Balmoral in August 1856. He went again to Balmoral with the Queen in August 1857.[48] Clarendon did not enjoy these visits to Scotland—he disliked the cold rooms, the Scottish weather, the long sermons and the outdoor walks which the Queen required of her guests and which prevented him reading Foreign Office despatches. He refused to wear a kilt and had no enthusiasm for Highland games.[49] Nevertheless, he established a close personal friendship with the Queen—keeping his comments on Balmoral for his private correspondence and telling the Queen jokes at dinner to keep his mind off the cold.[50] This personal friendship was strengthened by Clarendon's views on foreign affairs which, like the Queen's, frequently conflicted with those of Palmerston. Clarendon's disagreements with Palmerston went back many years and were intensified by Palmerston's suspicion of Clarendon's possible ambitions. To Palmerston, Clarendon's frequent decline of high office seemed only another indication of devious intrigue and an attempt to raise the price of co-operation.

In 1840, for example, when Clarendon had been Lord Privy Seal in Melbourne's administration, he had clashed with Palmerston over Britain's policy towards France and the Eastern question.[51] The disagreement, which nearly led to Palmerston's resignation, left relations between the two men strained. Palmerston vetoed a letter from Clarendon to Thiers, attributed Cabinet leaks to him and suspected him of intrigue.[52] In 1840 Granville had been Under-Secretary for Foreign Affairs with Palmerston, but their relationship had also been marked by some personal animosity—partly because of Palmerston's casual and abrasive approach to Foreign Office business, partly because of disagreements over policy and partly because Granville allied himself with Clarendon.[53] Like Clarendon, Granville was concerned about the risk of war with France over Egypt and Syria and he supported Clarendon and Lord Holland in their opposition to Palmerston.[54] In December 1840 Granville wrote to his father in Paris that the Palmerstons were 'angry with Clarendon and talk too much at him . . . Lady Palmerston said she was convinced that Clarendon had getting into the Foreign Office himself for an object and that he was an intriguer'.[55] When Granville attempted to support Clarendon and dispel suspicions about his motives, he was told by Lady Palmerston that he was too good-hearted to realise 'the depth of the cunning' of his friend Clarendon.[56] Thus, as early as 1840, the political groupings had been formed that led in 1859 to the exclusion of both Clarendon and Granville from foreign affairs and their relegation to education. In 1840 Clarendon was already well-regarded by the Queen, and this added to Palmerston's mistrust for Clarendon, who 'was at the time *persona grata* at Court—Lord Palmerston was not so, and knew it; and he gradually became deeply incensed'.[57] When

Derby's government fell in 1859 and Palmerston formed an administration, the Foreign Office was offered to neither Granville nor Clarendon—partly because Russell's support was essential for the formation of a new government and he insisted on becoming Foreign Secretary, but also because they both once more disagreed with Palmerston's foreign policy.

The Queen was particularly displeased that Clarendon was not to be Foreign Secretary and had declined to accept any other post in the government. She sent for and spent two hours with him, but he expressed his own 'dislike of office' and once more declined any government post.[58] His reluctance was influenced by the knowledge that Palmerston's policy on Italy, with which he disagreed, was supported by Russell and Gladstone, and that Palmerston's view would inevitably prevail.[59] But in spite of his protestations about being happily free from office, Clarendon attempted to influence British policy unofficially through private correspondence—particularly with Lord Cowley, Ambassador to France—and came once more under suspicion of intrigue.[60] When Russell heard of the letters, he sent instructions to all British diplomats, forbidding private correspondence on public affairs.[61] Cowley stopped writing for a time, but soon resumed the correspondence, 'unmindful or neglectful of the injunction he had received from the Foreign Office'.[62] In his letters, he was frequently critical of the government's policies, as Cowley, like Clarendon, 'remained convinced that real Italian unity was impossible, or, if by some miracle it were to be brought about, that it was contrary to British interests to encourage it'.[63]

Clarendon was thus an influential critic of the government, once more suspected of intrigue, who disagreed with the Palmerston administration in its major area of foreign policy. His intrigue, and his opposition to Palmerston's policies, was made particularly significant by the fact that Palmerston met opposition both from within his Cabinet and from the Queen, with whom Clarendon became increasingly influential while her relationship with Russell quickly deteriorated. She frequently objected to his despatches and at one point brought him to the brink of resignation, commenting about him that 'we might as well live under a despotism',[64] while Clarendon wrote to Granville that the Italian situation had 'considerably abated the *veni, vidi, vici* feeling with which Johnny had taken possession of that bed of roses, the Foreign Office'.[65] Nevertheless, both Russell and Palmerston 'treated with unconcern the constant apprehension of their colleagues as well as of the Queen and the Prince Consort'.[66] As difficulties increased between Russell and Palmerston on the one hand and the Queen and Prince Consort on the other, the unofficial influence of Clarendon increased. When the Queen moved to Balmoral in September 1859, Russell—supported by Palmerston—carried on 'a sharp paper warfare with the Queen' and the Prince Consort told Clarendon that the Queen's stay has been embittered by this 'most painful paper warfare with the two men',[67] while the Foreign Office despatches, according to Clarendon, 'contained nothing but the revolutionary doctrines of Ivan Ivanovitch',[68] his own nickname for Russell.

The danger of war between Britain and France over Italy was finally averted in December 1859 after a division within Napoleon's advisors and a change of Foreign Minister in France early in January 1860.[69] Cavour became Prime Minister of Sardinia in January 1860 and, on 17 January 1860, issued the first of the despatches on Italian affairs that, he declared, were 'worth a dozen victories in the field'.[70] The first despatch asked France and Austria not to intervene in the affairs of Italy and suggested that the Italian states should decide for themselves whether they wished to join Piedmont.[71] The policy of Russell and Palmerston, although seeming to be interventionist and dangerous, eventually led to the preservation of peace in Italy and its establishment as an independent nation. With hindsight, Clarendon and Granville were wrong to oppose progress towards Italian unity.[72] There also is no doubt that the peaceful settlement of the Italian question was one of the great diplomatic triumphs of the Palmerston administration and 'the most important and well-deserved success of British diplomacy between the Belgian settlement of Grey and the close of the Victorian era'.[73] At the time, however, the success of the government's policy was not immediately apparent and Clarendon continued to relish the government's difficulties, conduct a critical correspondence with his influential friends and maintain good relations with both the Queen and Prince Consort.[74] His active, if unofficial, involvement in the government's affairs continued until his appointment to the Clarendon Commission in July 1861.[75] He was, for example, in almost daily correspondence with Sir George Lewis, who often sent him full details of Cabinet discussions.[76]

Perhaps with the intention of reducing his influence and limiting his capacity for intrigue, in January 1861 Russell asked Clarendon to lead a mission to Vienna. This was to discuss the ceding of Venetia to Italy, to ask for reforms for those Italians who were still Austrian subjects and to dissuade Austria from pursuing a war with Sardinia. On the way, he was to visit Berlin and present the King of Prussia with the Order of the Garter.[77] It is difficult to believe that Russell had much hope of Clarendon accepting the proposal; it would have been humiliating for Clarendon to have accepted the post of subordinate negotiator for a settlement that he bitterly opposed. Perhaps the offer was meant to humiliate him, as he thought he was being given an almost impossible task, as he pointed out in his letter of 20 January 1861 declining Russell's offer.[78] Moreover, Clarendon thought that Austria *did* have just cause for a war against Sardinia, and was particularly scornful about his suggested visit to Berlin.[79]

In the early months of 1861 Clarendon thus posed a difficult problem to Russell and Palmerston—what to do with him. He was too hostile to government policy to be involved in government business—even in an unofficial capacity. His hostility was greatest in foreign policy, where his experience, influence and probably ambition were greatest. He had refused Russell's offer of a token, if prestigious, involvement in foreign affairs. He was, however, too influential, particularly with the Queen, to be disregarded. The appointment of Clarendon to the Royal Commission in 1861 was thus a suitable opportunity to provide him with onerous but honourable employment in an area of government policy far removed from foreign affairs. The Queen would be gratified by his appointment, and Clarendon would both have less time for political intrigue and bring the prestige of the Queen's favour to the inquiries of the Commission. Through his discussions and correspondence with Granville and Sir George Lewis, he was known to be interested in the public schools and to be of a reforming mind. Granville, the minister responsible for Education, was a personal friend and a long-standing political ally. Palmerston and Russell must have hoped that Clarendon's initial mild interest in the reform of the public schools would be sufficient to divert him from other political involvement and his acceptance must have been received with some surprise and relief.[80] Clarendon's initial interest became more than a diversion; he became convinced of the need for fundamental reform and, after the *Clarendon Report* in 1864, supported and promoted Public Schools Bills with conviction and stubborn persistence.

Clarendon himself had not attended a public school. His formal education had been entirely as a day-boy at Christ's Hospital, where the custom of the school allowed the masters to take private pupils.[81] He was admitted as a commoner to St John's College, Cambridge in 1816 and left in 1820, having been admitted directly to the degree of MA, then a privilege of the nobility. He had little ability in logic or mathematics but, unusually, had concentrated on modern languages, continuing to study them at Cambridge after taking his degree.[82] When he left Cambridge, he went to St Petersburg as an attaché to Sir Charles Bagot, the British Ambassador, and remained there for three years.[83] Like Granville, Clarendon's education owed little to the public schools, was little concerned with the classics and owed much to his early experience in Europe. His interest in the public schools came from concern with his son's progress at Harrow. In 1859, for example, Clarendon wrote to Sir George Lewis about his son, who had just spent part of his summer holidays with Sir George at his country home at Harpton in Radnorshire. The letter thanked him for taking care of the boy, but went on to make more general comments on public school education which made clear Clarendon's support for reform.

> I wish the best years of his life were not spent in forgetting French, making bad Latin verses and acquiring nothing that will fit him to be a prominent or useful member of society. I have long been of opinion that our public schools do not keep pace with the requirements of the age; indeed they seem to ignore or be indifferent to them; and altho' of late years some reformation has been forced on them by public opinion, yet it is always unwillingly adopted by masters who seem to be as much attached to routine as they are to dead languages.[84]

When the Newcastle Commission had presented its report in 1861, Gladstone persuaded Palmerston to appoint another Commission to look at 'the great public schools' and Clarendon was asked to preside, 'which he was very willing to do, having long been painfully impressed by the methods of education at some of these schools, besides disapproving of instruction being confined almost exclusively to Latin and Greek'.[85] In the Commons, the appointment of the Commission was approved, remarkably, with no opposition. This was partly due, no doubt, to a general view that some reform was necessary, and to the many articles that had recently appeared in the press. The financial mismanagement at Eton made it difficult for Tory MPs to oppose an inquiry without appearing to condone impropriety. Another reason was the active Parliamentary lobbying by Grant Duff, the relatively unknown member for Elgin in Scotland, who described himself at this time as 'a very humble but a very steady supporter of Her Majesty's Ministers'.[86]

Grant Duff, along with Granville and Clarendon, was the third most influential politician in the appointment of the Commission and, like the others, in his own education owed little to the public schools and much to European influence. He was MP for Elgin from 1857 to 1881 and was a Liberal with radical tendencies. Educated in Edinburgh, he came to England to go to Oxford University, graduating with a Second Class degree in classics in 1850. He then studied law at London University and was later called to the Bar in 1854.[87] He approached English institutions with the astringent scepticism of a Scottish expatriate who believed that Scottish arrangements were more sensible and who thought that the casual inefficiency and traditional prejudices of England could be overcome with Scottish commonsense. He was an active reformer in educational matters and the reform of the English public schools was only one of the causes to which he was committed. He was concerned with the reform of educational charities, the abolition of religious restrictions at Oxford, the reform of the Inns of Court and the continuing improvement of education in Scotland. He later became Rector of Aberdeen University in 1866. Although he was a student of the classics himself, he did not want an exclusively classical curriculum; he wanted the classical curriculum widened to include the study of classical literature, culture and ideas as an introduction to the study of European affairs.[88] He travelled widely in Europe, knew and met many prominent Europeans and wrote knowledgeable, perceptive articles on European affairs. These articles, published together in 1866 as *Studies in European*

Politics, showed that his criticisms of English education and of the public schools derived from his awareness of European developments—the decline in importance of the classics, the introduction of new subjects, the importance of science and engineering, the acceptance of state responsibility for education and the direction of education towards economic objectives.[89] What Grant Duff wanted was an inquiry into all endowed schools so that, reformed, they could together provide the basis of a national system of public secondary education.

Throughout the early months of 1861, he was active in lobbying other Members and, in his diary for 9 April 1861, he noted, 'gave notice of my motion for a Royal Commission on the Public Schools'.[90] Later, on 29 May 1861, he gave a description of his personal campaign.

> All through this spring I was much occupied in urging the expediency of a Royal Commission into the Public Schools, circulating a paper of reasons in favour of it to all Members of the House of Commons, and communicating with Northcote, the two Russells, the Head Masters of Harrow and Rugby, etc. besides Gladstone and Sir George Lewis, who were the members of the Government who took most interest in the matter. After much negotiation all ended amicably and the Commission was issued.[91]

Grant Duff's descriptions of his activities in the early months of 1861 reveal the extent to which the schools were consulted before an inquiry was formally proposed, the preliminary discussion with members of the Government and with possible members of the Commission and the importance of Grant Duff's own efforts to organise support for his proposal. In September 1861 he gave another account of these events in a speech to his constituents at Elgin.

> Some of you are aware that I obtained from the Government in the month of June last, the promise of a Royal Commission to inquire into the public and chief endowed schools of England. When I put my motion on the paper in the early part of the session, I by no means expected to effect what I wished without much trouble and opposition, because, although the excellent articles which had appeared in the *Cornhill* and elsewhere had prepared the public mind for an inquiry into these institutions, I feared that as soon as the question was stirred in the House, the old *'Floreat Etona'* cry might be raised, and that the same bad success might attend my efforts, which proved fatal to those of Mr. Brougham in 1818. I was then much relieved when, a day or two before the motion was to come on, I ascertained that Ministers were

not unfavourable to my proposal; and my satisfaction was much increased when somewhat later I found that they were willing to go so far in the direction in which I wished to move, that I had nothing to do but to leave the matter in their hands.[92]

Grant Duff gave notice of his motion on 7 February 1861 'to move an Address for the Royal Commission to inquire into the state of the higher School Education in England and Wales'.[93] His notice of motion indicated the difficulties in attempting to define the 'public schools' as a separate group at this time. The schools later investigated by the Clarendon Commission were legally little different from hundreds of other endowed grammar schools, many of ancient foundation, throughout the country. The Clarendon schools were simply the most prestigious—Eton particularly so, because of its long-established aristocratic connections and its proximity to Windsor. There was public concern about all endowed grammar schools—that is, schools originally endowed to teach primarily Latin and Greek grammar—and Grant Duff clearly wanted all endowed grammar schools to be the subject of investigation. His notice of motion attempted to indicate the scope of his concern by using the phrase 'Higher school Education', which was an unusual one. He was clearly not happy with this phrase and, when he next raised the matter with Sir George Lewis on 23 April 1861, attempted a clearer definition by asking for 'an inquiry into the state, discipline, studies and revenues of the schools, commonly called public schools, as well as those Endowed Schools in which the Latin and Greek languages are taught'.[94]

This implied distinction between the 'public schools' and other endowed grammar schools was difficult to describe, as it was based on status—on opinion—rather than any legal difference. Clearly, all 'public schools' were endowed schools, but not all endowed schools were acceptable as 'public schools'. In his reply, Sir George Lewis agreed to an inquiry and made his own attempt to overcome the difficulties of definition:

The principal class of endowed school had . . . been brought under the jurisdiction of Parliament, and especially of the Charity Commissioners, whose powers were created by Act of Parliament. Under these circumstances the Government could not refuse to recognise the public endowed schools of England as a fitting subject for a public inquiry; and they were not unfavourable to the principle of such an inquiry . . .

into the public endowed schools in which the Latin and Greek languages are taught.[95]

His reply was interesting for two reasons. Firstly, he suggested that a distinction should be made on grounds of status—'the principal class of endowed school'. Secondly, he used a new phrase to describe the schools he had in mind—'public endowed schools'. This phrase recognised the claims of the more prestigious schools to separate treatment whilst acknowledging that the legal basis of their foundation, which was used to justify government intervention, was common to all endowed schools. Although the distinction was quite arbitrary and posed legal difficulties, it was clear that MPs understood well enough which schools were to be treated differently, for Sir George Lewis continued that these schools—which he still did not name—were to be asked if they would agree to an inquiry. Clearly the public school representatives in Parliament, who were mostly from Eton, had such influence that the reform of public education could not proceed without prior agreement with the public schools.[96]

It was now clear that what the Government and Sir George Lewis had in mind was not what Grant Duff had asked for. Sir George Lewis intended to select a few of the most prestigious from all the endowed grammar schools. Clearly Winchester was meant to be included, because Sir William Heathcote, a former pupil and the MP for Oxford University, immediately asked for the school to be exempt from any inquiry, claiming that it had already been dealt with under an Act relating to the University of Oxford in which the school was treated 'as one of the Colleges of Oxford for the purposes of the Act'.[97] Winchester was eventually included, but the question illustrated again the contemporary problem of definition—that the public schools existed as a separate group only in opinion, not in law; just as their separation from all other endowed schools posed political and legal difficulties, so also did their separation from the Universities, with which many schools had long historic connections and with which they sometimes claimed equality of status. Heathcote's claim that Winchester was legally an Oxford college was based on a recent Act of Parliament but originated, as did other similar claims, both from a long historical association and the legal and financial connections of their endowments.

These claims to parity were sometimes conceded by their most outspoken critics. Henry Sidgwick, for example, in a very critical article about Eton in *Macmillan's Magazine* for February 1861, equated Eton with Oxford and Cambridge. According to him, Eton could have been reformed by the Commissioners for Cambridge University had they not been more concerned with getting Eton's agreement to reform at King's College, Cambridge.[98]

Heathcote's objection was also interesting in that it gave an early indication of two main arguments that the schools were to use against the Public Schools Bills of 1865 and 1868, and which they were to pursue with the Public Schools Commissioners appointed by the Public Schools Act of 1868. Firstly, there was the argument that a school had already been reformed—by a Court of Chancery judgement, for example, or, as at Winchester, by a former inquiry. Secondly, there was the argument that a school was entitled to separate and special consideration. The first argument met with little success once a school had been included in the scope of the Commission. The second argument was more successful in that it contributed to the failure of the Public Schools Bill of 1865, led to the exclusion of St Paul's and Merchant Taylors' from the Public Schools Act of 1868 and led to separate consideration for each school in the Act of 1868 and the long, protracted negotiations with the Public School Commissioners afterwards.[99] Another main argument—that a school had been endowed to meet local needs—came later and, although vociferously pressed by local people and sometimes by local MPs, came to nothing, having already been rejected by the Clarendon Commission.[100]

When Grant Duff next asked Sir George Lewis about a Royal Commission on 4 June 1861, he suggested the names of some possible schools in an attempt to find out which were to be included. He wanted to see the report cover all endowed schools, as a preliminary step to a national reform of all secondary education, and attempted to widen the scope of the Commission as much as possible.

What Grant Duff wanted was an enquiry into 'the Colleges of Eton, Winchester and Westminster, as well as of Harrow, Rugby, Charter House, Christ's Hospital, and all endowed, collegiate, cathedral, and prebendal Schools in Great Britain and Ireland in which the Greek and Latin languages are taught, with a view to ascertain whether the great resources of these institutions may not be rendered more serviceable to education and learning'.[101]

It was clear from the reply of Sir George Lewis, however, that he had no intention of initiating an inquiry of the kind Grant Duff wanted and assumed already that the Commission would be concerned only with the 'principal public schools', although he still did not say which schools he had in mind.[102] He had however, been in communication with these schools and found that they would 'generally be disposed to give information to a Royal Commission'.[103] He added that he was still uncertain about Winchester. Grant Duff again tried to find out which schools were to be included, but received only a vague answer, that the Commission 'should inquire into all endowed public schools in which the Greek and Latin languages were taught'.[104]

His reply illustrated the difficulty of discussing the public schools as though they were a separate group when legally they were not, and when any distinction that existed was based almost entirely on subjective criteria—status, scholarship, a claim to famous old boys or a national reputation—or objective criteria that were common to many other old endowed grammar schools—like an ancient foundation or the teaching of Latin and Greek—or, finally, on objective criteria that they shared with many of the new private or proprietary schools—like being boarding schools or having parents of wealth and distinction. Certainly, Grant Duff had asked for an inquiry into all endowed grammar schools throughout Great Britain. Such was the contemporary confusion about what was meant by 'public school' that Sir George Lewis's reply *could* have meant what Duff had asked for. When the Letters Patent were issued in July 1861, however, it became clear that Grant Duff had not got the national inquiry that he had asked for. Instead, there was to be an inquiry into only nine schools: Eton, Winchester, Westminster, Charterhouse, St Paul's, Merchant Taylors', Harrow, Rugby and Shrewsbury. All were in England, most were near London, and in 1861 they had a school population of only 2,696 boys.[105]

At the time no explanation was given of how these schools were chosen, but Grant Duff, commenting on the Commission's Report in 1864, gave an insight into the discussion that must have gone on in private. The school under discussion was Shrewsbury, traditionally and significantly known as 'The Free Grammar School of King Edward VI at Shrewsbury',[106] which claimed inclusion on the grounds of its scholarship and its distinguished history.[107] The school was thought to be on the borderline between the schools of the Clarendon Commission and the other endowed grammar schools, and Grant Duff's comments illustrated the difficulties of defining the 'public schools' for the Commission on arbitrary social and political grounds.

> This foundation now lies at the boundary line, I think, we may say, between the public schools usually so called and the other endowed schools of the country, and some controversy has arisen in recent years as to whether its future should be that of a first-rate school, or whether it should be adequate rather to the wants of the middle class, as of course the majority of the endowed schools ought to be. The Commissioners have decided that it should remain a first-rate school, and I think they have decided wisely . . . The Commissioners say that the people of Shrewsbury should turn their attention rather to creating a good proprietary school in the town, than to making the present school fulfill the purpose of an institution for giving what is loosely called middle class education.[108]

The explanation that Sir George Lewis gave in 1861, and to which Grant Duff later refers, was that there were simply too many endowed schools to be considered by one Commission. This hardly explains, however, why only the most prestigious schools were selected or why there were only nine schools selected for the Clarendon Commission when the Taunton Commission later considered nearly 800. Clearly at this stage Grant Duff himself accepted the arbitrary selection of these schools for the Clarendon Commission, but his comments make clear two other important implications of this division—implications and assumptions that were to have a profound and pervasive influence on the development of English secondary schools—that secondary education had to be suited to the social class of those being educated, and that only the higher classes could, or should, expect to be educated in a 'first-rate school'. The perpetuation of class difference by the public schools is thus not an incidental consequence of family background, but rather the continuing expression of the conservative political rationale which created them.

Once the Commission was established, however, the Commissioners included other schools on their own initiative—writing to headmasters, meeting informally and persuading them to give evidence, somewhat against their will, by telling them that the Commissioners had to look at other schools in order to make a comparison with the public schools. It is clear that the Commissioners were interested in developments that existed hardly at all within the public schools; that they thought these developments to be of great importance, and that they had to go outside the public schools to find convincing evidence that these curricular developments were possible, desirable and compatible with high academic standards. They were especially interested in modern studies, science and the preparation of boys for government examinations, and the schools included unofficially were Cheltenham College, Marlborough, the City of London School and Wellington.[109] In August 1862 the Clerk to the Clarendon Commission wrote to the headmaster of Cheltenham College and, at the same time, sent a similar letter to Marlborough.

> It has occurred to them [the Commissioners] that though Cheltenham College is not one of those into which they are directed to inquire, similar Returns from a School so large, so carefully organised, and so successful would be useful for purposes of comparison and illustration.[110]

Correspondence followed with all these schools. There was particular interest shown in the modern studies at Cheltenham and Marlborough and in science at the City of London School.[111] The initiator behind the inclusion of these schools was probably the Hon. Edward Twisleton, who wrote to the Clerk of the Commission in August 1862 asking for more information about Marlborough.[112] The headmaster of the City of London School was persuaded to co-operate after a private conversation with the Clerk at the office of the Commission, and sent in a detailed account of the school's progressive and wide-ranging curriculum, in which science had particular prominence.[113] The headmasters of these schools at first seemed reluctant to become involved with the work of the Commission. Considerable work was involved in compiling the returns and dealing with the correspondence, there was the risk of adverse comment and they did not have the status conferred by official

inclusion. This natural reluctance perhaps explains the overtones of flattery in the letters of the Clerk. Nevertheless, the
correspondence makes clear that these schools were included
because they provided proof that what the Commissioners
wanted could be done.

The inclusion of these as comparable schools in the work of
the Commission provides yet more evidence of the arbitrary
way in which the Commission selected public schools. There
were, in fact, three categories of school investigated: there was
Eton, which was alone the point and purpose of the investigation; there were the other well-known schools officially
investigated, which were there by association with Eton; and
there were the other schools, unofficially investigated, which
were there by association with good education.

There were no serious attempts by the nine public schools
to avoid inclusion in the Commission's inquiry, but once the
matter had passed from Parliament to the Commission the
possibilities of criticism, control and even legislation began to
loom larger. Once the necessity or prestige of inclusion had
passed, there was determined lobbying to defeat the Public
Schools Bills, to resist government intervention and to delay
or obstruct many of the changes proposed by the Clarendon
Commission or by the Public Schools Commissioners appointed
under the Public Schools Acts. This was true, to some extent,
of all the schools. Both St Paul's and Merchant Taylors', for
example, attempted to use delaying tactics in answering the
Commission's questions. St Paul's and the Mercers' Company
were already involved in a long, legal battle with Baron de
Rothschild,[114] and applied similar tactics to dealings with the
Commission. In January and April 1862 the headmaster wrote
in to apologise about the delay in sending the returns required
from the school—'there being some holidays', he had been
unable to complete them.[115] The headmaster of Merchant
Taylors' wrote to the Commission in March 1861 to point out
that he could only answer questions with the approval of the
Merchant Taylors' Company. The information had not arrived
in January 1862 and in the following April the headmaster was
still corresponding with the Commission, complaining about the
small print of the questions and the confused presentation of
the information sent to him.[116]

Both St Paul's and Merchant Taylors' successfully argued

themselves out of any legislative control when the *Clarendon Report* went to Parliament. This apparent contradiction between the wish to be included among the schools investigated by the Commission and the reluctance to accept the changes that followed, reflected the ambiguous position of the schools themselves and their changing, often contradictory attitudes to government intervention. They were all, to some extent, publicly endowed and could hardly object outright to government interest. They competed for public esteem and could not afford to lose the opportunity to have their comparability with Eton confirmed officially. Eton could not object to a government investigation when the school's dubious financial practices had been exposed so publicly in the press. The schools wished, however, to preserve their independence and to maintain, or improve, their social status. They made no pretence, or an unwilling token pretence,[117] of catering for the general public— even within their own locality—or of giving an education that the general public either needed or could afford. Many of the schools, originally founded by private bequests or state endowments, had become vastly profitable institutions—either from the increased value of the original endowments or from an increase in fee-paying pupils—so that endowments originally provided for public benefit had been engineered to provide capital funding for private fee-paying education and to provide large, sometimes unearned, incomes for headmasters, senior staff and other functionaries.[118] For all the schools apart from Eton, the objective to be gained from inclusion in the Clarendon Commission was neither change nor reform, but the preservation or confirmation of their status. Once included, this objective was gained, as there is no evidence that either St Paul's or Merchant Taylors' lost their claim to public school status after they evaded the provisions of the Public Schools Acts.

The composition of the Clarendon Commission, when appointed, aroused little comment. There were seven members, including Clarendon as President. These were Lord Clarendon, the Earl of Devon, Lord Lyttelton, the Hon. Edward Twisleton, Sir Stafford Northcote, William Thompson and Henry Vaughan. The Commission was markedly aristocratic in tone; four were members of established aristocratic families and another, Sir Stafford Northcote, was eventually to become an Earl. The members were predominantly products of the schools to be investigated.[119]

Commenting on the *Clarendon Report* in the Commons on 6 May 1864, Grant Duff gave a sketch of the Commission's members. Lord Clarendon was 'a man of the world', Lord Devon was 'a man of business' and Lord Lyttelton was 'a scholar'; William Thompson was 'now Professor of Greek at Cambridge' and Henry Vaughan was 'late Professor of Modern History at Oxford'. The Hon. Edward Twisleton was a man 'whose learning and high culture are well known to all'.[120] Clarendon gave a more vivid description of the members in a letter to Granville in August 1864. He declined the offer of presiding over a Royal Commission into the other endowed schools but, in declining, commented on the members of the Clarendon Commission and discussed their suitability:

> At the moment it would be impossible for me to fix the sum that would induce me to get upon a Middle School drag . . . I am very glad, however, that you meditate such a commission as I know it is wanted and will give satisfaction. Lyttelton would make a very good chairman—the only one of the late lot who would. Devon is weak, Northcote pedantic, Thompson idle, Twisleton quirky, Vaughan mad; yet they all had merits and worked usefully together, except Vaughan who, tho' a man of real genius, is unmanageable.[121]

Granville evidently approved of the work of the Clarendon Commission for he wrote to many former members, offering them places on the next Royal Commission—now known as the Taunton Commission.[122] He offered the chairmanship to Clarendon and Lord Devon, after first asking Lord John Russell, but all refused. He then offered the post to Lord Lyttelton, who declined on the grounds that his handwriting was too bad.[123] In his letter to Granville, Lyttelton in his turn gave a picture of the members of the Clarendon Commission. 'Lord Clarendon . . . sinned by making jokes which annoyed the witnesses; while Lord Devon sinned by not being able to joke at all. He can laugh sometimes . . . but a joke you might as well expect from a bell-wether or a Newfoundland dog.' Sir Stafford Northcote was 'the ablest and most serviceable of the lot' but 'he is devoured by political ambition, and if your rickety Government tumbles to pieces, he becomes Chancellor of the Exchequer and exit'. Mr Edward Twisleton was 'a queer man, who had long fits of silence and torpor alternating with great vivacity'. Professor Hepworth Thompson—afterwards Master of Trinity—

was 'a man of most polished and philosophical intellect, of great wit and humour, but over-refined and fastidious, somewhat too satirical and constitutionally very indolent, though if you poke him up he will do a fair share of work'. Lyttelton thought there was something to be said for all of these, but the one man to be avoided was Henry Vaughan.

> He is a marvel of subtle and minute industry, power of elaborate investigation, and long-drawn out and luminous statements and arguments, at least as luminous as his labyrinthine processes of thought admitted of; but much of it far too artificial and theoretical; and his practical results, though not to be despised, by no means in proportion to the quantity of matter out of which they came. He used to rule his own statistical tables, and do all kinds of work down to that of the merest clerk for himself. But with all this as a colleague he was intolerable. He would puzzle any witness out of his wits with metaphysical cross-questioning; and so disputations, prolix, unmanageable a man in council, it was hardly possible to meet with. He quarrelled, I believe, with all his friends, and lives a sort of hermit life at the top of Hampstead Heath.[124]

The Commission started work in the autumn, sending out printed questions to the schools in October 1861. The schools were visited in May, June and July 1862 and, between May 1862 and May 1863, the Commission examined 130 witnesses and held 127 meetings, many separately noted in *The Times*.[125] The Report was finally issued in March 1864.[126]

Notes

1 See, for example, Jasper Ridley, *Lord Palmerston*, London, 1970, pp. 508–9. Henry John Temple (1784–1865), 3rd Viscount Palmerston, was Whig/Liberal MP for Newport, Isle of Wight, 1807–11, for the University of Cambridge 1811–31, for South Hampshire 1832–4 and for Tiverton 1835–65. He was Secretary for War 1809–28, Secretary of State for Foreign Affairs 1830–4, 1835–41 and 1846–51 and Prime Minister 1855–8, 1859–65. The Queen's Speech of 1864, for example, contained a reference to only one domestic topic—'a report of a commission on clerical oaths'. See D. Southgate, *The Most English Minister: The Policies and Politics of Palmerston*, London, 1966, p. 527.

2 For his views on reform, see Southgate, *Palmerston*, p. 528. For Parliamentary reform in 1860, see K. Robbins, *John Bright*, London, 1979, p. 150. For his support for education, see *Hansard*, CXXIV, 30 June 1854, col. 960, quoted E. E. Rich, *The Education Act, 1870: A Study of Public Opinion*, London, 1970, p. 70. For his reconciliation with Palmerston, see R. A. J. Walling (ed.), *The Diaries of John Bright*, London 1930, 6 June 1859, p. 240; G. Saintsbury, *The Earl of Derby*, London, 1906, p. 122; Robbins, *John Bright*, p. 146. See also the *Morning Star*, 7 June 1859.

3 His great budget was introduced on 10 February 1860 and passed on 24 February 1860. See Walling, *John Bright*, pp. 247, 248. For his commercial treaty with France, signed on 24 January 1860, see Walling, *John Bright*, p. 244. For his

lukewarm interest in education and his reluctance to provide government money for state education, see P. Magnus, *Gladstone: A Biography*, London, 1978, pp. 203, 430. See also, Lord Edmond Fitzmaurice, *The Life of Granville, George Leveson Gower, Second Earl Granville K.G. 1815–1891*, London, 1906, I, pp. 415–16.

4 See Walling, *John Bright*, pp. 237–43. See also D. P. Krein, *The Last Palmerston Government: Foreign Policy, Domestic Politics, and the Genesis of 'Splendid Isolation'*, Iowa, 1978, pp. 10–17. Richard Cobden (1804–65) was Liberal MP for Stockport 1841–7, for Yorkshire (West Riding) 1847–57 and for Rochdale 1859–65.

5 See Southgate, *Palmerston*, p. 527.

6 See Rt Hon. Sir Herbert Maxwell, *The Life and Letters of George William Frederick, Fourth Earl of Clarendon K.G., G.C.B.*, London, 1913, II, pp. 185–8. See also Walling, *John Bright*, pp. 237–43 and Fitzmaurice, *Life of Granville*, I, pp. 320–46. For his grandson's account of these events from Clarendon's viewpoint, that 'a Government was built on Clarendon's self-suppression', see George Villiers, *A Vanished Victorian: Being the Life of George Villiers, Fourth Earl of Clarendon 1800–1870*, London, 1938, pp. 300–2.

7 Granville George Leveson Gower (1815–91) was elected for Morpeth, as Lord Leveson, at a by-election and retained his seat in the General Election of 1837. See Fitzmaurice, *Life of Granville*, I, p. 26. He is referred to throughout, for simplicity, as Lord Granville, although he only took the title in 1846 on the death of his father.

8 See Fitzmaurice, *Life of Granville*, I, p. 43.

9 Fitzmaurice, *Life of Granville*, I, p. 44.

10 See Fitzmaurice, *Life of Granville*, I, pp. 181–217.

11 See Fitzmaurice, *Life of Granville*, I, pp. 332–8.

12 See Fitzmaurice, *Life of Granville*, I, p. 3.

13 See Fitzmaurice, *Life of Granville*, I, p. 4.

14 See Fitzmaurice, *Life of Granville*, I, pp. 4–5.

15 See Fitzmaurice, *Life of Granville*, I, p. 11.

16 Fitzmaurice, *Life of Granville*, I, p. 12.

17 See Fitzmaurice, *Life of Granville*, I, pp. 14–15.

18 Hon. F. Leveson-Gower (ed.), *Letters of Harriet, Countess Granville 1810–1845*, London, 1894, I, p. 406, quoted Fitzmaurice, *Life of Granville*, I, p. 19.

19 Fitzmaurice, *Life of Granville*, I, p. 23.

20 'The Maecenas of Liberalism', *World*, 10 February 1875, quoted Fitzmaurice, *Life of Granville*, I, p. 23.

21 See Fitzmaurice, *Life of Granville*, I, p. 415.

22 See Fitzmaurice, *Life of Granville*, I, pp. 415–16.

23 Granville to the Prince Consort, 14 and 17 January 1853, quoted Fitzmaurice, *Life of Granville*, I, p. 417.

24 See Fitzmaurice, *Life of Granville*, I, p. 418.

25 See Fitzmaurice, *Life of Granville*, I, p. 418.

26 Granville to Lord Canning, 28 November 1855, quoted Fitzmaurice, *Life of Granville*, I, p. 128. See also pp. 418–20.

27 See Fitzmaurice, *Life of Granville*, I, p. 420.

28 See Fitzmaurice, *Life of Granville*, I, p. 421.

29 See Fitzmaurice, *Life of Granville*, I, p. 421.

30 See Fitzmaurice, *Life of Granville*, I, p. 421. Henry Pelham Fiennes Pelham-Clinton (1811–64), 5th Duke of Newcastle, was Whig MP for South Nottinghamshire 1832–46 and for Falkirk 1846–51. He was Secretary of State for the Colonies 1852–4, 1859–64 and Secretary of State for War 1854–5.

31 Fitzmaurice, *Life of Granville*, I, p. 434. Clarendon's interest in education was well known to his political contemporaries. In 1859, for example, Lord Aberdeen corresponded with him about the appointment of a new headmaster at Harrow. See Aberdeen to Clarendon, 29 September, 7 November and 8 November 1859, Clarendon Papers, MSS Clar. Dep. c. 525 (3).

32 Little is known of his early education but he attended Christ's Hospital, probably as a day boy. He attended also Thomas Hill's school in Kensington where his brothers Hyde and Charles were also day boys. See Maxwell, *Fourth Earl of*

Clarendon, I, pp. 14–15 and Villiers, *Earl of Clarendon*, p. 35. When Grant Duff asked for a Royal Commission, he included Christ's Hospital with Eton, Winchester, Westminster, Harrow, Rugby and Charterhouse but also included 'all endowed, collegiate, cathedral and prebendal schools'. See *Hansard*, CLXIII, 4 June 1861, col. 546. The school was not included in the Clarendon Commission and was, like Shrewsbury, a borderline case.

33 Clarendon had three sons and three daughters. The sons were Edward Hyde Villiers (1846–1914), George Villiers (1847–91) and Francis Hyde Villiers (1852–1925). All three sons were educated at Harrow. The eldest son was at Harrow 1858–63. See Villiers, *Earl of Clarendon*, pp. 157, 183, 211.

34 See Maxwell, *Fourth Earl of Clarendon*, I, pp. 28, 47–67 and Villiers, *Earl of Clarendon*, pp. 43, 52–83.

35 See Maxwell, *Fourth Earl of Clarendon*, I, pp. 67–165 and Villiers, *Earl of Clarendon*, pp. 83–114.

36 See Maxwell, *Fourth Earl of Clarendon*, I, pp. 169, 170, 176.

37 See Maxwell, *Fourth Earl of Clarendon*, I, pp. 214, 267.

38 See Maxwell, *Fourth Earl of Clarendon*, I, pp. 276, 325.

39 See Maxwell, *Fourth Earl of Clarendon*, I, p. 344.

40 See Maxwell, *Fourth Earl of Clarendon*, I, pp. 335, 363 and II, pp. 57–8.

41 See Maxwell, *Fourth Earl of Clarendon*, II, pp. 60, 61.

42 See Maxwell, *Fourth Earl of Clarendon*, II, pp. 62–3.

43 See Maxwell, *Fourth Earl of Clarendon*, II, pp. 89–91, 116–21.

44 See Maxwell, *Fourth Earl of Clarendon*, II, p. 121.

45 See Maxwell, *Fourth Earl of Clarendon*, II, p. 161.

46 See Maxwell, *Fourth Earl of Clarendon*, II, p. 186. For Clarendon's description of these events, see his letter of 17 June 1859 to Henry Reeve in Clarendon Papers, MSS Clar. Dep. c. 535 (4).

47 See Maxwell, *Fourth Earl of Clarendon*, II, pp. 301–4.

48 See Maxwell, *Fourth Earl of Clarendon*, II, pp. 89, 127–31, 148.

49 See Maxwell, *Fourth Earl of Clarendon*, II, pp. 148–9.

50 See Maxwell, *Fourth Earl of Clarendon*, II, p. 128. Clarendon was one of the few people with whom the Queen would joke, even on official occasions. See, for example, the arrival in November 1857 of the Siamese ambassadors who crawled the length of the Throne Room with their noses on the floor, in Maxwell, *Fourth Earl of Clarendon*, II, p. 157.

51 See Maxwell, *Fourth Earl of Clarendon*, II, pp. 182–201.

52 See Maxwell, *Fourth Earl of Clarendon*, II, pp. 182–201.

53 See Fitzmaurice, *Life of Granville*, I, p. 29.

54 Henry Richard Fox (1773–1840), 3rd Baron Holland, was Lord Privy Seal 1806–7 and Chancellor of the Duchy of Lancaster 1830–4 and 1835–40.

55 Granville to his father, 11 December 1840, quoted Maxwell, *Fourth Earl of Clarendon*, I, p. 200.

56 Lady Palmerston, quoted Maxwell, *Fourth Earl of Clarendon*, I, p. 200.

57 Fitzmaurice, *Life of Granville*, I, p. 30.

58 See Lady Clarendon, *Journal of the Fourth Countess of Clarendon*, unpublished, quoted Maxwell, *Fourth Earl of Clarendon*, II, pp. 185–6.

59 See Fitzmaurice, *Life of Granville*, I, p. 346.

60 See Villiers, *Earl of Clarendon*, p. 270. Henry Richard Charles Wellesley (1804–84), 1st Earl of Cowley, was Ambassador to France 1852–67 and Clarendon's deputy at the Peace of Paris negotiations in 1856.

61 See Maxwell, *Fourth Earl of Clarendon*, II, p. 186. Cowley's indiscretion ran to more than correspondence. In 1859, for example, he twice copied his own 'private' letters to Russell and sent the copies to Clarendon. See Cowley to Clarendon, 25 August and 9 October 1859, Clarendon Papers, MSS Clar. Dep. c. 536 (a).

62 Maxwell, *Fourth Earl of Clarendon*, II, p. 219.

63 Maxwell, *Fourth Earl of Clarendon*, II, p. 231. See also Cowley's letters to Clarendon on 12 November 1860 and 6 December 1860, quoted Maxwell, *Fourth Earl of Clarendon*, II, pp. 230–1.

64 The Queen, quoted Fitzmaurice, *Life of Granville*, I, p. 357.

65 Clarendon to Granville, 27 September and 6 October 1859, quoted Fitzmaurice,

Life of Granville, I, p. 359.

66 Fitzmaurice, *Life of Granville*, I, p. 359.

67 Fitzmaurice, *Life of Granville*, I, p. 360.

68 Clarendon to Granville, 23 November 1859, quoted Fitzmaurice, *Life of Granville*, I, p. 360.

69 See Fitzmaurice, *Life of Granville*, I, p. 368 and Maxwell, *Fourth Earl of Clarendon*, II, p. 198.

70 Cavour, quoted Fitzmaurice, *Life of Granville*, I, p. 368.

71 For the despatch of 27 October 1860, see Maxwell, *Fourth Earl of Clarendon*, II, p. 203.

72 'Lord Clarendon held strong views on the Italian question, which subsequent events have proved to be mistaken. He was sceptical about the possibility of a united kingdom of Italy, differing *toto coelo* from Palmerston on that matter.' Maxwell, *Fourth Earl of Clarendon*, II, p. 188. Maxwell could not find in Clarendon's subsequent correspondence any admission that he had been wrong. See Maxwell, *Fourth Earl of Clarendon*, II, p. 235. For an account of events from Clarendon's viewpoint, which links the decline of Austria with the establishment of German supremacy in Europe, see Villiers, *Earl of Clarendon*, pp. 300–7. For a general summary of events in Italy at this time, and the government's reaction to them, see G. M. Trevelyan, *British History in the Nineteenth Century and After: 1782–1919*, London, 1965, pp. 318–21 and David Thomson, *England in the Nineteenth Century (1815–1914)*, London, 1955, pp. 160–2.

73 Trevelyan, *British History*, p. 319.

74 See, for example, Clarendon to the Duchess of Manchester, 7 January 1860 and Clarendon to Sir George Lewis, 16 July 1860, quoted Maxwell, *Fourth Earl of Clarendon*, II, pp. 206–7, 220.

75 Letters Patent were issued on 18 July 1861 and the Commission first met on 20 July 1861. See *Clarendon Report*, I, p. 338.

76 See, for example, Maxwell, *Fourth Earl of Clarendon*, II, p. 228.

77 See Maxwell, *Fourth Earl of Clarendon*, II, pp. 234–5.

78 Clarendon to Russell, 20 January 1861, quoted Maxwell, *Fourth Earl of Clarendon*, II, p. 234.

79 See Maxwell, *Fourth Earl of Clarendon*, II, p. 234. He did eventually go to Berlin in October 1861 to attend the coronation of King William I of Prussia but he went as the Queen's representative and at her personal request. See Maxwell, *Fourth Earl of Clarendon*, II, p. 246.

80 Clarendon's relationship with the Queen continued to be close after his appointment to the Commission—particularly after the death of the Prince Consort on 14 December 1861. He fell from favour in 1863, however, when, on returning from a conference in Frankfurt, he greatly offended the Queen by his comments on Germany. She remained bitterly opposed to him afterwards and objected to his appointment as Foreign Secretary in 1868. She was also offended by his manner and by his close friendship with the Queen of Holland. See Maxwell, *Fourth Earl of Clarendon*, II, pp. 258, 261–2, 282, 353–5.

81 See Maxwell, *Fourth Earl of Clarendon*, I, pp. 14–15.

82 See Maxwell, *Fourth Earl of Clarendon*, I, pp. 15–17 and Villiers, *Earl of Clarendon*, pp. 37–42.

83 See Maxwell, *Fourth Earl of Clarendon*, I, p. 28. Sir Charles Bagot (1781–1843) was the second son of the 1st Baron Bagot. He was Minister Plenipotentiary to France in 1814 and to the USA 1815–20. He was Ambassador to Russia 1820–4, to Holland 1824–35 and to Austria in 1835. He was Governor-General of Canada 1841–3.

84 Clarendon to Sir George Lewis, 28 August 1859, quoted Maxwell, *Fourth Earl of Clarendon*, II, p. 196. During the work of the Commission Clarendon continued to correspond with Lewis on such matters as the educational system in Prussia, the failings of Eton and a confidential paper for the Commission prepared by Lyttelton. See Clarendon to Lewis, 16 October 1861 and 6 October 1862, Clarendon Papers, MSS Clar. Dep. c. 533 (2).

85 Maxwell, *Fourth Earl of Clarendon*, II, p. 261. See also Villiers, *Earl of Clarendon*, p. 316. Clarendon held strongly critical views about 'the time honoured corruption and deep rooted prejudice' of Eton. See Clarendon to Sir

George Lewis, 16 October 1861, Clarendon Papers, MSS Clar. Dep. c. 533 (2).

86 Grant Duff, *Hansard*, CLXIV, 28 June 1861, col. 135.

87 Mountstuart Elphinstone Grant Duff (1829–1906) was educated in Edinburgh and at Balliol College, Oxford. He then studied in London, gaining an LlB and being called to the Bar from the Inner Temple in 1854. He was Liberal MP for Elgin 1857–81. He was Rector of Aberdeen University 1866–72, Under-Secretary of State for India 1868–74, Under-Secretary of State for the Colonies 1880–1 and Governor of Madras 1881–6. He was a member of the Commons Select Committee appointed in March 1868 to consider the *Public Schools (No. 47) Bill.*

88 For his other interests in education, see the following: for educational charities, see *The Times*, 12 June 1863, p. 6 and 29 October 1864, p. 6; for Oxford University, see *The Times*, 17 March 1864, p. 8 and 29 October 1864, p. 6; for the Inns of Court, see *The Times*, 2 July 1864, p. 9 and 29 October 1864, p. 6; for Scottish education, see Rt Hon. M. E. G. Duff, 'First rectorial address at Aberdeen, 1867', partially reprinted in *Some Brief Comments on Passing Events made between February 4th 1858 and October 5th 1881*, Madras, 1884, pp. 236–8. See also, Mountstuart E. Grant Duff, *Inaugural Address delivered to the University of Aberdeen on his Installation as Rector*, Edinburgh, 1867, esp. pp. 4–14.

89 See Mountstuart E. Grant Duff, *Studies in European Politics*, Edinburgh, 1866, esp. pp. 50–1, 118–19 and 300–21.

90 Rt Hon. Sir Mountstuart E. Grant Duff, *Notes from a Diary, 1851–1872*, London, 1897, 9 April 1861, I, p. 155.

91 Duff, *Notes from a Diary*, I, 29 May 1861, pp. 157–8.

92 Duff, 'At Elgin, September 18th, 1861', *Some Brief Comments on Passing Events*, pp. 229–30.

93 Grant Duff, *Hansard*, CLXI, 7 February 1861, col. 146.

94 Grant Duff, *Hansard*, CLXII, 23 April 1861, col. 983.

95 Sir George Lewis, *Hansard*, CLXII, 23 April 1861, cols. 983–4. The phrase 'public school' has remained confusing, sometimes even for professional historians. G. M. Young, for example, wrote that 'in the eye of the law the public schools were nine in number' but this was never so. See G. M. Young, *Victorian England: Portrait of an Age*, London, 1966, p. 97. There were about 800 public endowed grammar schools before the *Public Schools Act, 1868* and the same number after the Act. The Act made separate legal arrangements for seven of these schools.

96 See Sir George Lewis, *Hansard*, CLXII, 23 April 1861, col. 984.

97 Sir William Heathcote, *Hansard*, CLXII, 23 April 1861, col. 984. Sir William Heathcote (1801–81) was the son of a former Prebendary of Winchester and a former pupil of the school. He was Conservative MP for Hampshire 1826–32, for the North Div. of Hampshire 1837–49 and for Oxford University 1854–68. He was a member of the Commons Select Committee appointed in March 1868 to consider the *Public Schools (No. 47) Bill.*

98 'Eton', *Macmillan's Magazine*, 3 February 1861, p. 292, attrib. H. Sidgwick, *Wellesley Index*, I, p. 561.

99 See Chapter 6, pp. 191, 204–5.

100 For Shrewsbury School, see Chapter 5, p. 157.

101 Grant Duff, *Hansard*, CLXIII, 4 June 1861, col. 546.

102 Sir George Lewis, *Hansard*, CLXIII, 4 June 1861, col. 546.

103 Sir George Lewis, *Hansard*, CLXIII, 4 June 1861, col. 546.

104 Sir George Lewis, *Hansard*, CLXIII, 4 June 1861, col. 547.

105 See *Clarendon Report*, I, pp. 7–11.

106 'Libera Schola Grammaticalis Regis Edwardi Sexti', School Charter of 10 February 1552, Shrewsbury Sch. Arch., quoted J. B. Oldham, *A History of Shrewsbury School 1552–1952*, Oxford, 1952, p. 1. See also Grant Duff, *Hansard*, CLXXV, 6 May 1864, col. 125.

107 For the school's scholarship, see Oldham, *A History of Shrewsbury School*, pp. 192–200 and G. W. Fisher, *Annals of Shrewsbury School*, London, 1899, pp. 482–94. For distinguished pupils, see Oldham, *A History of Shrewsbury School*, pp. 286–307. See also Chapter 5, pp. 149–151.

108 Grant Duff, *Hansard*, CLXXV, 6 May 1864, cols. 125-7.
109 For the complete correspondence, see HO73/58/10, 11 and 12, PRO.
110 Clerk of the Commission to the headmaster of Cheltenham College, 22 August 1862, HO73/58/11/1, PRO.
111 For correspondence with the City of London School, see HO73/58/10, PRO.
112 Twisleton to the Clerk of the Commission, 29 August 1862, HO73/58/11/1, PRO.
113 The Clerk of the Commission wrote to the headmaster of the City of London School on 15 October 1862. They met on the following day and, on 23 October 1862, the headmaster sent a detailed account of the work of the school, including a summary of its history from 1442. The curriculum included reading, writing, English grammar, arithmetic, English history, the Bible, Latin, Greek, French, natural philosophy and chemistry. The headmaster's aims were 'that no pupil of the City of London School shall look upon the world around him and find it a sealed book' and to 'enable those who go into the business life of London, to understand something of those processes which are in daily use amongst us'. See HO73/58/10, PRO.
114 The legal battle centred around an original agreement with Rothschild to exchange estates in Buckinghamshire belonging to the Mercers' Company with estates belonging to Rothschild in Northamptonshire. See *Answers to Questions Relating to the Nature and Application of the Endowments, Funds and Revenues of St. Paul's School*, HO73/58/5/4, PRO. See also, *The Attorney-General and Baron de Rothschild v The Mercers' Company. Amended Information and Bill of Complaint. Filed 19th May 1860. Amended 10th April 1861*, HO73/58/5/4, PRO.
115 Headmaster of St Paul's School to the Clerk of the Commission, 3 January 1862 and 29 April 1862, HO73/58/5/5, PRO.
116 See headmaster of Merchant Taylors' School to the Clerk of the Commission, 23 March 1861 and 24 April 1862, HO73/58/6/1, PRO.
117 Evidence given to the Lords Select Committee in 1865 suggested that some headmasters actively and unscrupulously discouraged local children. See Chapter 6, Note 49.
118 For the example of Eton see Chapter 2, pp. 41-2.
119 There were seven members of the Clarendon Commission. George Frederick William Villiers (1800-70), 4th Earl of Clarendon, was educated at Christ's Hospital and Cambridge. William Reginald Courtenay (1807-88), 11th Earl of Devon, was educated at Westminster and Oxford. George William Lyttelton (1817-76), 4th Baron Lyttelton, was educated at Eton and Cambridge. The Hon. Edward Turner Boyd Twisleton (1809-74) was educated privately and at Oxford. Sir Stafford Henry Northcote (1818-87) was educated at Eton and at Oxford. William Hepworth Thompson (1810-86), Professor of Greek at Cambridge, was educated privately and at Cambridge. Henry Halford Vaughan (1811-85), Professor of Modern History at Oxford, was educated at Rugby and at Oxford. Apart from the last two, all the members were experienced in public service. Apart from Clarendon, all the members had first class degrees in the classics. Most had a public or professional interest in education but none were scientists or engineers, nor were they businessmen or industrialists. For detailed information about their education and experience, see C. J. Shrosbree, 'The origins and influence of the Clarendon Commission (1861-1864), with special reference to Shrewsbury School', PhD thesis, Birmingham University, 1985, Appendix I.
120 Grant Duff, *Hansard*, CLXXV, 6 May 1864, col. 106.
121 Clarendon to Granville, 12 August 1864, quoted Maxwell, *Fourth Earl of Clarendon*, II, pp. 294-5.
122 See Fitzmaurice, *Life of Granville*, I, p. 432.
123 See Fitzmaurice, *Life of Granville*, I, p. 433.
124 Lyttelton to Granville, undated 1864, quoted Fitzmaurice, *Life of Granville*, I, pp. 434-5. When the Taunton Commission was finally set up in December 1864, only two members of the Clarendon Commission were included—Lyttelton and Northcote. 'Mr Halford Vaughan was left in the retirement of his hut on Hampstead Heath'. See Fitzmaurice, *Life of Granville*, I, p. 435.

125 See, for example, *The Times*, 7 June 1862, p. 11. The notices were brief and
factual; for a more detailed list, see Shrosbree, 'Origins of the Clarendon Commission', p. 164.
126 For a contemporary description of the Clarendon Commission's work see
'Public schools—report of the Commission', *Fraser's Magazine*, June 1864,
p. 655.

4 *The Clarendon Report*

The period between the appointment of the Commission in 1861 and the Commission's Report in 1864 was one of relative calm in the politics of national education. There were few articles in the periodicals and no discussion in Parliament as all awaited the results of the Commission's inquiries. Both in the House of Commons and outside, Grant Duff continued to promote educational reform in many areas of national life and occasional correspondence about the public schools, particularly about Westminster, continued in *The Times*.

Grant Duff was a tireless campaigner for reform in many English educational institutions and, having introduced public school reform into Parliament, continued to strive for reform elsewhere. He wanted to reform all endowed schools and criticised their defects in the Commons in June 1863, suggesting that the Charities Commission should become a department of the Privy Council so that there could be centralised and unified direction of all public education.[1] He supported the attempt to abolish religious tests at Oxford, and spoke for the *Tests Abolition (Oxford) Bill* in March 1864.[2] He supported the reform of legal education in the Inns of Court, the provision of better accommodation for London University and, later, the reform of education in India.[3] His passionate commitment to reform arose from both his belief in rationality and his awareness of progress in Europe. When speaking of reform, whether of the public schools, of the English universities or of science education, his standard of comparison and of criticism was always European. He was particularly concerned, for example, that the Scottish universities should maintain their excellence and look to Europe for their standards, rather than to England.[4] In 1862 he visited Holland with a particular interest in education and, between 1861 and 1864, published a number of articles in the *North British Review*, the *National Review* and *Fraser's Magazine* about contemporary developments in European politics, literature and education.[5]

The correspondence in *The Times* about Westminster was, by comparison, not about whether the school could emulate educational progress in Europe, but about whether it could provide suitable basic accommodation. The correspondence showed a tendency for some reforms that had already begun in the schools to continue while the Commission was sitting. The correspondence was also interesting in that it revealed once more the common legal basis of all endowed grammar schools and the arbitrary way in which some of these schools had been selected for the Commission. Just as Harrow, Rugby or Shrewsbury were simply well-known examples of grammar schools founded and supported by Royal or private endowments, so Westminster was simply a grammar school founded and endowed with the cathedral.

The correspondence began in February 1861, when *The Times* reported that Westminster School was not to move but was to improve its accommodation.[6] Additional schoolrooms had been built and there were plans to build a gymnasium and a fives court. The school was also attempting to improve conditions for day-boys by modifying the timetable and providing new buildings.[7] The report summarised the pressure on the school to reform and was optimistic about the possibility of progress—seen, however, only in terms of better accommodation and increased numbers, if the school was to 'compete with other public schools, most of which are fast bringing their foundations and statutes into working order with the wants of the age'.[8] One of the 'wants of the age' that Westminster had some difficulty meeting was the provision of healthy, adequate buildings, particularly because the school's endowment income was linked to that of the cathedral and too much money tended to be diverted for ecclesiastical purposes. In December 1863 a letter to *The Times*—after the *de rigueur* mention of distinguished old boys who included Lord Raglan, Lord Russell and the Archbishop of Canterbury—expressed hope that the new buildings would help Westminster shake off its reputation as an unhealthy school and 'rise to its former eminence'.[9] The choice of old boys was somewhat unfortunate, for Lord John Russell had been unable to endure the school and was taken away after less than a year.[10] Nevertheless, the writer blamed low numbers on poor accommodation and, in this, Westminster illustrated another difficulty of supporting public education entirely through endowments. If the value of endowments rose, the extra money might be creamed off—for private profit, perhaps, or to support other purposes. If the value of endowments fell, more money might be found through fee-paying pupils, and the school's public obligations again become a marginal consideration of little account. If either tendency went too far, then both public service and educational priorities might become burdens best disregarded, in the absence of either government funding or government control. Like many other endowed grammar schools, Westminster was originally part of an ecclesiastical institution, but began a separate existence at the time of the Dissolution. The school's endowments were, however, still linked with those of the cathedral; as the value of these endowments had increased, more money was diverted away from the school to the cathedral. Other schools were in a similar position. A letter to *The Times* in May 1864 claimed that all cathedral schools should have a greater share of money; at Rochester, Durham and Canterbury, the schools' share of the money had been raised, but this had not happened at Westminster, Ely or Chester.[11]

With the cathedral schools, as with all the endowed grammar schools, a legal uniformity was obscured by differences in reputation and status. In the period before the publication of the *Clarendon Report*, Grant Duff stressed the essential uniformity of the endowed schools and advocated the use of their endowments to create a reformed, national system of secondary education. He wanted to make the Charities Commission a department of the Privy Council so that the Committee of the Council for Education could become the Committee of the Council for Education and Charities, thus bringing all school education within the jurisdiction of one government department.[12] In June 1863 he spoke in the Commons about all endowed schools, suggesting that their great income—which he estimated at £1,500,000 for England and Wales—should be used to establish a national system of secondary education, and criticising all endowed grammar schools as they then operated—without government control or direction, without inspection and without regard for the wealth of many parents using public endowments.

In the first place, parents were continually aided in the education and maintenance of their children. The leading case of abuse in this respect was Christ's Hospital, where £5,104 per annum was devoted to dressing the boys in an antiquated costume, and probably there was not one of those boys whom his parents could not afford to dress in a respectable manner . . . The second vice of those schools was that in many cases the education which they provided was not that which was wanted in their district. In many the masters claimed to teach only Latin and Greek and it not infrequently happened that there was not a boy in the parish that desired to learn either the one or the other. The third vice applied to all the schools in general and was the irremovability of incompetent masters. The fourth vice was that they were subjected to no regular inspection. The fifty vice . . . was that generally they were so small it was impossible to manage them properly, and it was very much to be desired that some means might be adopted for . . . applying them [the endowments] in a more useful way than was possible at present.[13]

When the *Clarendon Report* was finally published in March 1864, Grant Duff's hope that it would create a speedy move towards reform, even in the small number of endowed grammar schools investigated, was disappointed. The relative calm that had prevailed in discussion about the public and the other endowed schools was replaced by controversy about the *Clarendon Report* itself—and there was some hostility towards the Commission's recommendations—both from within Parliament and from the public schools themselves. It was thus by no means inevitable that the *Clarendon Report* would be followed by an attempt at legislation or that any such attempt would be successful. It seemed even less likely that any legislation would implement the recommendations of the Report. This was particularly because the progress towards legislation was slow and tortuous, and was at times bitterly opposed by the public schools themselves through petitions, by legal counsel, and by peers and MPs who, because of family or local connections, were prepared to act as the schools' agents in obstructing the passage of the Public Schools Bills. The legislation was further delayed by political circumstances; between 1864 and 1868 there were four Prime Ministers—Palmerston, Russell, Derby and Disraeli—and if the period is extended to the last Public Schools Act in 1873 the number rises to five, with Gladstone.[14] Throughout 1867 Parliament was largely preoccupied with Parliamentary reform. Ten different Public Schools Bills were introduced between 1864 and 1873, and seven Publis Schools Acts were passed.[15]

It was clear from the debates in Parliament on the *Clarendon Report* that opposition to legislation was going to be considerable. The Commission made detailed recommendations for reform in three main areas: the governing bodies of the schools, their statutes and the curriculum.[16] The second and third recommendations were dependent on the first in that reformed governing bodies—with more members appointed by the Crown and other prominent national institutions, and with more members eminent in science or literature—could be given greater powers over the school statutes and finance and over the reform of the curriculum. The proposals for reform were bitterly opposed by the schools. Headmasters did not wish to see governing bodies with greater powers to intervene in the work of their schools, and did not wish to see men, however distinguished, appointed as school governors without necessarily having any knowledge of a school or its traditions. School governors saw an end to their influence and, usually representing local interests, were incensed that new school statutes might mean the end of some free education for local children. The schools were jealous of their autonomy and were particularly angered that the Public Schools Bill of 1865—the first major Bill that attempted to implement the Report's recommendations—imposed a degree of uniformity on the schools by attempting to legislate for them all collectively. Opposition to this principle led ultimately to the idea that the actual reform of the school governing bodies should be left to an 'Executive Commission' and thus to the Special Commissioners appointed by the Public Schools Act of 1868.[17] The schools were thus given an opportunity to negotiate the composition of their new governing bodies with the Special Commissioners—a process that often led to protracted wrangling which made necessary an extension of the original time limits set by the Public Schools Acts of 1869, 1870, 1871 and 1872. By this time, the reform of the public schools had been reduced to a series of prolonged disputes between the schools and the Special Commissioners about the precise composition of the new governing bodies and the details of new school statutes.[18] By this time the discussion of curricular reform had also virtually ceased, for there was no direct concern with such educational matters in the Public Schools Bills. In practice, such matters were left to the headmasters. The new men on the governing bodies, who were, in theory, to bring new ideas on the curriculum into the schools, finally found themselves with general control over the education provided in the schools but were not, in any case, generally 'new' men in the sense of being outside the established public school tradition. The great majority of new governors appointed under the Public Schools Acts—whether they were appointed by the Crown, by Oxford and Cambridge or by the Lord Chief Justice—were men who had once been pupils at a particular school before being appointed as governors to the same school.[19] They were therefore unlikely to introduce new educational ideas or to challenge the assumptions of the educational system that had brought them to eminence. The expressed purpose of the introduction of these new governors was to introduce new educational ideas; the effect of their appointment was to ensure the continuation of the existing classical tradition. There was nothing in the Public Schools Acts which suggested that they should be former pupils but, almost invariably, this was the case. The new governors often also had other personal associations with the school. Since the Public Schools Acts clearly placed responsibility for reform upon them, this policy also ensured that little reform of the curriculum took place.

The *Public Schools Act, 1868* was almost entirely concerned with the government and finance of the schools and the appointment of the Special Commissioners. The education to be given in the schools was mentioned briefly, once, and was to be left entirely to the discretion of the new governors.

> It shall be lawful for the new Governing Body of every School to which this Act applies . . . to make, alter, or annul such Regulations as they may deem it expedient to make, alter, or annul with respect to any of the following Matters . . .
> (7) With respect to the Introduction of new Branches of Study, and the Suppression of old ones, and the relative Importance to be assigned to each Branch of Study.[20]

This briefest of references to the curriculum comes in a list of the governors' routine responsibilities and is listed after their responsibility for sanitary conditions.

The Special Commissioners, appointed to negotiate with the schools over their new governing bodies and new school statutes, were also in entirety products of the public schools. Attempts in Parliament to specifically include men eminent in science or literature mainly failed, even when those nominated were public school men of irreproachable respectability. Lord Lyttelton's attempt to nominate Sir Roundell Palmer, formerly Attorney-General, and the Rev. Joseph Blakesley—an eminent theologian who was Almoner of St Paul's School and a Tutor at Trinity College, Cambridge—failed when his amendment, which had been approved by the Lords, was rejected in the Commons in July 1868 on the grounds that, by then, too many other Special Commissioners had been appointed.[21]

When the amendment came to the Commons on 28 July 1868, it was opposed by Spenser Walpole on behalf of the government. His argument had nothing to do with the 'eminent fitness' of the two men, but was based solely on the view that 'nine was too large a working number; and that by the addition, the balance of the Commission, both political and professional, would be very materially disturbed'.[22] What was revealing, however, was the suggestion by a supporter of the amendment that the Rev. Blakesley's name had been omitted because St Paul's School had been omitted from the Bill, and so there was no longer a need for that school to be 'represented'.[23] Sir Roundell Palmer's name would then have to be omitted, to preserve an odd number of Commissioners for voting purposes. This suggestion, although denied, tends to confirm the view that members of the Select Committees in Parliament and of the Special Commission were chosen unofficially, but deliberately, to represent individual schools, that the precise representation of these schools and the almost total exclusion of former pupils from other schools was deliberate. Rather than considering the schools in the national interest, it seemed that the Parliamentary Committees and the Special Commissioners represented the interests of the schools, and were deliberately chosen to do so. Evidence for this is circumstantial, as it is for the selection of school governors, but such a precise representation of each school on each committee cannot have been accidental; what was revealing about the discussion of the Special Commissioners was that a member had been dropped because 'his' school had been omitted from the Bill and no longer needed a 'representative'. Sir Roundell Palmer too, although from Rugby and Winchester, was also a member of the Mercers' Company and, unfortunately, an amateur scientist.

The impetus for reform that had come from the Clarendon Commission was further lost during the long process of legislation. Opposition from the schools, from MPs and from peers was encouraged by the long legislative process, which encouraged hopes that the Public Schools Bills might be stopped altogether,[24] by the majorities which public school men had at all times on all Parliamentary committees concerned with the Public Schools Bills,[25] and by the frequent changes of government—especially the change of government in June 1866 when Russell's Liberal government was replaced by a Conservative government under Lord Derby. This not only meant that Clarendon, who introduced the Public Schools Bills of 1864, 1865 and 1866, was replaced by Lord Derby, who introduced the Public School Bill of 1867, but that the Bill of 1865 which, much amended, eventually became the *Public Schools Act, 1868*, was introduced and amended three successive times in the Lords before it was discussed in the House of Commons.[26]

The *Public Schools (No. 32) Bill* of 1865 was introduced into the Lords in March 1865, and passed through the second reading, a Lords Select Committee and the Lords Report Stage in June 1865, but failed to reach the Commons.[27] In 1866 virtually the same Bill, as previously amended, was again introduced into the Lords in May as the *Public Schools (No. 110) Bill*.[28] Once more the Bill passed through the Lords, being further amended, and did not reach the Commons until July for a formal first reading.[29] No debate took place in the Commons until August 1866, when the Order for the second reading was discharged, after a brief debate, for lack of time.[30] No amendments were made at this time. Derby's government introduced a *Public Schools (No. 4) Bill* into the Lords again in February 1867 and once more the Bill progressed, with yet more amendments, through the Lords and received its third reading in March 1867.[31] This Bill received its first reading in the Commons in March, but the Order for the second reading was again discharged in August 1867 because of lack of time.[32]

The Lords thus had opportunities in 1865, 1866 and 1867 to discuss and drastically amend the Bills that had begun as the *Public Schools (No. 32) Bill* in 1865 before the Commons had an opportunity to begin any serious discussion of the Bill's proposals or to make any amendments. These opportunities given to the Lords were particularly important because it was here that opposition to the Bills was concentrated. The Lords gave the schools and other local petitioners an opportunity to be heard by counsel before the Lords Select Committee in 1865, and there is no doubt that these hearings in May and June 1865 were used by the schools and their supporters to obstruct and delay the Bill, to nullify its provisions, to disparage the claims of local people to free education and to argue that some schools should be exempt from the Bill's provisions—an exemption claimed successfully by St Paul's and Merchant Taylors'.[33] The introduction of the Public Schools Bills into the Lords was thus especially helpful for those who wished to prevent or delay government intervention, or to minimise the effect of any intervention, for it was in the Lords that public school men and conservative supporters of the established order were in the greatest majority and here that the bishops, uniformly conservative on this issue and including amongst their number two former public school headmasters, had most political influence.[34] The Lords Select Committee, although containing some members favourable to reform—Granville, the Prince of Wales and three members of the Clarendon Commission—had a large majority of public school men and, of these, most had been to Eton.[35]

By the time the *Public Schools (No. 24) Bill* reached the Commons in December 1867, the conservative amendments had been made and the Commons Select Committee, appointed in March 1868, was left with amendments that can be best described as technical, administrative and marginal.[36] Unlike the Lords, the Commons Select Committee did contain some radical reformers—men like Ayrton, Neate, Forster and Grant Duff himself—but still contained, nevertheless, not just the inevitable Conservative majority, but a large majority of public school men, including four from Eton. Eight public schools were represented on the Commons Committee by their former pupils—the seven schools mentioned in the Bill plus St Paul's.[37] The correspondence of Clement—a member of the Committee, MP for Shrewsbury and a former pupil of the school—made it clear that 'representation' meant looking after the interests of the school with which an MP was associated.[38] There can be little doubt that, although some radical members of the Committee were nominated because of their general interest in education, the majority were appointed specifically to protect the interests of their own schools. Such a precise representation of each school on the Committee can hardly have been fortuitous. Certainly, the Special Commissioners named in the Bill were nominated on that basis. If the successive Lords' amendments had made the Public Schools Bills finally acceptable to the schools and their supporters, the Commons Select Committee made the Bill conform to the particular, detailed demands of each school.

The role of MPs as representatives, or spokesmen, of particular sectional interests was well established in 1868, persisting long after the extension of the franchise in 1896, but there can be few examples of ostensibly reforming legislation which was so completely controlled throughout by the representatives of the institutions to be reformed and of the social class whose interests they served. The European impetus towards reform, the need for a national system of secondary education, the national interest in scientific and technical education which had underlined the public criticisms of 1860 and 1861 and the work of Granville, Clarendon and Duff, vanished in the Lords' amendments. The public schools were left confirmed by legislation in the status and privileges they had acquired by tradition and appropriation. The Public Schools Acts conferred upon them a separate legal identity which had been negotiated by their Parliamentary representatives.

The *Clarendon Report* received considerable publicity in 1864 and general, though qualified, approval in the periodical press. Descriptions of the Report, with comments, appeared in *Blackwood's Magazine*, in the *Cornhill Magazine*, in the *Edinburgh Review*, in the *Quarterly Review*, in *Chamber's Journal* and, some time later, in the *Fortnightly Review*.[39] The general concensus of these articles was that the Commission's inquiry had been justified and that, although much had been found that was praiseworthy, much more had been found that needed reform—particularly at Eton, where the need to reform the curriculum and the school's statutes was overshadowed by the need to reform the school's governing body to prevent financial misappropriation and to regularise and reform the school's financial arrangements. A comment from *Chamber's Journal* sums up the general view:

Upon the whole, then, it may be considered as fully made out, that these public schools might do much more than they now do, both in

amending the work which they profess to undertake, and by introducing other subjects of study which have not been introduced or ...
giving them far greater weight than is at present attached to them.[40]

The same point of view was put forward in the Parliamentary
debates on the Report. The Commons debate took place on
6 May 1864 on an Amendment to a Supply Resolution, introduced by Grant Duff, that 'the state of the higher School
Education is not satisfactory and calls for the early attention
of Her Majesty's Government'.[41] In his speech, Grant Duff
described the assertions of those who, like himself, supported
reform:

> That the education given to average boys at the public schools was very
> bad and secondly, that the education given to the most successful
> boys was, when compared with the requirements of the age, sadly
> inadequate. On both these counts of the indictment, the Commissioners
> have found, so to speak, a verdict for the prosecution, as they have also
> upon a hundred other counts.[42]

After speaking of the need to reform the constitution of the
schools, to improve the teaching of the classics and to broaden
the curriculum to include modern languages, geography, history,
English literature and science, he went on to recommend
entrance fees and the imposition of entrance qualifications
which, he said, had hitherto been of little importance to the
public schools.[43] Reform the schools in this way, he argued,
and 'the demand to enter such a school as Eton will become
so great, that you will be able to dictate what conditions you
please'.[44] Such schools, he said, would have a European importance—emphasising his view that reform should be seen in a
European context and that excellence ought to be established
by European standards.[45]

All the speakers in the debate which followed had close
connections with the public schools, mostly with Eton and—
although nobody disputed the accuracy of the Report or the
fairness of its comments—each speaker disagreed with Duff
in some way.[46] They regretted his criticisms, praised the schools,
stressed the co-operation that the schools had given the Commission and suggested that reform could best be left to the
schools themselves. Gladstone, who first replied, did not agree
with Duff's limited approval of the classics, regretted his

criticisms of Westminster School, disputed the value of modern languages for 'gentlemen' and, in a curiously modern comment, blamed the faults of the schools on the parents and on society.[47] He was particularly disparaging about the value of Italian and German in the education of a gentleman. The student and the author, he argued, were different in kind from the gentleman; other European countries might have authors and students, but they did not have gentlemen.[48] Once more, as in the public discussion before the Clarendon Commission, the public schools were defended on almost mystical social grounds for which measurable educational success was irrelevant. He praised the schools for having done their work well, 'namely, the work of rearing the English gentleman, and the fitting him for the discharge of those various duties which in this country have always been inseparable from his position in life'.[49]

The supposed ability of the schools, whatever their faults, to produce gentlemen was a powerful argument against change when the *Public Schools (No. 32) Bill* was introduced in 1865, as this ability was supposedly found most at Eton—the school for which the Bill was primarily introduced.[50] This ability was said to be so delicate that it would not survive government intervention or too-enthusiastic reform.

> In deciding, therefore, upon the results which have been obtained from our . . . public schools, do not let us forget, what is more import- ant than their teaching power, their training power . . . Whatever faults, therefore, we may be disposed to find with these institutions . . . let us remember that the country owes them a debt of gratitude for the work which they have performed . . . I feel confident, however, for my part, that there will be no violent or precipitate legislation upon the subject. I think rather that Parliament will approach it in a spirit of mistrust.[51]

The following speakers, Spenser Walpole and Sir Stafford Northcote, were both concerned to limit the extent of Parlia- mentary control over the schools, although both recognised that some Parliamentary action was unavoidable.[52] Walpole, who, like Gladstone, had been to Eton, suggested that the matter should be left to the Government to initiate 'a proposition founded on this Report'.[53] He continued Gladstone's argument that government control should be limited, suggesting that the schools had already begun to reform themselves and that they therefore, by implication, should be left alone as much as possible. This argument was much used by the schools and their Parliamentary representatives during the progress of the Public Schools Bills, perhaps in the hope that an expressed, active willingness to reform themselves might make legislation seem unnecessary. He had clearly discussed tactics with Eton in preparation for his speech.

> I, like my right hon. Friend [Gladstone] am connected with one of those great public schools. I mean Eton. I happen to know from the highest authorities there—indeed, I have their permission to say so—that since this Report has been in their hands they have taken all the recommendations of the Commissioners *seriatim* into their consideration, with the view of introducing as many of the improvements therein suggested as they believe will be advantageous to the institution. If, therefore, the Government are to take this matter in hand during the recess, they would do well . . . to put themselves in communication with the authorities of these schools as to the course they are inclined to pursue.[54]

Since the Report had only been issued in March 1864, and since Walpole himself confessed that he had not yet the time to read all of it or to form a judgement upon it, it was remarkable that Eton, within a period of about a month, could demonstrate such determination to reform practices and traditions that had continued for centuries.[55] Nevertheless, Walpole's suggestion that the government should take Eton's advice before proceeding was clear.

Sir Stafford Northcote, one of the Commissioners and another of the schools' supporters, thanked the schools for their co-operation, but this comment was rather a polite gloss on the situation.[56] It was clear that the schools had agreed to co-operate with the Clarendon Commission only because they knew that, if they did not, there would have been a public demand for an inquiry with full legal powers to obtain information.[57] Neither was a readiness to provide information always shown. As Grant Duff pointed out earlier in his speech, the Commissioners had been unable to conduct their own examinations within the schools to obtain evidence about the general education of the average boys.[58] All the schools had been reluctant to allow this; Shrewsbury and Rugby had finally agreed, but the others had refused. All the schools preferred to be judged by university results which, although not always creditable, enabled them to demonstrate the attainments of their ablest pupils. The education they provided for boys of average ability was open to question, as Duff suggested.

> The average product is an even inferior article—an article so inferior
> that the head masters of all the schools, except Rugby and Shrewsbury,
> positively refused to allow the Commission to examine them for them-
> selves, lest they should see how bad it was. The correspondence with
> regard to this is given at length, and should be read.[59]

The rest of Northcote's speech indicated other lines of
argument that were to be used by the schools and their supporters in their attempts to prevent or limit legislation. He argued,
for example, that any legislation should deal solely with the
government and finance of the schools, avoiding any control
over the curriculum. This was a curious argument, for the
Report had clearly indicated that curricular reform was necessary
and that the schools were generally unwilling to undertake it.
In asking for the schools to be left to determine their own
curriculum, he fell back upon the familiar argument that they
should not be interfered with too much, lest their ability to
develop character was impaired.

> He earnestly hoped . . . that Parliament should not attempt to deal
> directly with the subjects of study or the management of the schools . . .
> These public schools were national institutions, and had an important
> bearing on the formation of the national character; and not only so,
> but they were themselves the product of the national mind of
> Englishmen.[60]

Once again, the word 'public' was used in an ambiguous way
to suggest that these schools were so important for the public
good that they should be left as free as possible from public
accountability. Unlike Duff, Northcote did not want the schools
changed to accord with European ideas, for the English schools
produced 'men' (and the European schools, by implication,
did not).

> The English mind did not want the *lycées* and *gymnasia* which existed
> in other countries, but schools for the moral, physical and intellectual
> training of boys between the important years of twelve and eighteen,
> and which should make of these boys young men—men in every sense
> of the word.[61]

For the first time too, the argument was put forward that
Parliament should not attempt to legislate for all the schools

together, or, at least, should minimise this collective approach by appointing a separate Commission to negotiate with each school. This was eventually done. The *Public Schools (No. 110) Bill* of 1866 contained provisions for a Special Commission which was eventually appointed and which negotiated with each school the final details of its reform. Since the Commission was, in the event, composed entirely of public school men and concerned almost entirely with the details of governing bodies and school statutes, there was little educational reform to be expected of these men.[62] Northcote did envisage the new governing bodies being ultimately responsible for the internal management and curricula of the schools, but this roused exceptional hostility from headmasters and the powers of the governors were, in the end, severely restricted.[63] The appointment of a Special Commission and the limiting of legislation to matters of school finance and government were major subsequent changes from the *Public Schools (No. 32) Bill* of 1865 and the *Public Schools (No. 110) Bill* of 1866, and also represented major victories for the schools and their supporters, as all semblance of central government control or direction was thereby lost.[64] Northcote argued that the differences between the schools made any comprehensive legislation inappropriate and he hoped that 'the legislation which the House might adopt would effect the necessary improvements without destroying the great principle upon which our public schools had been conducted'.[65] He did not indicate which principle he meant. Perhaps it was the principle that character was more important than curriculum, or perhaps that the schools were best left to reform themselves—although both these principles, as the Clarendon Commission showed, had produced much that was discreditable and little in the way of educational progress.

One way for the schools to avoid Parliamentary intervention, however limited, was to claim legal exemption from Parliamentary jurisdiction. In a general sense, of course, all were subject to the sovereignty of Parliament but, in a more specific sense, this might be possible if a school could claim that its endowments were not 'public' or that its income came from private sources. It was clearly difficult for Parliament to impose new governing bodies and new statutes on a school that was legally 'private', since such a school could be closed if the private individuals or institutions supporting it withdrew financial support. As well as these practical difficulties, there would also be legislative problems because the statutes of such a school could only be changed by a private, rather than a public, bill. The procedure for a private bill—that is, a bill affecting only the rights or property of certain private bodies or individuals—allowed persons opposing or affected by the bill to be heard by counsel, and such a bill could not be introduced by the government. Some schools were later to claim that the Public Schools Bills themselves were of a hybrid, or partly private, nature, in the hope that Parliamentary proceedings would thereby be delayed.[66] Two schools however, St Paul's and Merchant Taylors', were able to claim successfully that their constitutions made them legally 'private' schools, in spite of some public endowment, and that these constitutions could not be legally altered by 'public' legislation. It was for this reason that the *Public Schools Act, 1868* concerned itself with only seven schools while the Clarendon Commission had investigated nine. Once again, during the initial debate in May 1864 there was an indication of the tactics that would be used by the schools to limit or prevent legislation. Grant Duff, in his comments on individual schools, mentioned the particular legal claims made for St Paul's and Merchant Taylors'.

> The evidence relating to St. Paul's is peculiarly interesting . . . It is now doing very little, whereas it is quite clear that it might be the first day-school not only in London, but in England. Its surplus revenue amounts to a very large sum, its accumulated capital is very great, and in little more than twenty years it will become very much richer. Surely it should be made what Dean Colet evidently intended it to be—an institution yielding to none in giving a really high class of education. There is, or is said to be, a question of law relating to the property of this school, about which a judicial decision should be immediately taken. What the decision will be, one can hardly doubt, as it is scarcely credible that Dean Colet, who was extremely anxious for the promotion of learning, should have wished the Mercers' Company to have been beneficially interested in the surplus revenues of his property, and only obliged to maintain the school as a charge upon them.[67]

The legal position of St Paul's and the school's endowments had been further complicated by litigation between the Mercers' Company and the solicitors of Baron de Rothschild during the period from 1858 to 1862.[68] In 1858, the Mercers' Company entered into negotiations with Baron Rothschild about the exchange of property in Buckinghamshire that belonged to St Paul's School for an estate belonging to Rothschild in Northamptonshire. This agreement was never completed, and the Mercers' Company declined to continue negotiations. Rothschild then took legal action against the Mercers' Company through the Attorney-General in the Court of Chancery—seeking to have the alleged agreement put into effect, claiming that the agreement was beneficial to the charity, arguing that the Mercers' Company was the trustee of Dean Colet's endowments and attempting to compel the Company to obtain powers from the Charity Commissioners to complete the contract. The argument of the Company was that, although it had an obligation to maintain St Paul's School, it had no obligation to devote the whole of Colet's endowments to this purpose. The view of the Mercers' Company was put very clearly to the Clarendon Commission: 'The Mercers' Company do not admit themselves trustees, in the legal meaning of the term, of the Coletine estates, but they acknowledge that they are bound to maintain the school.'[69]

The Mercers' Company eventually won the dispute with Baron Rothschild, but the Court declined to give a judgement on the Company's claim to be owner of the Colet estates and not merely the trustee. Soon after, however, the Attorney-General again commenced legal proceedings in the Court of Chancery—this time seeking to have the Mercers' Company declared the trustee, not the owner, of these endowments. This action was proceeding in 1864 and carried on until 1870, when the Court held that the Company did act as trustee for the whole of the Colet estates for St Paul's School, and was bound to account for the whole of the income from those estates which were held in trust for the school. The school was included in the *Public Schools (No. 32) Bill* of 1865, but the Mercers' Company appeared by counsel before the Lords Select Committee in May of that year and asked for St Paul's School to be excluded from the Bill because the Company was then engaged in litigation to determine the legal title to Dean Colet's estates. In June the Committee voted to exclude the school, although Clarendon, Granville and the Prince of Wales voted to keep it in.

The view of St Paul's School may be deduced from the comment of the school's historian that 'from every point of view it must be admitted that the school may congratulate itself that the recommendations of the Commissioners were not carried into effect'.[70] Very few of the Commissioners' recommendations were to be carried into effect, however, even for the schools that remained within the scope of the Public Schools Acts. St Paul's suffered the even worse fate of coming under the jurisdiction of the Endowed Schools Commission, set up by the Endowed Schools Act of 1869. As the school historian put it, 'the decision of the Court of Chancery that the Mercers' Company were in no sense the beneficial owners of the estates of the school, and its omission from the schedule to the Public Schools Act of 1868 brought it, by mere operation of law, within the mischief of the Endowed Schools Act of the following year'.[71] The school did not, therefore, escape government intervention, and was eventually included in less exalted company.[72]

The situation of the Merchant Taylors' School, which Grant Duff also referred to in his comments on the Report, was even more curious than that of St Paul's. The governors denied any legal obligation to maintain the school at all, and claimed the right to close it at will, whatever the wishes of Parliament. Grant Duff summarised the position as: 'The Merchant Taylors' Company . . . hold themselves free from all legal obligations whatever, and say that they might abolish their school altogether if they pleased.'[73] The school was more successful than St Paul's in excluding itself altogether from Parliamentary control, for it was never again discussed in debate and no mention of it appeared in the *Public Schools (No. 32) Bill* of 1865, although it had been included in the preliminary Public Schools Act of 1864.[74]

The Lords' discussion of the *Clarendon Report* was briefer than the debate in the Commons. Only two peers spoke, neither of whom had been educated in the public schools—one speaker was Clarendon and the other was Lord Stanhope, who had been educated privately.[75] The discussion was formally on an 'Address for Papers' and no division took place. Clarendon indicated that 'the government thought there was no time this year to go into a full discussion on the subject with respect to the governing bodies of schools, and the other points of the system'.[76] Stanhope, after some comments on the classics and after expressing some doubts about the advisability of introducing any advanced mathematics or any science into the schools, went on to raise more fundamental objections to the Report's recommendations. Like the objections in the Commons discussion, Stanhope's objections provided an indication of the objections that were later to be raised more forcefully against the Public Schools Bills, especially the *Public Schools (No. 32) Bill* of 1865. He objected to two recommendations that he thought would undermine the authority of headmasters: that parents should have some choice in their child's course of study and that formal arrangements should be made for headmasters to consult their staff about the running of their schools.

The Report recommended that 'arrangements should be made for allowing boys, after arriving at a certain place in the school, and upon the request of their parents or guardians, to drop some portion of their classical work (for example, Latin verse and Greek composition), in order to devote more time to modern languages, mathematics or natural science'.[77] Stanhope thought that parents did not know enough to make such judgements. He scornfully dismissed the claims of parents, especially mothers, to have any influence and wanted headmasters to be completely independent of them.

> He entirely objected to this reference to parents or guardians who would tend to assimilate the practice of public to that of private schools. Many of their Lordships knew that the main difficulty with which the heads of private schools had to contend was injudicious interference on the part of parents. An anxious mother wrote to the head master of a private school, 'I hope you will not think it necessary to teach my dear boy arithmetic, because it always gives him a headache;' or 'I trust you will not push him any further in Greek, for he declares the Greek alphabet is very hard'. It is extremely difficult for the head master of a private school to maintain an independent course in the teeth of such requests . . . Surely their Lordships would not wish to see such a system introduced into the public schools? It was the duty of the heads of those great establishments to prescribe themselves the course of study, and then to permit parents to send their boys or not, as they thought fit. Besides, he asked their Lordships to reflect how inadequate parents often were to form an intelligent opinion upon such points.[78]

It is difficult to understand how Stanhope's argument could be taken seriously when it was clear from the fees required of most parents, from the standard of education expected of boys on entry and from the general social standing of most public school parents that the majority of boys came from educated homes. Clearly, the public schools and their supporters wanted headmasters to be free from parental influence just as they wanted their schools to be free from Parliamentary influence. The ease with which Stanhope was able to dismiss the *Clarendon Report*'s support for more parental influence was perhaps partly a consequence of the kind of education provided, partly of its classical obscurity and partly perhaps of his choice of examples, in which women were said to be particularly incapable of making sensible judgements about their sons' education.

> Their Lordships might know instances in which mothers, left widows in straitened circumstances, had voluntarily deprived themselves of all the luxuries, and many even of the comforts, of life to obtain for their sons the advantages of a public school education; such cases were not infrequent and they were exceedingly meritorious and honourable to all parties concerned. Let their Lordships suppose a lady in such circumstances receiving the following letter from a headmaster: 'Dear Madam, I wish to learn your opinion of Greek iambics, and whether you judge it best that your son at this school should go on with Latin alcaics'. What answer could the poor gentlewoman return to such inquiries, and what would be its value when received?[79]

This dismissive attitude, in which women were typified as worthy but innocent, ignorant and helpless, had at least the merit of recognising that some mothers might have definite views about the education of their sons. The attitude of Parliament towards the education of women in endowed schools was totally dismissive. At no time in the debates on the *Clarendon Report* or the Public Schools Bills was the education of women mentioned at all, and nobody asked why it was that these great public endowments should be devoted exclusively to the education of men. The public schools had a tradition of educating only boys, which derived in part from the long association of the Church with education and the ecclesiastical origin of many foundations. The period from 1864 to 1868, when the main Public Schools Bills were before Parliament, was, however, a period when women's education received much discussion in the press, when girls were already being educated with boys in other state-aided schools and when much progress was being made in women's education at Oxford and Cambridge.[80] There were no inherent reasons why the public schools could not admit girls, particularly 'day girls', after appropriate legislation by Parliament—in fact, some schools did not even need this. The will of Lawrence Sheriffe, the London grocer who founded Rugby School, left money for 'a free Grammar Schoole . . . to serve cheifly [sic] for the children of Rugby and Brownesover' although no girls seem ever to have attended.[81] The attitudes of Victorian society towards women were complex and ambivalent, but the complete absence of any thought for women's education must have been due, in part, to the dominance of public school men in Parliament, who were determined to preserve the public school traditions and the schools' traditional function of producing the English 'gentleman', for whom there was no feminine equivalent.

The public schools, which were mostly boarding schools and usually far away from parents, also had a tradition of restricting parental influence over or knowledge of school life and a complementary tradition of committing much influence and authority to the headmaster. Such authority was naturally enhanced when the subjects taught were of such a scholarly and specialised nature that parents might feel reticent about entering into a thorough discussion of their child's progress, just as today's parents might feel some reticence in discussing modern mathematics. In any case, the nature of boarding school life made any close and informed contact with the schools difficult for most parents. The relative lack of parental protest over, for example, the excessive punishment frequently inflicted in these schools suggests that parents knew very little about what was going on and there can be little doubt that headmasters were content to enjoy their authority unrestricted by parents' views. One difficulty that headmasters faced was that foundation boys were usually local with parents nearby who were better placed to criticise both the curriculum and the headmaster's conduct of the school. It was from these local parents that complaints about the conduct of headmasters and attempts to reform the curriculum usually came.[82] One motive behind the desire of many headmasters to discourage foundation boys, and sometimes day-boys generally, was perhaps to limit local, well-informed criticism. Evidence given to the Lords Select Committee in 1865 suggested that, in spite of Stanhope's comments, many local parents were quite capable of making clear and well-informed judgements about their local school and the education that it offered.[83] In the years before the appointment of the Clarendon Commission the conflicts in many schools between local parents and local governors (who wished to reform the school curriculum to meet the wishes of local parents) and the school headmasters (who generally wished to preserve the classical curriculum and their schools' prestigious national reputation) made it clear that many local parents did wish to have more influence in their children's schools and made clear to the Lords Select Committee their view that the Clarendon Commission had not adequately consulted local parents and local interests.[84] One probable motive behind the wish of some headmasters to move their schools away from sites in the towns to new sites out in the country was the desire to be virtually free of parental oversight. At Shrewsbury, for example, both Butler and Kennedy met with much local criticism—both of the school's curriculum and of their severity. Moss was determined to move the school to a new site outside the town from the time of his appointment in 1866.[85] No doubt there was a need for new buildings and more space, but the experience of his predecessors with local parents must also have weighed with Moss.[86] The scandal at Shrewsbury in 1874, when Moss severely flogged a boy called Loxdale, was exacerbated by the fact that Loxdale was a local day-boy whose parents lived close enough to the school to know of the affair and to make an immediate protest.[87]

Clarendon's reply to Stanhope in the debate was surprisingly modern in its acceptance of the importance of parental views in a child's education. He had himself taken an active interest in his own son's education at Harrow.

> There was another reflection which his noble Friend had made, and in which he was hardly justified, with reference to the interference of parents. But their Lordships should observe that what the Commissioners proposed was this—that parents might be allowed to suggest some change, because, after all, a parent was likely to be better acquainted with the disposition of his own son than the headmaster. What they recommended, therefore, was that arrangements should be made for allowing boys, at the request of the parents, after arriving at a certain place in the school to drop some portion of the school business . . . in order to give the spare time to other studies.[88]

This proposal from the Commission would no doubt have

had a profound effect on the curriculum, since the obligation to provide choice for parental discussion would have encouraged diversity of provision and the growth of parental influence—not only in the endowed schools affected by the Public Schools Acts, but also in all the other schools for which the public schools provided a model and an example. As it was, the Lords' opposition prevented the inclusion of this recommendation in the Public Schools Bills and the Commission's concern for parental views remained a pious suggestion, being left—like curricular reform—to headmasters who had hitherto shown little enthusiasm for the idea. No mention of parental views was made in the Public Schools Bills and no provision made for parent representation on the new governing bodies.

The other of the Commission's suggested reforms to which Stanhope objected in the Lords was the introduction of some formal provision for consultation between a headmaster and his staff on matters concerning the conduct and organisation of the school. The Commission had found these 'school councils' in existence at Harrow and Rugby, and considered that they contributed to the welfare of these schools.[89] Stanhope objected to this proposal, as did most headmasters, on the grounds that the necessity to consult with his staff would undermine a headmaster's authority.[90]

> That appeared to him to be a very dangerous innovation, inasmuch as it would weaken the authority of the head master. Such a council, like other legislative bodies, would soon become subject to divisions; and when the boys once learnt, as they would be sure to do, that there were so many masters on one side and so many on the other, their confidence in and respect for the central authority would be weakened.[91]

Clarendon pointed out that this system already existed at Harrow and Rugby, but what the headmasters were objecting to, of course, was the possibility of provision in the new school statutes for a consultative body of staff whose advice they could not easily ignore.[92] What the discussion of these two recommendations in the Lords and the views of the head-masters revealed was the extent to which the practices of the schools in their internal government, and the views of the headmasters about school government, starkly reflected Conservative political attitudes, which saw authority as hierarchical and directive, not participatory or consultative, and which scorned and distrusted leadership based upon concensus. There was a close political parallel between opposition to consultation with parents and staff in schools and the opposition in Parliament to the extension of the franchise.

The political purpose of the Public Schools Bills—the preservation of educational, political and economic advantage for the 'higher classes' by the adaptation of the public schools to this end—and the reservation of these schools for the 'higher classes', was clearly and frankly indicated by many speakers in the Lords debates. Lord Houghton, for example, expressed these purposes forcefully in 1865 to an apparently approving House.

> The present question . . . is not only a question of the moral and intellectual character of the higher classes in this country, it is a question, I may say, of their political supremacy. The very lowest classes of the community are making advances in education, and with the eagerness shown on this subject, the generation to come may be still more active. It will be impossible, I believe, for the wealth, property and rank of this country to keep themselves in the same right government, and to have the same influence which they now exercise, unless great reforms be made in the public school system.[93]

However, as Houghton admitted, not all members of the 'higher classes' would have great ability, so 'with the majority education must be the means of making them fit to govern their fellow men'.[94] It was perhaps for this reason that so many speakers in both Houses stressed how important it was for the schools to produce 'gentlemen' and seemed relatively unconcerned about academic education, often regarding it as a desirable but secondary matter. Indeed, some members of the Lords showed much concern for the stupid but indigent members of the 'higher classes' and did not want them excluded by competitive examinations.

> He did not . . . think it would be well to rely entirely on competitive examinations for introducing the sons of persons in narrow circumstances. There was a tendency to think that it was their duty to educate clever boys only, whereas the object of these schools was to educate stupid boys as well. He was not clear that Sir Walter Scott or the late Duke of Wellington would have succeeded in such an examination. He was anxious to see these schools made available to the largest portion of the upper classes of this country.[95]

It was this view of the public schools as the places where, above all, attitudes acceptable to the 'higher classes' were formed, which led to such emphasis on the importance of the headmasters' powers as the symbol within the schools of the Conservative values of order, hierarchy and respected authority and which led to such disparagement of other school staff, of parents and of governors, all of whom had a reasonable claim to some influence. Such influence was characterised as 'interference' and such claims to influence as were admitted, were so only on the understanding that the claim was acceptable in theory but unacceptable in practice. The powers of governing bodies proved the most difficult to disparage because their legal powers already existed and their claims to influence over school policy were indisputable. However, Conservative speakers suggested that sensible governors never used this influence, and suggested that even the discussion of reform in Parliament did the schools a disservice because it encouraged governing bodies to 'interfere'.

> In fact, they [the new governing bodies] will have nothing else to do but to interfere, and they are called upon by Act of Parliament to interfere as much as possible . . . Now, no doubt these rights of interference are probably possessed by the governing bodies at this moment; but then they are not stirred up by Act of Parliament to interfere, and no doubt you wish by this Bill to stir them up to do so.[96]

Later, some speakers in the Lords wanted to give headmasters absolute authority over some aspects of school life by law, but were prevented from doing so by the legal difficulties of giving statutory powers to headmasters, who were legally the servants of their governing bodies. It was only these legal difficulties which prevented the Lords from giving headmasters unchallengeable powers.[97]

The initial debate in the Lords, although it revealed some major objections to the Clarendon Commission's proposals, ended without a division and the government merely indicated its intention to introduce a major Public Schools Bill in the next session. The *Public Schools (No. 168) Bill* was introduced in May 1864, but this was of a purely technical, legal nature, designed to prevent the appointment of new school governors that would make forthcoming legislation more difficult. Clarendon made the purpose of this Bill clear at the end of the first Lords debate.[98] It was introduced into the Lords in May 1864 and passed quickly through Parliament, receiving the Royal Assent on 29 July 1864 as the *Public Schools Act, 1864.* The main proposals of the government for the public schools were contained in the *Public Schools (No. 32) Bill* which was introduced into the Lords in March 1865.[99] It was this Bill against which the public schools and their supporters concentrated their opposition and which, much changed, eventually formed the basis of the *Public Schools Act, 1868.*

Notes

1   See Grant Duff, *Hansard*, CLXXI, 11 June 1863, cols. 712–17. See also Chapter 3, Note 88.
2   See Grant Duff, *Hansard*, CLXXIV, 16 March 1864, cols. 116–21. The Bill of 1864 was lost in July 1864, but Duff seconded another Bill in June 1865. He supported a similar Bill in 1868 with a plea for parity with Europe. See *Hansard*, CLXXVI, 1 July 1864, cols. 639–46; also, *Hansard*, CLXXVIII, 14 June 1865, cols. 207–10; also, *Hansard*, CXCIII, 1 July 1868, cols. 428–32. See also, Rt Hon. Mountstuart E. Grant Duff, *Some Brief Comments on Passing Events made between February 4th 1858 and October 5th 1881*, Madras, 1884, p. 278 and Rt Hon. Mountstuart E. Grant Duff, *Notes from a Diary, 1851–1872*, London, 1897, I, 1 July 1864, p. 282. See also Chapter 3, Note 88.
3   In 1864 he introduced but lost an amendment calling on the government to act on the findings of the *Report of the Commission of the Inns of Court*, appointed in 1854, which reported in August 1855. See *Hansard*, CLXXVI, 1 July 1864, cols. 639–46. For London University, see Grant Duff, *Hansard*, CLXXIX, 2 June 1865, cols. 1209–16. For India, see Grant Duff, *Hansard*, CXCII, 18 May 1868, col. 426. See also Chapter 3, Note 88.
4   At Aberdeen University in 1867 he reminded the students that Scotland 'was a member of the European commonwealth before it formed a portion of the United Kingdom'. Duff, *Some Brief Comments on Passing Events*, p. 237. See also Chapter 3, Note 88.
5   These articles are brought together in Mountstuart E. Grant Duff, *Studies in European Politics*, Edinburgh, 1866.
6   See *The Times*, 16 February 1861, p. 9.
7   See *The Times*, 13 August 1860, p. 9.
8   *The Times*, 16 February 1861, p. 9.
9   Unsigned letter to *The Times*, 8 December 1863, p. 3.
10   Lord John Russell (1792–1878) was at Westminster 1803–4; see *Dict. Nat. Biog.*, XVII, pp. 454–64. The other famous men were Lord Somerset (1788–1855), the 1st Baron Raglan of Crimean War fame, and Charles Thomas Longley (1794–1868) who was Archbishop of Canterbury 1862–8.
11   See *The Times*, 18 May 1864, p. 19.
12   See Note 1 above.
13   Grant Duff, *Hansard*, CLXXI, 11 June 1863, cols. 712–17.
14   The Prime Ministers were Palmerston (1859–65), Russell (1865–6), Derby (1866–8), Disraeli (1868) and Gladstone (1868–74).
15   The Bills were the *Public Schools (No. 168) Bill* of 1864; *Public Schools (No. 32) Bill* of 1865; *Public Schools (No. 110) Bill* of 1866; *Public Schools (No. 4) Bill* of 1867; *Public Schools (No. 24) Bill* of 1867; *Public Schools (No. 135) Bill* of 1868; *Public Schools (No. 217) Bill* of 1869; *Public Schools (No. 200) Bill* of 1870; *Public Schools (No. 204) Bill* of 1871 and the *Public Schools (No. 27) Bill* of 1872. This number includes only the Bills introduced anew into Parliament or after substantial changes in Select Committees. If all the

Bills were included and the timespan extended to the end of 1873, the number of Bills would be over twenty. The Acts were those of 1864, 1868, 1869, 1870, 1871, 1872 and 1873. For a detailed chronological summary of Parliamentary proceedings, see C. J. Shrosbree, 'The origins and influence of the Clarendon Commission (1861–1864), with special reference to Shrewsbury School', PhD thesis, Birmingham University, 1985, Appendix II.

16 For a contemporary discussion of the *Clarendon Report* and a comment on the Bill of 1865, see A. Trollope, 'Public Schools', *Fortnightly Review*, 2, 1 October 1865, pp. 481–7.

17 For a concise summary of the *Public Schools (No. 32) Bill* of 1865, see *The Times*, 20 March 1865, p. 5. For discussion about an 'Executive Commission', see *Hansard*, CLXXVIII, 3 April 1865, cols. 630, 644–5, 658–9 and 667. For discussion of the Special Commissioners, see *Hansard*, CLXXXIII, 29 May 1866, cols. 1410–16. For detailed information about the Special Commissioners, see Shrosbree, 'Origins of the Clarendon Commission', Appendix VII and Chapter 6, Note 103.

18 One reason for the number of Public Schools Acts after 1868 was to allow an extension of time for the settlement of these details. For Shrewsbury School as an example, see Chapter 5, p. 156. For other schools, see Chapter 6, Note 154.

19 For the importance of this in Parliament, see Chapter 6, p. 202. For Rugby, as an example, see Chapter 5, Note 130. For governors of Shrewsbury School before and after the Public Schools Acts, see Chapter 5, pp. 142, 157 and Chapter 2, Notes 47 and 48.

20 *Public Schools Act, 1868*, Section 12(7).

21 See *Public Schools Bill: Amendment to be moved by the Lord Lyttelton, (262a), 17th July 1868*, in *Hansard*, CXCIII, 23 July 1868, col. 1658. Sir Roundell Palmer (1812–95), a barrister, was Liberal-Conservative MP for Plymouth 1847–52 and 1853–7, and for Richmond 1861–72. He was Solicitor-General 1861–3 and Attorney-General 1863–6. Created 1st Baron Selbourne in 1872, he became Lord Chancellor 1872–4 and 1880–5. Rev. Joseph William Blakesley (1808–85) was Tutor at Trinity College, Cambridge 1839–45, Vicar of Ware 1845–72 and Canon of Canterbury Cathedral 1863–72. His career was promoted by Palmerston, who approved of his Whig views. He later became Dean of Lincoln. The son of a London merchant, he attended St Paul's School, became a governor of the school and, in 1864, was made Master of the Mercers' Company.

22 Spenser Walpole, *Hansard*, CXCIII, 28 July 1868, col. 1904. Spenser Horatio Walpole (1806–98) was Conservative MP for Cambridge University 1856–82 and a member of the Commons Select Committee on the Public Schools Bill.

23 'The reason why his name . . . was struck off, was because St. Paul's School . . . having been exempted from the operation of the Commission, it was supposed that his name, as representing the School, ought no longer to be retained.' Edward Bouverie, *Hansard*, CXCIII, 28 July 1868, col. 1905. See also *Hansard*, CXCIII, 28 July 1868, cols. 1903–8.

24 As late as June 1868 the governors of Shrewsbury heard from W. J. Clement, MP for Shrewsbury, that he would not be surprised 'if the Bill after all comes to nothing'. Clement to J. J. Peele, probably 7 July 1868, Bailiff's Bundles No. 122. William James Clement (1802–70), Liberal MP for Shrewsbury 1865–70, was a member of the Commons Select Committee on the Public Schools Bill. Joshua John Peele was Shrewsbury School Bailiff 1839–69. See also Chapter 5, Notes 99 and 120.

25 See Chapter 6, Notes 63, 103 and 110.

26 In 1865, 1866 and 1867. See Chapter 6, pp. 181, 191, and 195.

27 For the first reading, see *Hansard*, CLXXVII, 13 March 1865, col. 1533. For the second reading, see *Hansard*, CLXXVIII, 3 April 1865, cols. 630–68. For members of the Lords Select Committee, see *Hansard*, CLXXVIII, 3 April 1865, cols. 1304–5 and for the proceedings of the Select Committee, see the *Lords Select Committee Report, 1865*. For the Report Stage, see *Hansard*, CLXXIX, 22 June 1865, col. 626.

28 For the first reading, see *Hansard*, CLXXXIII, 11 May 1866, col. 743. For the

second reading, see *Hansard*, CLXXXIII, 29 May 1866, cols. 1408–16. For the
Committee Stage, see *Hansard*, CLXXXIII, 5 June 1866, cols. 1923–33 and
for the third reading, see *Hansard*, CLXXXIV, 18 June 1866, cols. 525–9.

29   See *Hansard*, CLXXXIV, 16 July 1866, col. 820.

30   See *Hansard*, CLXXXIV, 7 August 1866, cols. 2149–51.

31   For the first reading, see *Hansard*, CLXXXV, 7 February 1867, col. 80. For the
second reading, see *Hansard*, CLXXXV, 14 February 1867, cols. 333–4. For the
Committee Stage, see *Hansard*, CLXXXV, 26 February 1867, cols. 1002–3.
For the Report Stage, see *Hansard*, CLXXXV, 7 March 1867, col. 1428 and for
the third reading, see *Hansard*, CLXXXV, 8 March 1867, cols. 1546–7.

32   See *Hansard*, CLXXXV, 15 March 1867, col. 1914 and *Hansard*, CLXXXIX,
10 August 1867. (Recorded in General Index but not shown in transcript of
proceedings.)

33   See Note 68 below.

34   The predominance of Eton men in the Lords and in the government was overwhelming. Of the 458 members of the Lords listed at the opening of Parliament in February 1867, for example, 172 were Eton men. Of the remainder,
23 had been to Westminster, 8 to Winchester, 7 to Charterhouse, 2 to St Paul's,
39 to Harrow, 4 to Rugby and one to Shrewsbury. None had been to Merchant
Taylors'. See 'Roll of the Lords Spiritual and Temporal' given before the Queen's
Speech at the opening of Parliament, *Hansard*, CLXXXV, 5 February 1867. Of
the 13 peers who spoke in the Lords during the first week of the new Parliament,
9 were Eton men (Beauchamp, Delamere, Derby, Belmore, Wharncliffe,
Redesdale, Somerset, Dudley and Ellenborough). Of the others, one was from
Westminster (Russell), two were educated privately (St Leonards and Grey) and
one at Dr Burney's School, Greenwich and the naval academy at Gosport
(Chelmsford). See *Hansard*, CLXXXV, 5 February 1867, cols. 1–42; *Hansard*,
CLXXXV, 7 February 1867, cols. 79–82; *Hansard*, CLXXXV, 8 February 1867,
cols. 119–44. Of the 15 members of Derby's Cabinet in February 1867, 9 were
Eton men (Derby, Buckingham, Malmesbury, Walpole, Carnarvon, Cranborne,
Pakington, Northcote and Manners), 2 were from Rugby (Stanley and Peel),
one was from Shrewsbury (Hardy), 2 were educated privately (Disraeli and
Naas) and one at Dr Burney's School, Greenwich and the naval academy at
Gosport (Chelmsford). See the preamble to the Queen's Speech at the opening
of Parliament, *Hansard*, CLXXXV, 5 February 1867. The former public school
headmasters were the Archbishop of Canterbury and the Bishop of London.
Charles Thomas Longley (1794–1868), Archbishop of Canterbury 1862–8,
was headmaster of Harrow 1829–36. Archibald Campbell Tait (1811–82),
Bishop of London 1856–69 and Archbishop of Canterbury 1869–82, was headmaster of Rugby 1842–50. For a comment in the Lords, see Stanhope, *Hansard*,
CLXXV, 27 May 1864, col. 699.

35   See Chapter 6, Note 63.

36   See *Hansard*, CXC, 5 December 1867, cols. 634–5; *Hansard*, CXC, 20 March
1868, cols. 1982, 2052–3; *Hansard*, CXC, 14 February 1868, cols. 742–75.

37   See Chapter 6, Note 110.

38   See Chapter 5, p. 155.

39   See W. L. Collins, 'The Public Schools Report (No. I): Eton', *Blackwood's
Magazine*, 95, June 1864, pp. 707–31; W. L. Collins, 'The Public Schools Report
(No. II): Harrow and Rugby', *Blackwood's Magazine*, 96, August 1864, pp. 219–
40; W. L. Collins, 'The Public Schools Report (No. III): the London schools',
Blackwood's Magazine, 96, October 1864, pp. 449–71; W. L. Collins, 'The
Public Schools Report (No. IV): Winchester and Shrewsbury', *Blackwood's
Magazine*, 96, December 1864, pp. 696–718. See also 'Paterfamilias' (H. J.
Higgins), 'On some points on the Eton report', *Cornhill Magazine*, 10, July
1864, pp. 113–28, a letter from Lord Lyttelton on p. 639 and a reply signed
'Ed. C.M.', attrib. Higgins, on pp. 639–40. See also Goldwin Smith, 'Public
schools', *Edinburgh Review*, 120, July 1864, pp. 147–88; R. H. Cheney, 'Public
schools', *Quarterly Review*, 116, July 1864, pp. 176–211; 'The Public Schools
Commission', an unsigned article in *Chamber's Journal*, Fourth Series, 42, 15
October 1864, pp. 659–62; A. Trollope, 'Public schools', *Fortnightly Review*,
2, 1 October 1865, pp. 476–87.

40 'The Public Schools Commission', *Chamber's Journal*, p. 662.
41 Grant Duff, *Hansard*, CLXXV, 6 May 1864, col. 105. For the whole debate, see *Hansard*, CLXXV, 6 May 1864, cols. 105–43.
42 Grant Duff, *Hansard*, CLXXV, 6 May 1864, col. 106.
43 Grant Duff, *Hansard*, CLXXV, 6 May 1864, cols. 106–17. By history and geography, he meant modern history and modern geography; ancient history and ancient geography were generally taught as minor, complementary parts of the classical curriculum.
44 Grant Duff, *Hansard*, CLXXV, 6 May 1864, col. 118.
45 Grant Duff, *Hansard*, CLXXV, 6 May 1864, col. 118.
46 The speakers in the debate, apart from Grant Duff, were Gladstone (Eton), Spenser Walpole (Eton) and Sir Stafford Northcote (Eton). See *Hansard*, CLXXV, 6 May 1864, cols. 127–43.
47 Gladstone, *Hansard*, 6 May 1864, cols. 127–9. Evidence had been given to the Commission about brutality at Westminster School by a parent, Mr Meyrick, and his son. This was one of the very few instances when the Commission commented adversely on school discipline and the reaction of both Gladstone and Northcote was regret, not that the incidents had taken place, but that Grant Duff should mention them publicly in Parliament. The reaction of Gladstone and Northcote illustrated the social code on such matters—the expectation of silence, the antagonism which such criticisms brought from the public schools' supporters and the difficulties, for boys particularly, in giving evidence to the Commission. For Northcote's comments, see *Hansard*, CLXXV, 6 May 1864, cols. 139–40. See also, *Clarendon Report*, III, pp. 474–95. For another contemporary comment, see 'The Public Schools Commission', *Chamber's Journal*, pp. 662–3.
48 See Gladstone, *Hansard*, CLXXV, 6 May 1864, col. 129.
49 Gladstone, *Hansard*, CLXXV, 6 May 1864, col. 134. Gladstone had tried himself 'to lay down what is nowadays required for the education of an English Gentleman' in the *Clarendon Report*. See Clarendon to Sir George Lewis, 16 October 1861, Clarendon Papers, MSS Clar. Dep. c. 533 (2).
50 'Without intending any offence, I think I may say that this Bill is especially framed for the reform of Eton.' Bishop of London, *Hansard*, CLXXVIII, 3 April 1865, col. 648. See also Note 34 above. The Bishop of London was a member of the Lords Select Committee on the Public Schools Bill.
51 Gladstone, *Hansard*, CLXXV, 6 May 1864, col. 134.
52 Sir Stafford Northcote (1818–87) was Liberal-Conservative MP for Dudley 1855–7, for Stamford 1858–66 and for North Devon 1866–85. He was a member of the Clarendon Commission and of the Commons Select Committee on the Public Schools Bill; see also Chapter 3, Note 119 and Chapter 6, Note 110. For Spenser Walpole, see Note 22 above.
53 Walpole, *Hansard*, CLXXV, 6 May 1864, col. 137.
54 Walpole, *Hansard*, CLXXV, 6 May 1864, cols. 137–8. For another example of this argument about Eton, see Derby, *Hansard*, CLXXVIII, 8 April 1865, col. 653. See also a letter from 'A Reformer' in *The Times*, 31 March 1865, p. 12; see also a comment in *The Times*, 15 February 1868, p. 8 and an article about the reforms at Eton already introduced in the *Eton Chronicle*, 21 May 1868, quoted in *The Times*, 23 May 1868, p. 9. For the failure of the Public Schools Bill of 1865, see Trollope, 'Public schools', p. 487.
55 See Walpole, *Hansard*, CLXXV, 6 May 1864, col. 137.
56 See Northcote, *Hansard*, CLXXV, 6 May 1864, cols. 138–9.
57 See *Hansard*, CLXII, 23 April 1861, col. 984.
58 Grant Duff, *Hansard*, CLXXV, 6 May 1864, col. 108.
59 Grant Duff, *Hansard*, CLXXV, 6 May 1864, col. 108.
60 Northcote, *Hansard*, 6 May 1864, cols. 139–40.
61 Northcote, *Hansard*, 6 May 1864, col. 140.
62 Of the 7 Special Commissioners, 5 had been to Eton, one to Harrow and one to Shrewsbury. See Chapter 6, Note 103.
63 See, for example, Kennedy's views on governors' powers in B. H. Kennedy, *Shrewsbury School: A Letter to His Grace the Archbishop of York on the Public Character of Shrewsbury School, as Affected by the Public Schools*

Bill, Cambridge, 1865, pp. 1–6. For a similar, succinct, forceful expression of headmasters' views, see the Bishop of London, *Hansard*, CLXXVIII, 3 April 1865, col. 651.

64   See Chapter 6, pp. 189–91.
65   Northcote, *Hansard*, CLXXV, 6 May 1864, col. 192.
66   For the Shrewsbury governors' use of this Parliamentary tactic and the precedent on which it was based, see Chapter 5, pp. 154–5.
67   Grant Duff, *Hansard*, CLXXV, 6 May 1864, cols. 123–4. John Colet, Dean of St Paul's, was the founder of St Paul's School in about 1509 and left the school considerable endowments on his death in 1519. See M. F. J. McDonnell, *A History of St. Paul's School*, London, 1909, pp. 7–27.
68   See McDonnell, *St. Paul's School*, pp. 416–18 and Chapter 3, Note 114. See also Derby, *Hansard*, CLXXVIII, 3 April 1865, cols. 631–2; also Lyttelton, *Hansard*, CLXXVIII, 3 April 1865, col. 666. In 1868 Spenser Walpole gave a clear explanation of the omission of St Paul's and Merchant Taylors' from legislation—that the schools were 'more or less schools of a private and not of a public character'. See Walpole, *Hansard*, CXC, 14 February 1868, cols. 742–3. For the case for the exclusion of St Paul's, as presented to the Lords Select Committee, see *Lords Select Committee Report, 1865*, 15 May 1865, p. 75. For the Committee's vote, see 'Order of reference', *Lords Select Committee Report, 1865*, 16 June 1865, p. ix.
69   *Clarendon Report*, IV, p. 72.
70   McDonnell, *St. Paul's School*, p. 415.
71   McDonnell, *St. Paul's School*, p. 415.
72   The school continued to resist the proposals of the Endowed Schools Commission and subsequently of the Charity Commissioners, even after a new scheme drawn up by the Endowed Schools Commission had been approved by the Queen and Privy Council in 1876. Another scheme for the school was introduced in 1879 and yet others in 1893 and 1894. The schemes of 1893 and 1894 were particularly resisted, the first because it proposed to introduce boys from other local elementary and secondary schools and therefore 'to benefit an arbitrarily defined class at the expense of the rest'. The second was resisted because it proposed to introduce representatives of the London County Council onto the school's governing body. Agreement on a scheme, which both excluded boys from other local schools and the London County Council, was not reached until 1900. An attempt to introduce English grammar instead of Latin grammar into the school's entrance examination was also defeated at this time. The school's attempts to defeat the wishes of Parliament are described in some detail, and with some pride, in McDonnell, *St. Paul's School*, pp. 414–25.
73   Grant Duff, *Hansard*, CLXXV, 6 May 1864, col. 124.
74   See the *Public Schools (No. 168) Bill. 1864. Ordered by the House of Commons to be printed 23rd June 1864.*
75   See *Hansard*, CLXXV, 27 May 1864, cols. 699–718; also Note 41 above. For Clarendon's education, see Chapter 3, Note 32. Philip Henry Stanhope (1805–75), 5th Earl Stanhope, was educated privately and at Christ Church, Oxford. He was Conservative MP for Wootton Bassett 1830–2 and for Hertford 1835–52. He was a member of the Lord Select Committee on the Public Schools Bill.
76   Clarendon, *Hansard*, CLXXV, 27 May 1864, col. 718.
77   *Clarendon Report*, I, pp. 35–6, quoted *Hansard*, CLXXV, 27 May 1864, col. 702.
78   Stanhope, *Hansard*, CLXXV, 27 May 1864, col. 709.
79   Stanhope, *Hansard*, CLXXV, 27 May 1864, col. 709.
80   See, for example, A. Maclaren, 'Girls schools', *Macmillan's Magazine*, 10, September 1864, pp. 409–16; J. Davies, 'Female education', *Quarterly Review*, 119, April 1866, pp. 499–515; Dorothea Beale (attrib.—signed A. Utopian), 'On the education of girls', *Fraser's Magazine*, 74, October 1866, pp. 509–24; Anne Clough, 'Hints on the organisation of girls' schools', *Macmillan's Magazine*, 14, October 1866, pp. 435–9; 'Women's education', *Fraser's Magazine*, 79, May 1869, pp. 537–52. The 1860s saw a prolonged campaign for the improvement of women's education 'as a gateway to other rights and opportunities'.

See J. Lawson & H. Silver, *A Social History of Education in England*, London, 1973, p. 306. One important result of this campaign was the inclusion of girls' schools in the work of the Taunton Commission. See Lawson & Silver, *Social History of Education*, pp. 306-7. The period saw also much progress made in academic and higher education for women. In 1858, for example, Dorothea Beale became principal of Cheltenham College for Young Ladies, following the earlier work of Frances Buss at the North London Collegiate School. A college for girls, founded at Hitchin in 1869, moved to Cambridge in 1874 as Girton College. At Oxford University, the first lectures and classes for women were organised informally in 1866. See Lawson & Silver, *Social History of Education*, pp. 304-7 and C. E. Mallet, 'Modern Oxford', in *A History of the University of Oxford*, III, London, 1927, p. 431. In these contemporary circumstances, it is arguable that a powerful though unspoken motive for the priority given to the public schools in Parliament, for the defence of the schools' traditions and for the insistence on a separate Act for the most well-known schools was to preserve the schools for men and to pre-empt the claims of women to a share in the schools' great public endowments.

81 'The true Copy of the intent of Lawrance Sheriffe, concerning the Parsonage of Brownesover, which intent was sealed, subscribed, and delivered by Lawrance Sheriffe, George Harrison, and Barnard Field, as by the same intent appeareth. Copyed the 20th of December, 1580. E. Harrison', quoted in *The Book of Rugby School: Its History and Daily Life*, Rugby, 1856, p. 37.

82 See, for example, the criticisms of Dr Arnold made by M. H. Bloxam in evidence to the Lords Select Committee in 1865. See *Lords Select Committee Report, 1865*, 12 May 1865, p. 46. See also the criticism of Dr Butler and Dr Vaughan at Harrow made by William Winkley, a house agent and bookseller of Harrow, in the *Lords Select Committee Report, 1865*, 15 May 1865, pp. 132-4. For local criticism at Shrewsbury under Kennedy and Moss, see Chapter 5, pp. 140-1. For earlier local criticism of Dr Butler at Shrewsbury, see J. B. Oldham, *A History of Shrewsbury School 1552-1952*, Oxford, 1952, pp. 74-8.

83 See Note 82 above. See also the evidence of J. W. Cunningham, a Churchwarden in Harrow, a Director of the Waterworks and Treasurer of the Parochial Schools, in the *Lords Select Committee Report, 1865*, 15 May 1865, pp. 95-8.

84 See, for example, the evidence of William Winkley of Harrow in the *Lords Select Committee Report, 1865*, 15 May 1865, p. 133. A deputation from the parish of Harrow-on-the-Hill met Clarendon on 25 March 1865. The deputation, which consisted of the vicar and fourteen others, was reported in *The Times*, 27 March 1865, p. 9. Another complaint about the Commission's lack of consultation was made by W. H. Bateson, Master of St John's College, Cambridge, who complained that the public was not aware of the implications for some university colleges, alleged that his own College, which had close legal and historical links with Shrewsbury, had not been consulted at all, and drew attention to the implications of the division that was to be made between the grammar schools of the Public Schools Bills and the other endowed grammar schools. See *The Times*, 28 March 1865, p. 7. William Henry Bateson (1812-81), a former pupil of Shrewsbury, became the first Chairman of the new governing body for Shrewsbury under the Public Schools Acts. See Chapter 5, Note 129.

85 See Note 82 above and Chapter 5, p. 158.

86 See, for example, Samuel Butler's comment that he had 'all the mammas in Shrewsbury' against him, in Samuel Butler, *The Life and Letters of Samuel Butler*, London, 1890, II, p. 124, quoted Oldham, *A History of Shrewsbury School*, p. 75. Moss himself had been a day-boy at Shrewsbury. See Mrs Moss, *Moss of Shrewsbury: A Memoir 1841-1917*, London, 1932, pp. 64-5.

87 See Chapter 5, pp. 163-4.

88 Clarendon, *Hansard*, CLXXV, 27 May 1864, col. 717.

89 *Clarendon Report*, I, pp. 53, 209, 227-8, 233.

90 'A bishop who had been for many years at the head of a great public school told him that during the whole of the time he had never had a single difference with any of his masters, but that, nevertheless, if an order had been issued directing such a council . . . to take effect on Monday, he would have sent in

his resignation on Tuesday.' Stanhope, *Hansard*, CLXXV, 27 May 1864, col. 710. See also B. H. Kennedy, *Notes on Public Education: A Paper read, by the Rev. Dr. Kennedy, at the Meeting of the National Association for the Promotion of Social Science, York, September, 1864*, Bailiff's Bundles, No. 122, p. 1. Also, R. H. Cheney, 'Public schools', *Quarterly Review*, 116, July 1864, p. 179.

91 Stanhope, *Hansard*, CLXXV, 27 May 1864, col. 710.

92 See Clarendon, *Hansard*, CLXXV, 27 May 1864, col. 718.

93 Houghton, *Hansard*, CLXXVIII, 3 April 1865, col. 662. Robert Monckton Milnes (1809–85), 1st Baron Houghton, was MP for Pontefract 1837–52 and a member of the Lords Select Committee on the Public Schools Bill.

94 Houghton, *Hansard*, CLXXVIII, 3 April 1865, col. 662.

95 Houghton, *Hansard*, CLXXV, 6 June 1864, col. 1253.

96 Bishop of London, *Hansard*, CLXXVIII, 5 April 1865, col. 651. See also Note 34 above.

97 For these proposals, and the legal difficulties, see *Hansard*, CXCIII, 23 July 1868, cols. 1654–8.

98 Clarendon, *Hansard*, CLXXV, 27 May 1864, col. 718.

99 See *Hansard*, CLXXVII, 13 March 1865, col. 1533.

5 Shrewsbury and the Clarendon Commission

In 1861, when the Clarendon Commission was appointed, Shrewsbury was a small but ancient grammar school with a reputation for classical scholarship. The school contained 131 boys of whom 60 were day-boys. Of these day-boys, 22 were entitled to free education as the sons of Shrewsbury burgesses.[1] The school was founded in 1551, after the dissolution of the monasteries, by the 'bailiffs, burgesses and inhabitants of Shrewsbury' and by 'many other subjects of our whole neighbouring country there', who petitioned the King to grant some of the estates of the local dissolved collegiate churches for this purpose.[2] King Edward VI granted the school the appropriated tithes of the churches of St Mary and of St Chad in Shrewsbury for the foundation of a 'Royal Free Grammar School'.[3] Queen Elizabeth subsequently added the tithes of Chirbury in 1571 and income from tithes remained the school's main source of income until long after 1868.[4] The school was established in the centre of the town, on a hill by the castle close to the parish church of St Mary.

The fortunes of the school fluctuated greatly during its history, the number of pupils at one time falling to eighty under Dr Kennedy. This was not, however, the smallest the school had been: numbers had dropped to less than twenty in 1798 when his predecessor Dr Butler became headmaster.[5] These two men had revived the fortunes of the school and established its reputation for classical scholarship. The *Clarendon Report* praised the academic success of the school, but made twenty-nine recommendations for its reform, not including the more general recommendation which applied to all the public schools.[6] Both the need for reform and the influence of the Clarendon Commission can be seen in the history of the school, which has national significance in the history of English secondary education as it was here that the break was made, by the Clarendon Commission and the Public Schools Acts, between the old grammar schools of the country and the new public schools. Shrewsbury was the marginal school—a successful, ancient grammar school, but not one that could easily claim parity of esteem with Eton—and it was at Shrewsbury that an arbitrary line was drawn and the public school system created.

Contemporary comments about Shrewsbury illustrated the difficulty of making an arbitrary distinction between the more prestigious and the less prestigious grammar schools which the Commission, and the political protection of Eton, required and to which the Public Schools Acts gave legal confirmation. As a grammar school—that is, a school for grammatically teaching the learned languages—Shrewsbury was no different from hundreds of other endowed schools in the country and from other schools in its own area.[7] The King Edward VI School at Birmingham, for example, where Kennedy's father had been Second Master, was of an exactly similar foundation.[8] At Ludlow in Shropshire there was another Grammar School of King Edward VI whose headmaster was also a distinguished scholar and a Fellow of St John's College, Cambridge.[9] The term 'public school' had, however, been used for many years to describe endowed grammar schools and the association of the phrase in the public mind with the more well-known grammar schools provided the government with a convincing, if vague, basis for this arbitrary division between the schools that were, like Eton, thought suitable for the 'higher classes' and those that were not.[10] The inclusion of a school in the same group as Eton naturally conferred prestige and the head-master of Shrewsbury, Dr Butler, had argued earlier in the century that the two schools were comparable when two Bills by Henry Brougham—concerning endowed grammar schools—proposed to leave out the six best-known schools but to include Shrewsbury.[11] Confusion over which schools were to be included was evident in the Commons both in 1861, when the Commission was appointed, and in 1864, when the *Clarendon Report* was first discussed, but Shrewsbury was clearly regarded as the borderline school.[12] How arbitrary this distinction was legally may be seen in the case of St Paul's School, which was included in the Clarendon Commission, excluded from the Public Schools Acts on a legal technicality, but included in the Endowed Schools Act of 1869.[13] The arbitrary nature of a distinction made, in practice, on grounds of social status, may be seen in the case of Shrewsbury School, which had succeeded so well that it became, in the eyes of the Commission, too good to remain a middle-class school. It was suggested that 'the people of Shrewsbury should turn their attention rather to creating a good proprietary school in the town than to making the present school fulfil the purpose of giving what is loosely called a middle class education'.[14] The people of Shrewsbury, having established the school in 1551 and obtained the original endowments, were in effect told that they should give up the school, start again with no endowments, content themselves with a commercial school that would suit their social standing, break an association of 300 years and allow Shrewsbury to 'remain a first-rate school' within the Public Schools Acts, offering a gentleman's education in the classics in accordance with the ambitions of its headmasters and the wishes of the gentlemen in London. Just as English public education was dispossessed of these great schools by the Public Schools Acts, so was the town of Shrewsbury dispossessed of its great school and local education impoverished, so that in Parliament Eton could be protected amongst a hastily-gathered group of similar, and acceptable, schools. The *Clarendon Report* thus confirmed the new status of Shrewsbury and defined both its name—as a public school—and its function as a school for the 'higher classes' although its clientèle was no different socially from that of many other grammar schools, either at the time of the Clarendon Commission or for many years after. Shrewsbury's inclusion in the Public Schools Acts thus conferred status on a school which provided the classical education of the 'higher classes' to pupils of essentially middle-class origins, who perhaps aspired to a high social status but did not generally already possess it.[15] The reputation of the school for classical scholarship was particularly important politically because, although the school did not already educate the 'higher classes', it could claim that it was suitable to do so.

Having been included in the Commission's inquiry and obtained confirmation of its status, Shrewsbury did not, however, agree with all the *Clarendon Report*'s recommendations and did its best initially, as did other schools, to avoid inclusion in the Public Schools Acts—attempting to delay, limit or obstruct the Bills and subsequently the negotiations over the new school governors and the new statutes. Initially, opposition

came from both Dr Kennedy and the governors. Dr Kennedy
was opposed to many recommendations in the Report, but
particularly to those which concerned the powers of headmasters
and the nature of the curriculum; the governors opposed the
loss of their own powers, the consequent end of local influence
and the abolition of the school's responsibilities to local
children. Dr Kennedy's opposition dwindled after 1865, when
it became clear that the Public Schools Bills would be profoundly
conservative in educational matters and express the earnest
conservatism of the House of Lords, rather than the radicalism
of European experience. The classical curriculum would be left
intact, headmasters' powers unchanged and the Bills concerned
almost entirely with matters of finance and the new governing
bodies. The Shrewsbury governors, however, continued in Parliament, in the school and in the town their opposition to the Bills
and the Public Schools Acts, until after the new governors met.[16]

The original recommendations of the *Clarendon Report* for
Shrewsbury were concerned with six main areas of reform: the
governing body (Recommendations 1–4), the Exhibitions
(Recommendations 6–8), the Foundation boys (Recommendations 9–11), the fees (Recommendation 12), new buildings
(Recommendations 13–17) and the curriculum (Recommendations 12–26).[17] The new governing body was to consist ultimately
of thirteen members of whom six were to be nominated by outside bodies—three by Oxford and Cambridge colleges and three by
the Crown. The Corporation of Shrewsbury was to appoint
three members and the remaining four were to be elected by
the governors themselves. The Exhibitions were to be made
available at any Oxford or Cambridge college, were to be
consolidated and some funds from them were to be made
available for the provision of new buildings. The privileges of
the sons of burgesses, who approximated to the foundation
boys at other schools, were to be removed after twenty-five
years to be replaced by forty Free Scholarships, awarded by
competitive examination.[18] In the meantime, the number of
free places was to be limited to forty. The tuition fees were to
be increased to twenty guineas and the governors were to pay
the fees of the Free Scholars. Two new boarding houses were
to be built for not less than a total of 100 boys. These buildings
were to be part of 'a larger design, comprehending a plan for
school buildings hereafter to be raised when funds shall be

forthcoming, and the occasion for doing so shall seem to the Governors to have arrived'.[19] The recommendations about the curriculum were that a master for natural science should be appointed immediately, and that a 'Non-Collegiate' class should be more firmly established, offering modern subjects like science, modern languages, modern history, modern geography, mathematics, music and drawing, in addition to giving some classical education.[20] This 'Non-Collegiate' class, which already existed, was to be encouraged and given equal status with the rest of the school. Appropriate provision was to be made in this class for prizes and free places.[21]

Kennedy's objections were to the proposed new governing body and its increased powers at the expense of the head-master, the retention of free education and the changes in the curriculum. He put forward these views forcefully, in a public address at York in September 1864 and in a long letter to the Archbishop of York, written in May 1865 and published soon after.[22] He particularly objected to the proposal that governors should determine the relative importance 'to be assigned to each branch of study',[23] arguing that this was the proper concern of the headmaster alone and that such control would 'lower his professional character and impair the dignity of Education as a profession'.[24] He argued that such power would be dangerous, since a headmaster could be dismissed but a board of governors could not.[25] He accepted the need for new subjects, provided that the importance of the classics was recognised and retained, but with one reservation. This was that it was impossible 'to redistribute the boys of a Public School for distinct instruction according to proficiency in five subjects—Classics, Mathematics, Natural Science, French and Drawing . . . without such an increase in the staff of masters, as well as in other means and appliances, as few, if any schools could hope to achieve'.[26]

In his letter to the Archbishop of York, written when the *Public Schools (No. 32) Bill* was under consideration in the Lords, Kennedy made clearer his objections to the proposed changes in the governing body. The proposed new governing body was the same as that proposed in the *Clarendon Report*— the existing governors would remain, but would be gradually replaced by new nominees as the former governors retired or died. The immediate proposal in the Bill was that five new governors should be added.[27] Kennedy's objection was that the new governing body so formed would be dominated by the old, at least initially, and thus would not proceed to the other reforms required, particularly the gradual abolition of free education which the governors were then pledged to defend.[28] He praised the help and the 'uniform courtesy and personal kindness' he had received from the governors during the previous twenty-nine years but doubted their willingness to reform.[29] He had 'a settled and strong conviction' that 'the Governing Body of Shrewsbury School, as constituted in the seventh schedule of the Bill, would not be a suitable and efficient instrument to carry out the reforms suggested by the School Commissioners, and apparently contemplated by the author of the Bill'.[30] The governors of course, as Kennedy argued, had strong local connections and would therefore be opposed to changes which favoured and fostered the national, classical and fee-paying character of the school—all of which were contrary to local educational interests, but all of which Kennedy wanted.[31]

The difficulty was that Kennedy and the school governors did not agree about what was meant by reform. The governors, many of whom were appointed by Shrewsbury Corporation, wanted to introduce a more modern curriculum on terms of equality with the classics and to maintain local claims to free education—some governors even wished to extend free education to all ratepayers.[32] Kennedy disputed the meaning of the word 'free' in the school's title, arguing that it meant 'free from ecclesiastical control' and not 'gratuitous'.[33] To emphasise this view, and to prevent what he considered to be a misunderstanding about the nature of the school, he suggested changing the name of the school which, he said, was 'obsolete and misunderstood', from 'Free Grammar School' to 'a Public School of Liberal education', since the original title implied that the school should be one in which 'local boys are gratuitously educated'.[34] To most governors and many local people, however, the right of some local children to receive free, local secondary education was the one benefit that remained for the town from a school that owed its existence and foundation to the petitions of the townspeople. The number of children attending free was declining, but this was partly attributed to the unsuitable, almost exclusively classical, curriculum.[35] The governors, and many local people, wanted both to change the curriculum and to increase the number of local children—a prospect which filled Kennedy with alarm. It would, he said, 'utterly swamp this Royal and Public Foundation' for 'by what *abstract* right can every person claim to educate his son in a Public School without cost?'[36]

Conflict at Shrewsbury between the headmaster and the governors about free local education, about the curriculum and about the school's function, was not new.[37] The *Clarendon Report* and the first Public Schools Bills intensified this conflict, but only briefly for by 1866, when Kennedy retired, the Bill— as amended in the Lords—broadly coincided with Kennedy's views: the school was to be a national institution; its obligation to provide some free local education was to go, and the place of the classics was not immediately threatened as the curriculum was to be left to future governors, who would not in the main be spokesmen for local people. Moreover, there was to be a Special Commission, which Kennedy strongly supported, to negotiate with each school, so that each school's circumstances could be given separate consideration. Kennedy's successor, Henry Whitehead Moss, also came into conflict with the un-reformed governing body, but over the removal of the school to a new site rather than the proposals of the *Clarendon Report* or the Public Schools Bills.[38] Although the governors continued to oppose the Public Schools Bills and the Public Schools Acts until after the new governors were appointed in 1871, their struggle to maintain some local control over the school was fought, after 1865, in Parliament rather than within the school.[39] Their struggle of 1864–71 was merely the final continuation of the many disputes between headmasters and governors at Shrewsbury—disputes which had been endemic from the foundation of the school and were all fundamentally concerned with the relationship of the school to the local people.[40] The Public Schools Bills simply transferred this conflict from school politics, local politics and the courts to Parliament—but to an unrepresentative Parliament and a conservative House of Lords with little interest in curricular reform or secondary schools in general and much concern with the preservation of some schools, like Shrewsbury, for their own political purposes.

The general legal arrangements by which the school was regulated in 1865 were that the ordinances of the original foundation and the subsequent endowment by Queen Elizabeth had been superseded by an Act of Parliament in 1798. This Act, in turn, had been changed substantially by a scheme agreed with the Court of Chancery in 1853. The school was regulated by the terms of this Chancery Scheme at the time of the Clarendon Commission.[41] There were thirteen governors who were originally individually named in the Scheme.[42] These, as in the Act of 1798, were men of standing in Shropshire and had to be resident in the county. The Mayor of Shrewsbury was Chairman *ex officio*. Each new governor was appointed by Shrewsbury Corporation from three nominations submitted by the school governors. The Scheme maintained the governors' general control of the school, which had been established in 1798, against the claims of both the headmaster and the Corporation, but made specific provision for staffing, fees, regular academic examination of the boys by an outside examiner, maintenance of school records, stipends to be paid at the livings of St Mary's, Clive, Chirbury and Astley for which the school was responsible, and for small payments to the schools in each parish (and in St Chad's also) for 'the education of the children of poor parents'.[43] The Chancery Scheme maintained the school's local obligations—that had been regularised by the Act of 1798—and confirmed the right of free education for the legitimate sons of Shrewsbury burgesses.[44] Finally, the Scheme maintained the basic classical curriculum of the school, but gave the governors the right to introduce 'such other Modern Languages, Art and Sciences' as they thought proper, provided that they obtained the agreement of the Bishop of Lichfield, the School Visitor.[45]

The Chancery Scheme itself was the result of a protracted legal battle between the headmaster and the governors about the curriculum, and thus about the future of the school. In 1843 the borough council first suggested that the governors should establish a 'commercial' school for local children.[46] Nothing was done on that occasion, but in 1848 the governors resolved that 'an education more generally useful to the sons of Burgesses than the present classical one is desirable' and petitioned the Court of Chancery to use funds for that purpose.[47] The headmaster bitterly opposed the proposal and his relations with the governors became very strained, the governors referring on one occasion to the 'now threatened hostility' of Kennedy and writing to him at one time through the Bishop of Lichfield.[48] When the governors' petition was heard in court, it was opposed by counsel representing Kennedy and St John's College, Cambridge, which had a long historical association with the school.[49] The final Chancery Scheme was something of a compromise, for while the governors were not allowed to establish a separate 'commercial' school or to provide more modern subjects solely for the sons of burgesses, they were permitted to introduce new subjects and so the possibilities for curricular reform at the school after 1853 were almost unlimited. In addition to Greek, Latin, the Holy Scriptures and the Anglican liturgy, catechism and doctrines, the Scheme stipulated that the subjects of instruction should include English, French, mathematics, ancient and modern history and geography.[50] Such was the obstinate devotion of Kennedy to the classics, however, that these other subjects included in the Chancery Scheme were given merely a token and marginal place in the school's curriculum. The weakness of the Scheme was that it depended, in the last resort, on Kennedy's willingness to accept the reforms, to change his own attitude and to grasp the new possibilities that the Scheme opened up, both for the school and for the town. He never did this and so, for the ten years preceding the *Clarendon Report*, the school remained under his restrictive, classical influence until the Public Schools Bills brought the conservative politics of the Lords to his assistance. The Scheme did enable the governors to promote the formation of a 'Non-Collegiate' class, but this class remained in the shadow of Kennedy's preference for the classics and, under his influence, its studies remained discouraged and discouraging. The title of the class, which was one on which Kennedy insisted, was negative, implying as it did non-achievement, and refused the subjects of this class the dignity of academic recognition.[51] Kennedy had a 'deep conviction of the educational value of the classics'. There was undoubtedly a direct conflict of views between him and the governors about the school's curriculum and, unless both sides agreed, all plans came to nothing.[52]

An earlier attempt had been made to introduce science into the school before the Chancery Scheme. In August 1852 the Rev. W. Burbury—a master at the school—wrote to the Bailiff asking to be reimbursed for the money he had already spent on scientific apparatus.[53] Burbury was well-placed to introduce

new subjects, for he had married Kennedy's eldest daughter
Charlotte in June 1852.[54] His letter, however, has 'Postponed'
written across it. In about 1853 Kennedy wrote to the governors
to suggest 'the establishment of a class in the school, which
shall have lessons in Physical Science and Linear Drawing
instead of Greek and Classical Composition'.[55] He asked if the
governors would pay for scientific and drawing equipment
'which the government offers at a cheap rate to Public
institutions', suggested a charge of £5 each year for instruction
and asked about the position of burgesses' sons. Finally, he
asked the governors to advertise the new classes in the press 'as
at King Edward's School, Birmingham'.[56] In October 1853 the
governors agreed to meet the expenses of the 'suggested course
of scientific, etc. instruction' if sufficient boys enrolled and if
the Bailiff was instructed to make the proposals public.[57]
Nothing came of this agreement, however, and there is no
further mention of it in the minutes. No doubt these arrangements were overtaken by events for the Chancery Scheme,
which had just been agreed and which gave the governors the
legal power to introduce far greater changes into the school
curriculum. In July 1855 the governors appointed a committee
'to confer with the Head Master on the subject mentioned in
his letter, of allowing a new arrangement for Boys not intended
for College'.[58]

Such was the origin of the 'Non-Collegiate' class which aroused
the interest of the Clarendon Commission.[59] It was a small class,
consisting of never more than twenty boys, who were not
destined for university and whose curriculum 'omitted Latin
composition and all Greek, and included modern languages,
English composition, history and extra mathematics'.[60] Kennedy
had little enthusiasm for this class, and its boys could not rise
into the sixth form.[61] The school's historian suggests that the
formation of this class took place before the governors' petition
to Chancery but, in fact, its introduction was clearly the direct,
if delayed, result of the Chancery judgement and of parental
pressure.[62] Both Kennedy and T. A. Bentley, the master responsible for it, complained that the class attracted the idle and
those looking for a 'soft option', but the terms on which boys
were admitted were so unfavourable that it was hardly surprising
that it was avoided by the more able, hardworking boys.[63]
The *Clarendon Report* itself made clear how adverse these

conditions were—so much so that it seems surprising that the class was joined by any boys at all. Not only were they not admitted to the sixth form, but there was no entrance examination, no examination system within the class and no prizes. Kennedy refused to allow the words 'commercial education' to be used in the school.[64] The technique of 'killing off' an inconvenient class by the unobtrusive, methodical discouragement of those wishing to join is well-known in education, and it is perhaps part of the technique to express regret when the class eventually fails. It is in this context that the Clarendon Commission's comment, that 'Kennedy appears reluctant to abandon it', must be seen; there had been repeated requests from local parents over many years for such a class and, since the Chancery Scheme, no legal restraints on the introduction of new subjects. It is difficult to believe that Kennedy could not have established this class successfully, many years earlier, had he genuinely wished to do so. If the recommendations of the *Clarendon Report* had been followed, the class could have become an important and integral part of the school's work with the equality of treatment that the Clarendon Commission wanted.[65] But Kennedy expressed surprise at the importance attached to this class by the Commissioners; he exaggerated their reservations, ignored their general approval, disregarded their suggestions for improving it and immediately closed it down.

> The Commissioners in their Report, [he wrote] have given more prominence to an experiment of mine, called the Non-Collegiate Form, than I ever expected or meant it to obtain . . . being merely in this embryo condition, simple and inoffensive, and without much importance in the business of the school, I was exceedingly surprised, on reading the Report, to see the prominence which the Commissioners give to it . . . I have therefore ceased to include this Form in my prospectus of the school . . . It must therefore now be understood that there exists no such thing in the School as 'a Non-Collegiate Form'.[66]

Kennedy's deference to the views of the Commission was not usually so much in evidence and it was clear that, alarmed at the prospect of this class flourishing, he used an exaggerated and highly selective reference to the *Clarendon Report* to justify its immediate closure.[67] Nowhere does he mention the Commission's positive proposals for the encouragement of the class which, small and little-regarded as it was, was the only curricular reform to have come from the Chancery Scheme. What the Commissioners, governors and many parents clearly wanted was an alternative curriculum, but what Kennedy gave them was an inferior one, deliberately contrived to be so, which he abolished at the first opportunity. Here was a class which was kept humble in its expectations, unrewarded and of low status, a token provision both unexamined and undemanding, with immensely important subjects trivialised by clever school politics, which took away achievement, recognition or advancement. Here in Kennedy's 'Non-Collegiate' class, this practical expression of scholastic prejudice, may be found the origins of the English secondary modern school and the further divisions of the 1944 Education Act.

There was nothing unexpected about Kennedy's attitude towards non-classical studies, for the school's tradition was almost entirely classical; its reputation had been established in classical studies and Kennedy was arguably the leading classical scholar of his day. His attitude illustrated, however, the difficulty of introducing even moderate curricular reform, even when supported by parents and the governing body, against the wishes of an entrenched headmaster. Kennedy's attitude towards non-classical studies perhaps illustrates a truism of political sociology—that leaders tend to encourage activities in which they themselves excel, so that their claims to leadership may be maintained and their status enhanced. A headmaster who is good, for example, at administration will tend to stress the importance of administration in his school and in education generally, and judge the performance of other teachers by their level of achievement in activities in which he himself excels. Since the maintenance of dominance, in a sociological sense, is not usually a legitimate motive in a school—except in relation to the children—the sociological need for the headmaster to maintain acknowledged dominance may be expressed in terms of curricular guidance or educational priorities—'setting the tone of the school', for example, or 'concentrating on the important things in education'. Kennedy's opposition to new subjects of study cannot be explained solely in terms of his own academic interests or his educational philosophy, and underlines the difficulties faced by governors, parents and the Clarendon Commission in their attempts to introduce curricular reform into the public schools through headmasters whose reputation had been established in older, more established areas of study. The authority of the leader is weakened if the group's activities move into areas where the leader's excellence may be challenged, where his expertise is irrelevant (or even non-existent), and where his ability to initiate change is limited; the proposed extension of the work of Shrewsbury placed Kennedy in precisely this position. For any headmaster schooled in the classics, the situation would have been difficult, but for Kennedy it was particularly so—he was associated with the best in classical education, probably the most famous teacher of the classics in the country, a renowned classical scholar and the author of school text-books which were themselves to become classics of a different kind.[68] In the schools, the interests of headmasters like Kennedy joined forces with the conservative interests of the Lords in defence of the classics.

It would be a mistake, however, to suppose that Shrewsbury offered only the classics in the period before the Public Schools Acts. The traditional, formal school curriculum was, of course, heavily weighted towards the classics in theory, and was even more so in practice for, although French, mathematics and English essay appeared in the annual prize lists, the evidence of contemporaries suggests that these other subjects were given little time and considered of even less importance. W. E. Heitland, who entered the school in 1862 and moved into the sixth form in the summer of 1863, described Shrewsbury at that time as 'a quaint survival' with a curriculum 'one-sided to a degree now inconceivable and remarkable even then'. French was 'a mere figment' and time allocated for mathematics was 'often spent in pleasant conversation, in the doing of impositions . . . or sometimes in writing skits on topics of school interest'.[69] A whole week each Half was devoted to ancient geography, and any spare time at the end of each Half often given to history—Roman history written in Latin, which had to be translated and which was 'mere waste of time in the saddest fashion'.[70] There were no lessons in English language or in English literature, which entered the school mainly through impositions, as Milton was Kennedy's favourite source.[71] He was prepared to accept subjects other than the classics, but only as second-best alternatives for those boys who failed to make satisfactory progress in the classics. He was, he said, prepared to attempt the introduction of new subjects out of respect for the Clarendon Commission, but was somewhat gloomy and unenthusiastic about it.[72] The clearest expression of his views on the place of more modern subjects in the curriculum came, by implication, in his evidence to the Lords Select Committee in 1865 on the 'Non-Collegiate' class. He thought that 'it might be very well carried on and conducted as a subordinate element for the purpose of satisfying the lower class', but only if 'there was no danger of it growing so large that it should interfere with the more important purpose of the school'.[73] He had introduced mathematics and French into the formal school curriculum soon after his appointment in 1836, probably out of respect for the wishes of his predecessor Dr Butler, but did not seem to regard these subjects very seriously.[74] The upper sixth were not expected to continue French—even formally—and marks for French were not allowed to affect a boy's place in the school.[75] Mathematics was not introduced until three years later, as Kennedy 'took so little interest . . . that he is said to have become unable to do a simple sum correctly'.[76] In the sixth form twenty out of twenty-eight hours' tuition was devoted to the classics.[77]

Much, however, must have gone on at the school that did not appear in the formal curriculum. The *Clarendon Report* commented that 'boys should . . . continue to take advantage of the School of Design in the town'[78] and in 1851 Samuel Butler took lessons from Philip Vandyke Brown, a local artist.[79] Music flourished in the school, if informally. *Paget's Scrap Book* records numerous charades, balls and entertainments, and there was clearly much going on. In December 1848, for example, there was an entertainment in the school called *Comic Charades* and his pen and wash drawings show a small, well-lit stage, musicians and an enthusiastic audience.[80] Paget also kept a collection of twenty-six school songs, 'as sung by the RSS. Philharmonic Society' in 1848, which although comic and mock-serious does show that many activities now within the school curriculum were then pursued informally through individual enthusiasm.[81] The school's activities cannot, therefore, be wholly judged from the formal 'Subjects for Examination' or the life of the school as recreated wholly from time-tables and government reports. Music, particularly, seems to have flourished under Kennedy, although somewhat to his surprise and as a result of accidental circumstances, when the parish church was closed for repair and the services transferred, with music, to the school chapel.[82]

This sudden development of musical interest illustrates how enthusiasm and favourable circumstances could extend and enrich the informal curriculum. The disadvantage of this situation was that when circumstances became less favourable, such as when a particular teacher left or when enthusiasm waned, these subjects could easily disappear. Science, for example, although briefly encouraged by Kennedy and Burbury in 1852–3, then disappeared and did not reappear in the formal school curriculum until 1856. By 1880 the sixth form was studying dynamics, statics and Newton's *Principia*, but the general introduction of science as a regular and accepted part of the curriculum did not come until after the school moved to its new site in 1883.[83] Sometimes, no doubt, these informal, often brief innovations had an importance for the boys who took advantage of them which was not apparent at the time. In the 1850s, Kennedy introduced German and, for a time, taught the subject to the upper sixth form. Although the innovation did not last long, Samuel Moore was a pupil during this period, from 1852–8. He later became the first to translate Marx into English, and probably first began to learn German under Kennedy.[84] The encouragement of such interests that were outside the classical curriculum was largely a matter of luck. Charles Darwin, perhaps the school's most famous pupil, was not so fortunate and found little encouragement at Shrewsbury for his scientific interests.[85]

The classics were taught very successfully at Shrewsbury, for in terms of university prizes the school's record was remarkable. The *Clarendon Report* recognised this, concluding a summary of the school's examination successes with the comment that 'the extent to which this small school contributes to the teaching power of the Universities is remarkable'.[86] In four cases Shrewsbury boys won university prizes while still at school and 'each University altered the statutes to exclude . . . the unfair competition of schoolboys with resident undergraduates'.[87] Contemporary opinion of Shrewsbury scholarship was divided; some considered it too narrow even for classical scholarship, for the exactness of translation was stressed more than an appreciation of classical literature or an understanding of classical culture.[88] By the time of the Clarendon Commission, however, there was established a Shrewsbury 'method', of which Kennedy himself was a product.[89] Butler had introduced a policy of regular examinations and promotion on merit at the school, and to this Kennedy added the insistence that boys should think in Greek and Latin and treat classical history as though it concerned contemporary events.[90] In an account of Kennedy's teaching, written soon after his death by W. E. Heitland, a former pupil, there is an impression of drama, vigour and immense enthusiasm. 'He was never tedious: a lesson . . . was got through at a terrific pace . . . his tall and striking figure never—or hardly ever—at rest, his bright, piercing eye, his mighty voice echoing among the rafters, all combined to fix attention . . . He seemed to fill the room with his presence.' When he translated, 'he is not merely translating Demosthenes: he *is* Demosthenes speaking extempore in English'.[91]

The standard of classical scholarship, like the success of the school, depended on the teaching ability of the headmaster—on his scholarship, his enthusiasm and his vigour—for the school taught the classics almost exclusively and the headmaster himself invariably taught the sixth form, on whose university successes the reputation of the school depended. Butler saved the school from almost total collapse in 1798, but academic standards fell as he grew older and 'in the summer of 1836 Greek scholarship at Shrewsbury was . . . at a very low ebb'.[92] Kennedy raised academic standards again, declaring that 'my Sixth Form is the hardest . . . in England, and I intend it to be so', but they declined again as he neared retirement.[93] The personal influence of the headmaster was increased by the small size of the sixth form, which in Kennedy's day was usually about twenty boys, and by the number of older boys who came to the school late in their school career—sometimes straight into the sixth form—just to be taught by Kennedy and who had not progressed through the school in the normal way.[94] The Sidney Gold Medal, instituted in 1838 for the best classical scholar of the year, stipulated that candidates should have spent a specified time in the school in order to prevent newcomers from winning the prize too often.[95] Kennedy's success, and that of the school, was gained with 'promising scholars from other schools' rather than the result of consistent good teaching in all years.[96] The lower forms in Kennedy's time seem to have been largely untouched and uninspired by the influence of the headmaster and Heitland, writing of the Kennedy period, referred to the comparative inefficiency of the rest of the staff and the 'tiresome mill of the lower forms' which was a poor preparation for sixth form work.[97]

Kennedy left before the Public Schools Act of 1868 was passed, but was called upon to give evidence before the Lords Select Committee in 1865.[98] It was clear that the *Clarendon Report* and the Public Schools Bills had reopened the conflict between Kennedy and the governors that had been temporarily settled by the Chancery Scheme of 1853. In a letter to the School Bailiff in May 1865, he made it clear that he did not have the same objections to the Bill as the governors and warned them that he would express his views vigorously, both to the Lords Committee and in his letter to the Archbishop of York, which was soon to be published.[99] By this time, the governors of the school and the town council of Shrewsbury were actively campaigning against the Bill. In fact, the governors at this period were almost acting on behalf of the town council, for the Mayor was Chairman of the governors and all the governors lived locally. Just as Kennedy was concerned with maintaining the national character of the school, so the governors were concerned with preventing the immediate curtailment and eventual abolition of what Kennedy called 'privileges for the burgesses' and what the Borough of Shrewsbury called 'preferential rights'.[100] What the governors and the town were defending, as their Petition of April 1865 made clear, was not just the right of free education for the sons of burgesses, but also the right of preferential treatment in the award of exhibitions, scholarships and church livings connected with the school.[101] What lay behind the disagreement was the same fundamental question that had always caused conflict from the time of the school's foundation: was the school to serve local interests first, as the governors wished, or was it to be first a national 'public' school, as Kennedy wanted? This explains the school's apparently contradictory behaviour—that Shrewsbury fought to be included within the Clarendon Commission schools, but fought against the provisions of the Public Schools Bills. This was partly because the Clarendon Commission conferred a certain status which was, as in the case of

St Paul's and Merchant Taylors', irremovable by subsequent events, but also because the case for inclusion was fought primarily and traditionally by the headmaster, while the case against the Public Schools Bills was fought mainly by the governors and town council on behalf of local opinion. The case for inclusion could be argued privately by the headmaster, by letters or personal contacts, without the need to consult the governors—just as Kennedy argued against some specific provisions in the Bill—through peers or bishops who were over-whelmingly sympathetic to Kennedy's views and in direct, deliberate and sometimes critical opposition to his own governors. The governors' case was put more formally by petition, by counsel and by local MPs—using school funds to finance a protracted campaign.

In his public letter to the Archbishop of York in 1865, Kennedy made an astonishing attack on all local authorities and on 'municipal' school governors in particular, tracing the influence of borough councils in education back to the Reformation and the need for Edward VI to find political supporters in the country who could be trusted with the public endowments taken from the Church.[102] Borough councils were 'the very last Trustees to whose charge a Public School ought to have been committed. For such a purpose all narrowly local Trusteeship is bad: but municipal Trusteeship is worst of all'. He added, rather unconvincingly, that he did not mean 'to speak with any disrespect of municipal institutions . . . still less of the Corporation of Shrewsbury or its members'.[103] In the same letter, he argued that the preservation of the local obligations of the school tended to lower standards, although he was prepared to concede that some Exhibitions should be kept for poorer local children, provided they had ability. He would 'admit poverty to be a fair claim to preference when personal merit is high' but did not want 'to provide poor boys of small learning and ability with the means of going to College'.[104] The possibility that an appearance of 'small learning and ability' could be the result of poverty, of discouraging circumstances or of non-classical interests does not seem to have occurred to him. His pursuit of excellence within such a narrow, arbitrary boundary tended to discourage local boys and his own 'Non-Collegiate' class left other subjects discouraged and unrewarded. The classics must have been the subject least likely to interest local parents, especially those who could not afford to send their children to the universities, so that the maintenance of the classical curriculum, which the governors opposed and which to Kennedy was the only area of academic excellence, discouraged local parents. Kennedy could thus argue that there was little demand from local parents for the education the school provided, and that the free admission of more local children, or the introduction of new subjects, would threaten academic standards. That the governors wanted to do these things was only more evidence, according to Kennedy, of the irresponsibility of local governors and town councils. Yet the governors had tried for many years to introduce educational reforms at the school and Kennedy's own record of trusteeship, as headmaster, remains in English education an awesome record of complacency, obstruction, academic prejudice and indifference to the aspirations of local children.

The narrow classical curriculum must also have discouraged many fee-paying boys whose interests did not lie in that direction; Charles Darwin did not flourish in this classical environment and must have appeared 'of small learning and ability'.[105] Kennedy did not mention the fee-paying boys, also of 'small learning and ability', who attended the public schools and universities in large numbers, as the discussion of the *Clarendon Report* made clear. Kennedy wanted the pursuit of excellence to be selective and contrived—selective in that the test of excellence was to be applied more rigorously to the poorer scholarship boys, whose entry was to depend on excellence, and contrived in that excellence was to be recognised and encouraged only in the classics.[106] The subjects most likely to appeal to the poorer local children, and in which it was perhaps possible to acquire some excellence without an expensive preparatory education, were discouraged and then suppressed altogether with the closure of the 'Non-Collegiate' class.

The declining number of burgesses' sons attending in 1865, which was partly an inevitable consequence of the narrowly classical curriculum and partly also of the declining political importance of burgess rights after 1835, was taken by Kennedy as evidence that there were insufficient local boys of ability to support the academic ambitions of the school, as he saw them, and to enable the school to 'hold its Public rank unimpaired'.[107]

The governors, however, wanted the school to continue to serve
the local community and did not agree that it would serve the
country less by reverting to the status of a local grammar school
for, in their view, this was its original purpose. In spite of
Kennedy's views about local authority governors, they legally
and formally controlled the school and began a long campaign,
with school funds, against the Public Schools Bills. When
Kennedy retired in 1866 his own objections to the original Bill
had been met by amendments in the Lords and Moss, the new
headmaster, actively supported the inclusion of the school in
the Bill—in deliberate opposition to the policy of his own
governors.[108]

By April 1865 the governors were attempting to organise
support amongst their own contacts in the Lords, had written
to St John's College, Cambridge, asking for support and had
appointed J. R. Kenyon QC to represent them before the Lords
Select Committee.[109] They were also already deep in consultation with the governors of other schools, particularly Harrow
and St Paul's.[110] But neither in the Lords Select Committee of
1865 nor the Commons Select Committee in 1868 were they
able to substantially change the Bills, protect their own influence
or defend the interests of local children.[111] At first there was a
desperate attempt to have the school excluded from the Bill
on the grounds that Shrewsbury had already been reformed
by the Chancery Scheme of 1853, after Kenyon had been told
by Birmingham solicitors, probably mistakenly, that King
Edward VI School in Birmingham had been omitted from
legislation for this reason.[112] Kenyon then planned, in consultation with the Shrewsbury governors and with representatives of Harrow in London, to block the second reading in the
Lords in May 1866, with the argument that the Bill was
essentially a private bill and that therefore the correct Parliamentary procedure had not been followed. If this argument
had been successful, the Bill would have been thrown out, as
it had followed the normal procedure for a public bill. A
similar objection had been used successfully in 1863 to block
a proposal to amalgamate the City Police in London with the
Metropolitan Police, as Kenyon explained to the governors.[113]
But the Harrow representatives decided to reserve their
opposition for the Commons and, in the event, this tactic was
not required. The Bill did not reach the Commons until 16

July 1866, by which time there was no hope of it becoming law before the end of the Parliamentary session. Only a brief debate took place at the second reading on 7 August 1866.[114] The hope of using Parliamentary procedure in this way was probably a forlorn one, as the *Public Schools Act, 1864* had established a precedent. The Lords would certainly have been unsympathetic and, by the time the Bills reached the Commons, they had been discussed for so long in the Lords that such a legislative upheaval would have been unthinkable.

There was little the Shrewsbury governors could do during the autumn of 1866 and during 1867. The Public Schools Bill introduced into the Lords in February 1867 was merely a repetition of the previous Bill.[115] Although the Lords did not appoint another committee and the Bill was sent to the Commons in March, the second reading was not reached until 10 August 1867, when the Bill lapsed.[116] In December 1867, however, the *Public Schools (No. 24) Bill* went straight to the Commons, reached its second reading on 14 February and was referred to a Common Select Committee on 20 March 1868.[117] By this time, the Shrewsbury governors had no hope of excluding the school from the Bill or blocking the Bill's progress. They were still hopeful, however, of making some marginal but important amendments and turned to their local MPs for help—for the Commons committee would not hear counsel or accept further petitions. The governors hoped to bring about these changes through Dr W. J. Clement, who was a Shrewsbury MP and a member of the Select Committee.[118] The amendments to be proposed by Clement, if approved, would have maintained the influence of the borough council over day-boys and restricted the choice of any new site for the school to an area within half a mile of the town centre.[119] They were also still concerned with the preservation of local claims to free education.

Their attempts to change the Bill met with only limited success. Clement, a local surgeon who had been Mayor of Shrewsbury 1862–4 and also chairman of the school governors, fell ill and attended only one of the eight meetings of the Commons Select Committee.[120] The governors then approached other MPs, but these too met with only limited success. Francis Powell, the Conservative MP for Cambridge, agreed to help but saw little hope of changing the Bill to protect local interests.[121] He did manage to add one amendment, protecting the rights of existing burgesses to free education, but thought most of the governors' proposals 'at all times hopeless'.[122] Relations between Powell and the governors became strained; Powell perhaps thought many of the suggested amendments unreasonable because they were politically hopeless, and the governors perhaps thought that Powell was not pressing their case with sufficient vigour.[123] By the middle of June 1868 the governors had abandoned Powell and approached Jasper More, who had been a Shrewsbury School boy and was at that time Liberal Unionist MP for South Shropshire.[124] His efforts, too, were unsuccessful; the Report Stage was concluded on 7 July and given a third reading without further debate on 14 and 15 July 1868. On 31 July 1868, the Bill became law.[125] The most important change for all the schools was that the existing governors had to submit schemes for new constitutions before 1 May 1869. Each new governing body then had to submit new school regulations before 1 January 1870. The award of foundation places at all the schools could now be dependent upon a scholarship examination and, at Shrewsbury, the site of the school could be moved, but to a place not more than three miles from the town centre. The rights of Shrewsbury burgesses, and of local residents at Rugby and Harrow, were to continue only for the lifetime of those then living.[126] In October 1868 the governors of Shrewsbury met and expressed strong disagreement with many clauses of the Act which related to the school.[127]

There followed an extensive correspondence between the governors and the Special Commissioners about the new governing body and the new school regulations. Although the Act set a time limit for this, it could be extended, which meant that there was much scope for argument, obstruction and delay and agreement was not reached until 1871 for the new governing body, and until 1873 for the school regulations.[128] Delay had a special significance at Shrewsbury, for Henry Whitehead Moss, the new headmaster appointed by St John's College, Cambridge in 1866, wanted to move the school and had, on his own initiative, managed to have a clause allowing this put into the Bill of 1866. The existing governors were opposed to the move, and so delaying the implementation of the Act was a means of delaying the school's move. The new governors met in December 1871, however, and, despite much local opposition, agreed in

December 1874 to the removal of the school from the centre of the town.

For Shrewsbury School, the Clarendon Commission and the subsequent legislation led to increased conflict between the headmaster and the governors who, being local men appointed by Shrewsbury Corporation, tended to promote and protect local interests—particularly the rights of burgesses, the reform of the curriculum and the preservation of the school on its traditional site. The Public Schools Act of 1868 resolved this conflict by creating a new governing body, on which local interests were represented by only a small minority.[129] The majority of the new governors were eminent former pupils whose loyalty was to the school as a national, prestigious institution rather than as a school with local obligations. They thus shared and supported the national aspirations which Moss had for the school, and which Parliament itself, in general, supported. One of the most important changes introduced by the Act was that the new governors were, almost entirely, successful former pupils of the school who were unlikely to press for curricular reform or to have much concern for the school's local responsibilities which had, in any case, been virtually removed by the Act. The attempts by the Shrewsbury governors to retain for local children even nominal or residual benefits from the school largely failed, although these attempts were pursued with urgent desperation right up to the final consideration of the Bill in the Commons in 1868. Shrewsbury, like the other schools of the Act, was both separated from other endowed grammar schools and put beyond the reach of local children. The school's public endowments were given, in effect, to the 'higher classes' who then dominated Parliament, and who saw this opportunity to seize the country's most well-known schools.

That this legal seizure was presented in Parliament as being in the nation's interest does not necessarily imply that the discussions in Parliament were conducted in the language of cynicism. Parliamentary conservatism was the unashamed conservatism of men who found it impossible to imagine a country not governed by the 'higher classes' and who saw, in the appropriation of the public schools' endowments for expensive private education, the preservation of an established social order, with all appropriate deference. The massive buildings of Shrewsbury School which now overlook the town form a lasting monument to the oppressive and divisive consequences of Victorian class interests, just as Shrewsbury Castle forms a monument to feudalism and the wars with Wales. Yet the conservation of these schools, even in this national interest, left local interests entrenched—these were not the interests of local children, however, but rather the local interests and ambitions of the schools themselves. There was nothing in the Public Schools Acts to say that the new governors should be former pupils, but they usually were—not just at Shrewsbury, but at all the public schools.[130] At Shrewsbury, the new governors nominated by Oxford and Cambridge, by the Royal Society and by the Lord Chief Justice were all former pupils.[131] In this respect also, the Public Schools Act was a most conservative measure, for it created new governing bodies dominated by men who had themselves been successful in the unreformed schools. The radical reforms in school government and finance introduced by the Act were thus used to safeguard and maintain the schools' traditional curriculum and social position.

At Shrewsbury, the first consequence of the Act was to settle the conflict between Moss and the governors about the removal of the school to a new site. The *Clarendon Report* had criticised the school's buildings and suggested that expansion was slow because the buildings were too old and too small.[132] Moss had expressed his dissatisfaction with the buildings and the general situation of the school in the centre of the town in his first letter to the governors in 1866, and his motives were clear: he wanted to expand the school, to make 'the maintenance of proper discipline' easier and to foster the school's national reputation so that it could 'compete on equal terms with the other great schools of England'.[133] Moss wanted some urgent action because the Public Schools Bill of 1866 was at that point before Parliament and he wanted included a clause giving the governors the legal power to move the school. The governors were not enthusiastic but eventually agreed and the clause, limiting the move to within three miles, appeared in the *Public Schools (No. 78) Bill* of 1867.[134] From 1866 to 1871, the governors were almost wholly concerned with opposing the Public Schools Bills and then negotiating with the Special Commissioners, so that Moss's proposal received little attention. But the new governors first met in December 1871 and almost immediately made a move to end any of the school's remaining local obligations.[135] In 1872 the new governors began to consider the possibility of moving the school and formally resolved to do so in March 1874, after much opposition from Shrewsbury Corporation and from some former pupils, and after much controversy about the merits of possible alternative sites.[136] The present Kingsland site was bought in 1876 and the school moved in July 1882. For Shrewsbury School, the removal to a new site was a major consequence of the Clarendon Commission and the Public Schools Acts for, although Moss favoured the move, it seems unlikely that his wishes would have prevailed without the recommendations of the *Clarendon Report*, the appointment of a new governing body and the greater control over the school's finances given to the governors by the Act of 1868. The local politics of the move were, however, complicated by the other changes introduced by the Act. The move was associated in the town with an increase in the number of fee-paying pupils, with new governors mostly imposed from outside, with the end of free places for local children and with the end of local involvement. The removal of the school symbolised the end of its service to Shrewsbury and the local community and the beginning of a new educational rationale, imposed by Parliament for very different political purposes. The removal of the school to a new site in order to provide local children with a better education would not have been met with such bitter opposition or protracted controversy. It was not so much the move which provoked opposition, but the educational loss for local people that it both symbolised and expressed.

The history of the school after 1868, and particularly after 1882, was one of gradual expansion and general prosperity. Numbers grew slowly from 170 in 1868 to 199 in 1883, and increased more rapidly from then on in the new buildings. In 1893 numbers had risen to 299, and in 1894 to 309. Numbers continued to grow slowly, with some fluctuations, reaching 408 in 1919 and 505 in 1926.[137] The social background of parents changed slowly but significantly between 1868 and 1888. Although never high, the number of titled parents increased slightly, as did the number of parents with legal, military or medical backgrounds. The number of burgesses' sons, and therefore the number of boys from the homes of successful tradesmen, decreased sharply. The number of boys whose parents were in the Church or from the landed gentry remained high and constant. The main difference made by the Act was that before 1868 many children of local tradesmen went on to professional or university careers. After 1868, as the free education of local children fell into disuse, those boys who went on to professional or university careers came inevitably from families already well established—socially, financially and often professionally.[138] The geographical distribution of parents remained remarkably constant, with a large number of boys coming from Lancashire and the industrial towns of the north-west of England. The school continued to attract fee-paying day-boys from Shrewsbury, but very few boys from Shropshire generally. Although Shropshire was a very wealthy county throughout this period, with many very large estates, its landed families almost never sent their children to Shrewsbury School. Where these children went is not known, but it could be that the school, although socially mobile, was still not sufficiently accepted to attract children from the wealthiest families.[139] The school slowly grew more prosperous, as increased numbers meant an increased return from fees. The move depleted resources, but the school's income reached £6,132 in 1890, with an overall surplus of £261.[140]

The curriculum changes, so strongly urged by the Clarendon Commission, came but slowly. The examination syllabus and prize lists each year remained largely classical until well after 1890. The opposition of the Lords in 1865 to curricular reform and the headmasters' defence of the classics seem generally to have been successful, certainly so for Shrewsbury School.[141] Some modern history and modern geography was taught in the years after 1868, but mostly to the lower forms and not by specialist teachers. The prize list for 1874, for example, lists five classics teachers (including Moss) but only two teachers of mathematics, one teacher for modern languages and one for writing. These last two had no degrees. A specialist history teacher was not appointed until 1900 and, even then, the appointment apparently survived only by chance.[142] The first teacher of natural science appeared in 1883 and, although science and mathematics slowly gained ground in the school, the classics remained predominant and, as late as 1900, over a third of the staff were classics teachers.[143] In 1884 there was a modern division and in 1885 prizes given for chemistry.[144] In

1886 two teachers are listed for the modern side and German appears as an examination subject. In 1886 also, a natural science class is given with class lists for chemistry (chemical theory and inorganic chemistry) and for physics (sound, light and heat and electricity).[145] By 1889, as well as special classes for the Army and the Civil Service examinations, the school had 'an excellent laboratory for the study of practical Chemistry' and 'an advanced Science Class for boys who intend to compete for Science scholarships'.[146] By 1889 too, mathematics and science were taught throughout the school and the science staff by 1900 included a Fellow of Owens College, Manchester.[147] This was certainly evidence of progress, but it was twenty years after the Public Schools Act of 1868. English literature also made slow progress in the school. Although prizes were sometimes given for English essay as far back as 1849, there was no organised provision for the study of English language or English literature until 1872, when parts of Tennyson's *In Memoriam* appeared in work for the sixth form and the lower school read *The Talisman* by Sir Walter Scott.[148] Tennyson's works then appeared frequently, but Shakespeare did not appear until 1880 when the sixth form read *Hamlet*.[149] The astonishing and almost total neglect of English language and literature thus continued for many years after the *Clarendon Report* and the Public Schools Acts.

The monitorial system at Shrewsbury did change in the years after 1868, although it is difficult to judge how far this change was due to the Public Schools Acts and how far it was the result of other factors—the appointment of Moss in 1866, the tendency to conform with other public schools or perhaps the move to the new site in 1883 with the consequent increase in numbers and the greater geographical dispersal of the boys. In Kennedy's time, the monitorial system at Shrewsbury was unusual and the *Clarendon Report* commented favourably upon it.[150] The monitors, or praeposters, as they were called, were encouraged by Kennedy to do more than help the teachers maintain good order. They were, said Kennedy, 'representatives of the School' who sometimes negotiated with the headmaster on the school's behalf.[151] Another distinguishing feature of the Shrewsbury system was that the praeposters had no power to beat boys and 'would not be supported by the Headmaster were they to do so'.[152] This difference from the practice which had been made central to public school education by Dr Arnold indicated again perhaps that Shrewsbury was a marginal school and could not always easily claim equality with Eton and the other schools of the Clarendon Commission. The speed with which Moss changed the praeposters' powers in order to conform to what was done elsewhere suggests both a need to seek acceptance for the school and a willingness to sacrifice much that was valuable in the school's traditions in order to do so. It is perhaps not accidental that the great period of Shrewsbury School scholarship was before the Public Schools Acts and before innovation, in both teaching methods and school organisation, was constrained by what was expected in a public school. The Shrewsbury tradition fostered by Kennedy—in which praeposters were given great responsibilities, limited powers of punishment and a representative role in the school—had much to offer to other schools as a possible, progressive approach to school organisation. After the Public Schools Acts, while the representative character of the praeposters remained, their powers were changed to allow them to beat other boys, in conformity with the normal practice at other public schools.[153] Later headmasters confirmed this, for a circular from Alington to the praeposters provided rules for guidance and prohibited the use of canes tipped with metal.[154] The praeposters retained this power for many years, certainly until the Second World War.[155]

In Kennedy's time, the power to beat boys had usually been exercised by the headmaster alone, using a birch—a practice which Moss continued. The severity and number of floggings declined after 1868 although, as with the monitorial system, it is difficult to judge how far these changes were the result of the Clarendon Commission and how far the result of other changes in the school's circumstances. Kennedy's floggings were severe, although he reduced their frequency in his later years. In his evidence to the Clarendon Commission, he said that he flogged boys 'perhaps half a dozen times' in the half year.[156] Evidence given at a public inquiry, held by the school governors in 1874 into a flogging by Moss, supported those figures, although probably not all floggings were recorded. Kennedy was casual about school records and even Moss, usually so meticulous and methodical, admitted that 'once or twice, perhaps once a year at the outside' he had flogged a boy without entering his name on the list.[157] In comparison with Kennedy,

Moss seems to have been less severe for, as he admitted, he was not a strong man; figures given in evidence in 1874 showed a marked decline in the number of floggings.[158] At first sight therefore, it seems surprising that it was Moss, not Kennedy, who became the centre of a flogging scandal in 1874 when he gave a boy eighty-eight strokes of the birth for bringing beer into his study, but the circumstances suggest that this violent incident was the culmination of all the long conflict in the school between the headmasters and the governors, and the expression of the headmaster's anger and frustration provoked by the long struggle over the Public Schools Bills and the future of the school. For the boy flogged so severely in May 1874 was Geoffrey Loxdale, the son of John Loxdale—a school governor and the man who had most opposed, delayed and almost frustrated the plans and ambitions of Moss for the future of the school.[159]

This conflict between headmaster and governors had been a noticeable feature of the school's history from the time of its foundation but the conflict had been intensified by the *Clarendon Report*, the opposition of the governors and of Shrewsbury Corporation to the Public Schools Bills, the appointment of Moss in 1866, his immediate suggestion that the school should be moved and the opposition of the governors to this suggestion.[160] The governors continued to delay the implementation of the Act for some years after 1868 so that the new governors did not meet until the end of 1871. An attempt by Moss, earlier in 1871, to coerce the governors into an agreement to move the school had been peremptorily rejected with a pointed reference to the competence of his predecessors in the same situation.[161] Even when the new governors met, the two members elected by the Corporation continued to defend local interests and stubbornly opposed the removal of the school to a new site.[162] The most prominent of these men was John Loxdale, who had been Mayor of Shrewsbury in 1858 and a member of the old governing body since 1848.[163] Loxdale was also a leading opponent of the Public Schools Bills and a member of the governors' committee set up to oppose them.[164] The opposition of these two men to Moss's proposal to move the school was strengthened in December 1873 when an influential deputation, including the Earl of Powis, met the governors to oppose the move.[165] The deputation was unsuccessful; John

Loxdale resigned in February 1874 and the new governors finally approved the move in March 1874.[166]

For Moss, however, this must have been a time of great stress and anxiety when all his plans and ambitions for the school seemed threatened by the interminable intransigence of the old governors, who had influential local support. Throughout 1873 there was a virulent campaign in the local and even the London press, often aimed personally at Moss.[167] Geoffrey Loxdale's offence, coming when it did, must have released all the anger, distress and frustration that had probably built up in Moss's mind from the time of his appointment. That the offence involved beer must have seemed to Moss, with his dislike for strong drink and his fear of the corrupting influence of town life, to epitomise all that he was struggling against when he had just passed through a harrowing period of local criticism, antagonism and opposition led by the boy's father and for which the boy must have seemed partly responsible. That Moss flogged the boy for the faults of his father, from malice or for revenge, is too simple an explanation, but it is impossible to believe that Moss was not conscious of flogging John Loxdale's son, for the incident was out of character and otherwise inexplicable. The incident revealed perhaps both the prolonged distress and frustration of the headmaster and the extent to which the *Clarendon Report* and the slow progress towards legislation and change intensified the conflict between headmaster and governors. Although often expressed in terms of disagreement about discipline, free education or the curriculum, this conflict was essentially about the purpose of the school—was it a school for local children which others might also attend, or was it a national school to which local children were admitted in small numbers as a privilege?

The scandal, and the governors' inquiry which exonerated Moss, did, however, enable Shrewsbury Corporation to get its way over the school's new site. Moss and the governors favoured the Coton Hill site, but were less inclined to pursue this option after the scandal in face of determined local opposition. Kenyon and Lord Powis, who joined the governors early in 1874 as new nominees of Shrewsbury Corporation following the resignation of Loxdale and Dr Henry Keate, were no doubt anxious to prevent further public conflict and persuaded the governors to accept the Kingsland site, which was favoured by the Corporation. The Corporation was anxious to develop building land at Kingsland and saw the potential financial benefit to the town of siting the school there. The agreement by Parliament in 1873 to the building of a new bridge across the Severn by the Kingsland site added to the attraction of this proposal. Moss was not wholly in favour, however, for the buildings at Kingsland had previously been a workhouse, while the school had long associations with Coton Hill but, in the end, the school did move to Kingsland in 1882 and its success on the new site was perhaps a final contribution by the Corporation to the school's future.[168]

For Shrewsbury, the most important consequence of the Clarendon Commission and the Public Schools Acts was that Parliament settled the future of the school. It was to be a national, fee-paying school, which was what the headmasters wanted. The Public Schools Acts and the Special Commissioners provided a new governing body, with few local connections, that was likely to support the headmaster's view. Grant Duff, Granville and Clarendon had hoped that the Clarendon Commission and the Public Schools Acts would lead to the speedy introduction of more modern and more scientific subjects into the schools' curriculum, following the example of what they had seen in Europe. But at Shrewsbury, these new subjects came slowly, with little enthusiasm, and the school continued to offer a predominantly classical education for many years, although with reformed finances and improved premises. Local parents and governors, who had struggled for so many years under Kennedy to reform the school's curriculum and whose efforts had led to the Chancery Scheme of 1853 and the 'Non-Collegiate' class, now had no influence over the school because only two members of the new governing body were nominated by the town. The Public Schools Acts thus removed from a position of influence at Shrewsbury School the only group that had achieved significant curricular reform and took from the town, and the education of the town's children, a school that owed its foundation to the people of Shrewsbury.

Notes

1 These numbers are for October 1861. For school numbers, see the *Clarendon Report*, I, pp. 310–11 and C. J. Shrosbree, 'The origins and influence of the Clarendon Commission (1861–1864), with special reference to Shrewsbury

School', PhD thesis, Birmingham University, 1985, Appendix VIII. The most thorough, factual description of the school at this time is to be found in the *Clarendon Report* itself and the supporting evidence. See the *Clarendon Report*, II, pp. 303–26 and the *Clarendon Report*, IV, pp. 313–57.

2   *Letters Patent of King Edward VI*, quoted in the *Clarendon Report*, II, p. 303. For a detailed account of the earlier history of the school, see J. B. Oldham, *A History of Shrewsbury School 1552–1952*, Oxford, 1952, Chapters I–VII and for a brief account, see the *Clarendon Report*, II, pp. 303–6.

3   The formal title of the school was *The Free Grammar School of King Edward VI at Shrewsbury*, a title which continued in use after the *Public Schools Act, 1868* but which caused difficulties for the Clarendon Commission and much controversy locally because the meaning of the word 'free' was much disputed. See the *Clarendon Report*, II, p. 303. See also Chapter 1, Note 24.

4   On 22 May 1571, Queen Elizabeth granted the school the tithes of Chirbury Rectory which, together with other revenues from Chirbury and other parishes, amounted to £20. School accounts for 1578–9, the earliest that survive, show a total income of £186 5s 9d of which only £2 11s 0d came from entrance fees. See Oldham, *A History of Shrewsbury School*, p. 8.

5   For Shrewsbury School numbers 1830–1951, see Shrosbree, 'Origins of the Clarendon Commission', Appendix VIII. Samuel Butler became headmaster in 1798 after a distinguished academic career at St John's College, Cambridge and remained until 1836. For an account of his work at the school, see Oldham, *A History of Shrewsbury School*, pp. 72–103. For Kennedy, see Chapter 1, Note 27, and Note 91 below.

6   The recommendations concerned the governing body (Recommendations 1–5), school scholarships and exhibitions at Oxford and Cambridge (Recommendations 6–8, 10, 11, 28), foundation boys (Recommendations 9–10), fees together with the cost of new buildings and the rent of the playground (Recommendations 12, 13, 14, 15, 16, 17, 29), the reorganisation and encouragement of the 'Non-Collegiate' class, including the appointment of a science teacher (Recommendations 18, 19, 20, 21, 22, 23, 24, 25, 26), the ages of attendance (Recommendation 27) and the appointment of Examiners (Recommendation 28). The recommendations would have reduced drastically the influence of Shrewsbury Corporation by limiting its nominees on the governing body to a permanent minority. When the recommendations were fully implemented, there would be a governing body of thirteen members—three nominated by Shrewsbury Corporation, one by St John's College, Cambridge, one by Magdalen College, Cambridge, one by Christ Church, Oxford, three by the Crown and four by the governors themselves. The Chairman would no longer be the Mayor of Shrewsbury *ex officio* but would be chosen by the governors. The *Clarendon Report* proposed to change the governing body immediately by interim extra nominations of one member each from the Corporation, the three Colleges and the Crown, thus raising the number of members from twelve to seventeen. The numbers would then be gradually reduced by death or resignation. Scholarships were to be tenable at any Oxford or Cambridge college and local claims to preference were to go. Two new boarding houses were to be built and, in order to do this, some university scholarships were to be suspended, the fees raised to twenty guineas, some property sold and some money borrowed on the security of the school's tithes. The 'Non-Collegiate' class, which had a much-reduced classical curriculum and which offered instead modern languages, English, modern history and mathematics, was to be strengthened by the appointment of a science teacher and put on terms of equality with the classics classes. There were to be equal fees for this class, examinations, prizes, some free places awarded after a competitive examination and a regular, ordered curriculum. External Examiners for the school were to be appointed who would report to the governors. Boys were to attend only between the ages of nine and nineteen years. For these recommendations, see the *Clarendon Report*, II, pp. 323–5. For the detailed investigation of the school from which these recommendations are derived, see the *Clarendon Report*, II, pp. 303–23. For the general recommendations which applied with minor exceptions to Shrewsbury, see the *Clarendon Report*, I, pp. 52–5.

7 See Chapter 1, Note 64.

8 See Oldham, *A History of Shrewsbury School*, p. 104.

9 Sampson Kingsford (1825–90), who had a first class degree in classics and was a Fellow of St John's College, Cambridge, was headmaster of the Grammar School of King Edward VI at Ludlow 1857–65. See J. A. Venn (ed.), *Alumni Cantabrigienses*, II, 1752–1900, Cambridge, 1947, IV, p. 49 and *Eddowes's Shrewsbury Journal*, 9 July 1862, p. 4.

10 See T. W. Bamford, *The Rise of the Public Schools: A Study of Boys' Public Boarding Schools in England and Wales from 1837 to the Present Day*, London, 1967, pp. ix–xi. Even Grant Duff, a radical reformer in education, accepted that Eton was the most appropriate school for the 'higher classes' but wanted to make Eton a school for the 'higher classes' throughout Europe, offering a suitably reformed curriculum. See Grant Duff, *Hansard*, CLXXV, 6 May 1864, col. 118.

11 The six schools excluded were Winchester, Westminster, Harrow, Rugby, Eton and Charterhouse. See Bamford, *Rise of the Public Schools*, p. x.

12 In 1866, Westminster refused to play cricket against Shrewsbury because 'Westminster plays no schools except public schools' and because the Committee of the Public Schools Club recognised only Charterhouse, Eton, Harrow, Rugby, Westminster and Winchester. The reply of the Shrewsbury captain was that Shrewsbury was 'the most important school in England at a time when Westminster was unknown' and significantly, that Shrewsbury's inclusion in the Clarendon Commission put the school's status beyond dispute. See Oldham, *A History of Shrewsbury School*, pp. 239–40.

13 See Chapter 4, Notes 68, 70 and 72.

14 Grant Duff, *Hansard*, CLXXV, 6 May 1864, col. 125.

15 Until the appointment of the new governing body in 1871, the number of titled governors always exceeded the number of titled parents. It was common at Shrewsbury to have two or three titled members at a governors' meeting—a high proportion when the average attendance at meetings between 1855 and 1871 was only eight. On 5 April 1866 for example, the nine governors included Viscount Hill, Lord Berwick and Sir V. R. Corbet Bart. For Shrewsbury governors before 1871 and their attendance, see Shrosbree, 'Origins of the Clarendon Commission', Appendix XIII. See also Note 42 below. Titled parents were unusual at Shrewsbury, but became rather less so after 1868. See Shrosbree, 'Origins of the Clarendon Commission', Appendix XII.

16 The governors at Shrewsbury had particularly strong motives for delay: they wished to safeguard local claims, in spite of the Act, and they wished to oppose the removal of the school to a new site. Governors at other schools did not have these two particular motives, apart from the question of local claims at Harrow and Rugby, and were no doubt more concerned to settle their constitutions and their school regulations quickly, after such a long period of legislative uncertainty.

17 See Note 6 above.

18 For the definition of a Shrewsbury burgess, see Chapter 1, Note 24.

19 *Clarendon Report*, II, p. 324.

20 *Clarendon Report*, II, p. 325.

21 *Clarendon Report*, II, p. 325.

22 See B. H. Kennedy, *Notes on Public Education: A Paper read, by the Rev. Dr. Kennedy, at the Meeting of the National Association for the Promotion of Social Science, York, September, 1864*, Bailiff's Bundles No. 122 and B. H. Kennedy, *Shrewsbury School: A Letter to His Grace the Archbishop of York on the Public Character of Shrewsbury School, as affected by the Public Schools Bill*, Cambridge, 1865.

23 *Clarendon Report*, I, Recommendation III, p. 5.

24 Kennedy, *Notes on Public Education*, p. 1.

25 Kennedy, *A Letter to His Grace the Archbishop of York*, pp. 1–2. He argued also that a board of governors may be hindered by internal divisions and that, although a headmaster and a board of governors may both do harm, only a headmaster may have a positive influence for good.

26 Kennedy, *Notes on Public Education*, p. 2. He did not regard curricular innovation with enthusiasm but with a dismissive pessimism. While prepared to

encourage drawing, mapping or physical exercise for 'boys of a low intellectual grade', he did not think it possible to teach French or German effectively in a public school and confessed that he was himself 'unable to follow the rapid utterance of the foreigner'. See Kennedy, *Notes on Public Education*, p. 2.

27 See Note 6 above.
28 See Kennedy, *A Letter to His Grace the Archbishop of York*, pp. 5–6.
29 Kennedy, *A Letter to His Grace the Archbishop of York*, p. 4.
30 Kennedy, *A Letter to His Grace the Archbishop of York*, pp. 4–5.
31 See Kennedy, *A Letter to His Grace the Archbishop of York*, pp. 5–6.
32 See Kennedy, *A Letter to His Grace the Archbishop of York*, p. 6.
33 For the full development of Kennedy's argument about the original purpose of the school and the meaning of 'free', see Kennedy, *A Letter to His Grace the Archbishop of York*, pp. 8–20. See also B. H. Kennedy, *Letter to the Mayor and Town Council of Shrewsbury*, Shrewsbury, 1848, cited Oldham, *A History of Shrewsbury School*, p. 111. For Kennedy's evidence to the Clarendon Commission, see the *Clarendon Report*, II, p. 322. The *Clarendon Report*, although arguing that the school was for 'all classes' and that burgesses did not have an exclusive right to free education, could see 'no reason, so far as regards the Founder's intention, why, if any privileges at all are to be retained, they should not be shared by all natives, or even by all established inhabitants of the town'. *Clarendon Report*, II, p. 308.
34 Kennedy, *A Letter to His Grace the Archbishop of York*, p. 19.
35 There were twenty-five boys at the school receiving free education as the sons of burgesses at the time of the Clarendon Commission and, of these, twenty-two were day-boys. See the *Clarendon Report*, II, pp. 308, 321. The number of these foundation boys had declined from 'sixty to seventy' at the time of Kennedy's appointment, although accurate records and registers do not survive. See Kennedy, *A Letter to His Grace the Archbishop of York*, p. 7. Various reasons were given for this decline. Kennedy attributed it to the Municipal Corporations Act of 1835 which had made the title of 'burgess' merely nominal and mostly irrelevant. Others attributed the decline to the classical curriculum, the discouragement of more modern subjects and the inconvenience of the school hours for day-boys. See the *Clarendon Report*, II, pp. 306–7. The number of boys admitted free as sons of burgesses continued to decline after 1865 and particularly after 1871 as the residual rights of the *Public Schools Act, 1868* gradually became extinct. Although some foundation boys were admitted in most years between 1866 and 1890, the average number was only four and none at all were admitted in 1880–1, 1885–6 and 1888–9. See Shrosbree, 'Origins of the Clarendon Commission', Appendix X.
36 Kennedy, *A Letter to His Grace the Archbishop of York*, p. 6. For a more general comment on the conflict between local interests and the aspirations of headmasters, see Bamford, *Rise of the Public Schools*, pp. 197–203.
37 For an account of an early dispute in 1587 between John Meighen, the headmaster, and the burgesses over the appointment of the School Bailiff—which involved ultimately both the Lord Chancellor and the Queen's Council—see Oldham, *A History of Shrewsbury School*, p. 35. For other disputes 'in which Shrewsbury Headmasters seem to have been always involved', see Oldham, *A History of Shrewsbury School*, pp. 35–40, 63–5, 77–8 and 111–14. Moss always wanted to loosen the school's ties with the town. See John Byrne, 'The removal of Shrewsbury School 1866–1882', MEd dissertation, Birmingham University, 1983, p. 103.
38 Henry Whitehead Moss (1841–1917) was headmaster 1866–1908. He is chiefly remembered for three achievements: his association with the removal of the school to a new site in 1882, his long period of over forty years as headmaster and the infliction of the worst public school flogging on record in 1874. A full but fulsome account of his life may be found in the biography by his wife. See Mrs Moss, *Moss of Shrewsbury: A Memoire 1841–1917*, London, 1932. See also Oldham, *A History of Shrewsbury School*, pp. 130–54 and Byrne, 'The removal of Shrewsbury School'. See also J. B. Lawson, '1882 Genesis: Exodus', *Old Salopian Newsletter*, 92, May 1983.
39 When the new governors met on 12 December 1871, there was a last-ditch

attempt to defend local rights but this failed on 28 February 1872 when an amendment moved by John Loxdale and Henry Keate, the members nominated by Shrewsbury Corporation, was defeated. See *Trustees' Minutes*, 12 December 1871, p. 323 and *Trustees' Minutes*, 28 February 1872, p. 329. Until 1874, there was opposition to the move but this also failed. See *Trustees' Minutes*, 20 March 1874.

40 See Note 37 above.

41 The Chairman of the governors was the Mayor of Shrewsbury during his term of office which lasted one year. Shrewsbury Corporation selected each new member of the governors, as a vacancy occurred, from a list of three nominations submitted by the existing governors. For a summary of the governors' constitution, see the *Clarendon Report*, II, pp. 303–6 and 309. See also Oldham, *A History of Shrewsbury School*, pp. 70–1 and 111–13. For the details of the Chancery Scheme, see the *Clarendon Report*, II, Appendix Q and also *The Free Grammar School of King Edward VI at Shrewsbury. Order, Report and Scheme as made and settled by the Court of Chancery in 1853*, Shrewsbury, undated. See also the evidence of J. R. Kenyon QC, in the *Lords Select Committee Report, 1865*, 29 May 1865, pp. 269–70. Governors of Shrewsbury School were known formally as Trustees, but the governing bodies of all the Clarendon Commission schools are here referred to as 'governors', following the practice of Parliament.

42 The governors included members of the local gentry (Lord Hill, Lord Berwick and Sir Baldwin Leighton Bt, for example), prominent professional men from Shrewsbury (like banker William Butler Lloyd or solicitor John Loxdale), local clergy (Rev. Edward Warter and Rev. Robert Lingen Burton) and local businessmen (like John Nightingale, Mayor in 1866, the third generation of Shrewsbury barbers and the keeper of a toy shop and 'fancy repository' in High Street, Shrewsbury). Before 1871 the governors provided a wide experience of social, commercial and professional life and had a wide variety of educational backgrounds, including (in 1868 for example) Eton, Rugby, Westminster and Shrewsbury. For the attendance, occupation and education of Shrewsbury governors 1855–71, see Shrosbree, 'Origins of the Clarendon Commission', Appendix XIII.

43 See *Order, Report and Scheme as made and settled by the Court of Chancery*, pp. 22–3, 25–6, 31–3.

44 See *Order, Report and Scheme as made and settled by the Court of Chancery*, p. 22.

45 See *Order, Report and Scheme as made and settled by the Court of Chancery*, p. 22, quoted Oldham, *A History of Shrewsbury School*, p. 112.

46 See Oldham, *A History of Shrewsbury School*, p. 111.

47 *Trustees' Minutes*, 7 July 1848, quoted Oldham, *A History of Shrewsbury School*, p. 111.

48 Oldham, *A History of Shrewsbury School*, p. 111.

49 See Oldham, *A History of Shrewsbury School*, p. 112. The history of this association illustrates the long struggle of Shrewsbury headmasters to free themselves from local accountability. In 1561, Thomas Ashton—a Fellow of St John's College, Cambridge—was appointed as the first headmaster. As the result of his own efforts, the school obtained further endowments from Queen Elizabeth in 1571. As part of this settlement, Ashton obtained the right to draw up new school Ordinances, approved in February 1578. Before then, control of the school had been almost entirely in the hands of local people but the Ordinances gave the right to nominate masters, including the headmaster, to St John's College, Cambridge. The right to nominate the headmaster remained until the *Public Schools Act, 1868*. See Oldham, *A History of Shrewsbury School*, pp. 8–11 and the *Clarendon Report*, II, pp. 303–6.

50 See *Order, Report and Scheme as made and settled by the Court of Chancery*, pp. 31–2.

51 No formal recognition of this class was given in the annual school prize lists except a brief note in 1857 indicating that boys for the 'Non-Collegiate' class were drawn from other classes throughout the school. See *Shrewsbury School, 1857*, Bailiff's Bundles No. 122. No record exists of the boys who were in this

class except that the size of the class was about twenty and that the class was established as the result of pressure from parents. See the evidence of Edward Calvert and Armand Bentley in the *Clarendon Report*, IV, pp. 309, 349–50.

52 Oldham, *A History of Shrewsbury School*, p. 109.

53 See Burbury to the School Bailiff, 16 August 1852, Bailiff's Bundles No. 111. The Rev. William Burbury (1822–65) married Charlotte Amy May Kennedy on 10 June 1852 and remained at the school until October 1860. See Venn, *Alumni Cantabrigienses*, I, p. 448 and *Trustees' Minutes*, 10 October 1860, p. 228.

54 See Note 53 above.

55 Kennedy's proposals are undated. See B. Kennedy, *Proposition to establish a class for Physical Science and Linear Drawing*, Bailiff's Bundles No. 111.

56 Kennedy, *Proposition to establish a class for Physical Science*.

57 *Trustees' Minutes*, 31 October 1853.

58 *Trustees' Minutes*, 5 July 1855.

59 See the *Clarendon Report*, II, pp. 322–3.

60 See Oldham, *A History of Shrewsbury School*, p. 110.

61 See Oldham, *A History of Shrewsbury School*, p. 110.

62 Oldham described the formation of the 'Non-Collegiate' class without giving a date. He then went on to describe the negotiations between Kennedy and the governors which led to the Chancery Scheme of 1853. Oldham's treatment of this topic is doubly misleading for it suggests that Kennedy initiated the 'Non-Collegiate' class on his own initiative and that the governors went ahead with Chancery proceedings in spite of the reforms that Kennedy had already begun. Neither suggestion was true. For the discussion of the 'Non-Collegiate' class and his account of the Chancery proceedings, see Oldham, *A History of Shrewsbury School*, pp. 110–12.

63 Thomas Armand Bentley came to the school in 1842 and his name appears in the staff list preceding the report of the Chancery Scheme, where his subjects are given as French and German. See *Order, Report and Scheme as made and settled by the Court of Chancery*, Section 2. Bentley was responsible for the 'Non-Collegiate' class and gave evidence about it to the Clarendon Commission. Known as 'Bonk', he was the 'Punishment Master' for many years and responsible for checking that 'penals'—lines of verse written out as a punishment—were done. He remained at the school until 1893. See Oldham, *A History of Shrewsbury School*, pp. 171, 188 and the *Clarendon Report*, IV, pp. 349–50.

64 See Oldham, *A History of Shrewsbury School*, p. 110 and the *Clarendon Report*, II, pp. 322–3.

65 See the *Clarendon Report*, II, pp. 322–3 and Kennedy, *A Letter to His Grace the Archbishop of York*, p. 20.

66 Kennedy, *A Letter to His Grace the Archbishop of York*, p. 20.

67 From 'consideration of the deference due to their judgement', he decided to close the class at the earliest opportunity. See Kennedy, *A Letter to His Grace the Archbishop of York*, p. 20. Yet the Commissioners wished to offer 'such suggestions for the improvement of the class . . . to place it on a good footing'. They suggested that the work of the 'Non-Collegiate' class might 'afford a useful stimulus to the modern studies of the classical school' and recommended that school funds 'should be applied to the encouragement of merit' in the class. See the *Clarendon Report*, II, pp. 322–3.

68 For an introduction to the sociology of groups and group leadership, in which some of these insights are explored, see G. C. Homans, *The Human Group*, London, 1975, pp. 180–1 and W. J. H. Sprott, *Human Groups*, London, 1958, pp. 152–9.

69 W. E. Heitland, 'Dr. Kennedy at Shrewsbury', *Eagle*, XV, No. 89, June 1889, pp. 3, 12–13. This article, published soon after Kennedy's death, in the journal of St John's College, Cambridge, gave both a general account of the school's curriculum in the years before the *Clarendon Report* and a vivid, affectionate description of Kennedy's teaching.

70 See Heitland, 'Dr. Kennedy at Shrewsbury', pp. 12–13 and Oldham, *A History of Shrewsbury School*, p. 122.

71 Some examples of these impositions from Kennedy's time survive in *Paget's*

Scrap Book, an evocative and moving collection of drawings, notes, invitations and other souvenirs of school life collected by Alfred Tolver Paget who taught at the school 1840–55.

72 See Kennedy, *Notes on Public Education*, pp. 1–3.
73 Kennedy, evidence in *Lords Select Committee Report, 1865*, 26 May 1865, p. 254.
74 See F. D. How, *Six Great Schoolmasters*, London, 1904, p. 103, quoting G. W. Fisher, *Annals of Shrewsbury School*, London, 1899.
75 Separate classes were organised for French and separate prizes given. For a summary of the school curriculum in 1862, see the *Clarendon Report*, II, p. 311.
76 How, *Six Great Schoolmasters*, pp. 103, 104.
77 See Oldham, *A History of Shrewsbury School*, p. 116.
78 *Clarendon Report*, II, p. 325.
79 See H. F. Jones, *Samuel Butler: A Memoire*, London, 1919, pp. 41–2.
80 This entertainment took place on 6 December 1848 and the stage notes also are preserved. See *Paget's Scrap Book*.
81 See *Paget's Scrap Book*.
82 See Kennedy, *A Letter to His Grace the Archbishop of York*, p. 26. For music, see also Egerton's diary quoted in P. Cowburn (ed.), *A Salopian Anthology: Some Impressions of Shrewsbury School during Four Centuries*, London, 1946, pp. 176–8. J. C. Egerton was at the school 1844–8.
83 The school issued a prize list each summer, entitled *Shrewsbury School* with the appropriate date. Attached to the prize list each year was a detailed list of the work done by each form during the year. These lists were called 'Subjects for Examination' under Kennedy and later, under Moss, 'Subjects read during the Term'. The slow, gradual acceptance of science may be traced in the prize lists from 1880 to 1890. The first teacher specifically appointed for natural science, W. S. Ingrams, appeared in the Staff List for 1883. In 1885, two prizes for chemistry were offered and a separate class list for chemistry appeared, containing the names of thirty boys from the Shell Form. In 1887, there were two teachers for natural science and both German and science made a serious appearance in the curriculum. Even in 1887 there were only two teachers for science and two for the modern side; there were seven teachers for classics. For this and much more information about the curriculum, see the prize lists for 1880–90 in Bailiff's Bundles No. 122.
84 Samuel Moore was at Shrewsbury School 1852–8. After attending Trinity College, Cambridge and Lincoln's Inn, he became a cotton spinner in Manchester and an Equity Draftsman. For his life and his association with Marx and Engels, see Erhard Kiehnbaum, 'Samuel Moore', *Beiträge zur Geschichte der Arbeiterbewegung*, 17 January 1975, pp. 1074–81. (Herausgegeben vom Institut fur Marxismus–Leninismus beim Zentralkomitee der Sozialistischen Einheitspartei Deutschlands Redaktion, Berlin, East Germany). See also Venn, *Alumni Cantabrigienses*, II, p. 456.
85 See Francis Darwin, *The Life and Letters of Charles Darwin*, London, 1887, I, p. 35, quoted Oldham, *A History of Shrewsbury School*, p. 195.
86 The most concise summary of the school's academic record is to be found in the *Clarendon Report*, II, pp. 314–15. See also Oldham, *A History of Shrewsbury School*, pp. 192–4 and Kennedy, *A Letter to His Grace the Archbishop of York*, p. 25. Also, D. S. Colman, *Sabrinae Corolla: The Classics at Shrewsbury under Dr. Butler and Dr. Kennedy*, Shrewsbury, 1950.
87 Oldham, *A History of Shrewsbury School*, p. 193. Kennedy himself won the Porson Prize and the Browne Medal for Latin Ode at Cambridge in 1823—after matriculation but while still at school. Boys still at school won the Ireland Scholarship at Oxford in 1831 and the Craven Scholarship at Oxford in 1844.
88 See Oldham, *A History of Shrewsbury School*, p. 193 and Colman, *Sabrinae Corolla*, p. 6.
89 In Butler's time, the headmaster of Harrow and an assistant master came to Shrewsbury to hear Butler taking a lesson. See Colman, *Sabrinae Corolla*, p. 7.
90 See Colman, *Sabrinae Corolla*, p. 7.
91 Heitland, 'Dr. Kennedy at Shrewsbury', pp. 8, 10. It is a matter of interest that Kennedy did nearly everything that teachers now are told to avoid: he was

habitually late, encouraged boys to learn from each other, never gave fair copies, never went through a composition with a boy, sometimes kept an exercise for weeks and often gave an exercise back with no comments written on it. No record of exercises or marks was kept and boys in the Sixth were allowed to use translations. Assistance from teachers out of school hours was practically unknown. Kennedy was an original Latin poet, however, and was renowned for his translations of the most unpromising material. Oldham gives the example of a summons from 'Smith and Son, Solicitors' to a meeting of the Bridge Committee 'to consider Mr. Diffie's proposal for laying down gas pipes' which Kennedy translated into Latin elegiacs. See Oldham, *A History of Shrewsbury School*, p. 115. See also Heitland, 'Dr. Kennedy at Shrewsbury', pp. 3–15. Although the author of the well-known Latin primer, he made little reference to formal grammar. See Colman, *Sabrinae Corolla*, p. 9.

92 H. A. J. Munro, a pupil at the school 1833–8, quoted in Colman, *Sabrinae Corolla*, p. 8.
93 See Heitland, 'Dr. Kennedy at Shrewsbury', p. 6.
94 See Oldham, *A History of Shrewsbury School*, p. 119.
95 See Oldham, *A History of Shrewsbury School*, pp. 118–19.
96 Oldham, *A History of Shrewsbury School*, p. 119.
97 W. E. Heitland, quoted in Oldham, *A History of Shrewsbury School*, p. 188.
98 See the *Clarendon Report*, II, pp. 322–32 and the *Clarendon Report*, IV, pp. 313–25 and 329–39.
99 Kennedy to Peele, 13 May 1865, Bailiff's Bundles No. 122. Joshua John Peele was the School Bailiff 1839–69. His successor was De Courcy Peele. See *Trustees' Minutes*, 5 February 1869. The Bailiff acted as school secretary and accountant, kept the minutes of governors' meetings and implemented the governors' decisions.
100 See Kennedy to Peele, 13 May 1865, Bailiff's Bundles No. 122 and *To the Right Honourable the Lords Spiritual and Temporal, in Parliament Assembled. The humble petition of the Mayor, Aldermen, and Burgesses of the Borough of Shrewsbury in Council Assembled*, Bailiff's Bundles No. 122. For the presentation of this petition, see the *Lords Select Committee Report, 1865*, 29 May 1865, p. 269.
101 The petition was proposed originally by 'Resolution of the Committee of the Council of the Borough of Shrewsbury'. The proposal then came to the school governors who set up a committee to draft the petition in April 1865. See *Trustees' Minutes*, 1 April 1865, pp. 241–2.
102 See Kennedy, *A Letter to His Grace the Archbishop of York*, pp. 16–17.
103 Kennedy, *A Letter to His Grace the Archbishop of York*, pp. 16–17.
104 Kennedy, *A Letter to His Grace the Archbishop of York*, p. 18.
105 See Oldham, *A History of Shrewsbury School*, p. 93.
106 See Note 104 above.
107 Kennedy, *A Letter to His Grace the Archbishop of York*, p. 27.
108 See Moss, *Moss of Shrewsbury*, p. 62. Kennedy was particularly opposed to two recommendations of the *Clarendon Report*: curricular reform by Parliament or school governors and the appointment of a council of assistant masters in each school. The Public Schools Bills of 1865 made no specific recommendations about the curriculum and gave only a general oversight of it to the governors. The councils of assistant masters did not appear in the Bills. See Kennedy, *Notes on Public Education*, p. 1. The *Public Schools (No. 32) Bill* of 1865 proposed, with some variation for each school, the abolition of foundation rights at Harrow, Rugby and Shrewsbury and these clauses remained in spite of the appeals by counsel made to the Lords Select Committee on behalf of local inhabitants. For Kennedy's views, see *A Letter to His Grace the Archbishop of York*, pp. 6–14. For the clauses concerning foundation rights at Harrow, Rugby and Shrewsbury, see the *Public Schools (No. 32) Bill* of 1865, Clauses 20, 21 and 23, quoted in Shrosbree, 'Origins of the Clarendon Commission', Appendix III. See also the *Lords Select Committee Report, 1865*, 19 June 1865, p. xi.
109 John Robert Kenyon QC (1807–80), educated at Charterhouse, was Judge of the Chancellor's Court at Oxford University 1843–80 and Chairman of Shropshire Quarter Sessions 1871–80. A member of a well-known Shropshire

family, he became a governor of Shrewsbury School in March 1874. See Shrosbree, 'Origins of the Clarendon Commission', Appendix XIV. For the correspondence with Lord Powis, the Bishop of Lichfield and St John's College, Cambridge, see Bailiff's Bundles No. 122. Edward James Herbert (1818–91), 3rd Earl of Powis, was a prominent landowner in Shropshire and influential in local affairs. He was also a member of the Lords Select Committee and a governor of Shrewsbury School from 1874. See Shrosbree, 'Origins of the Clarendon Commission', Appendix IV. The Bishops of Lichfield were associated with the school from the time of its foundation and had some advisory powers. See Oldham, *A History of Shrewsbury School*, pp. 4, 9, 33, 37, 112, 119, 127. John Lonsdale (1788–1867), of Eton and King's College, Cambridge, was Bishop of Lichfield 1843–68.

110 See the Mercers' Company to the Mayor of Shrewsbury, 22 March 1865, Bailiff's Bundles No. 122, and G. E. Cottrell to the Mayor of Shrewsbury, 20 March 1865, Bailiff's Bundles No. 122. George Edward Cottrell, a barrister and a resident of Harrow, was a former Harrow pupil. See M. G. Daughlish & P. K. Stephenson (eds.), *Harrow School Register 1800–1911*, London, 1911, p. 112.

111 See Chapter 6, pp. 189–91, and 197.

112 See Kenyon to Peele, 11 May 1865, Bailiff's Bundles No. 122. The solicitors were Whateley and Whateley of 41 Waterloo Street, Birmingham.

113 Private bills relate to matters of purely local or private interest and follow a special quasi-judicial procedure. The Public Schools Bills followed the procedure for public bills, in which the second reading, when the principles of the bill are approved, is the most important stage. Opponents of the Public Schools Bills were given an opportunity to present evidence and objections, with the help of counsel, to the Lords Select Committee in 1865, but only after the Bill had already been approved in principle. Objections were thus unlikely to obstruct the progress of the Bill. The *Public Schools Act, 1864*, which followed the public bill procedure, had established a precedent and the successful objection to the Metropolitan and City of London *Police Amalgamation (No. 89) Bill*, to which Kenyon referred, was made at the first reading. See *Hansard*, CLXX, 21 April 1863, cols. 481–525 and *Hansard*, CLXX, 22 April 1863, col. 526. See also A. H. Birch, *The British System of Government*, London, 1969, pp. 221–31.

114 See *Hansard*, CLXXXIV, 7 August 1866, cols. 2149–55. See also Kenyon to Peele with enclosed correspondence, 7 June 1866, Bailiff's Bundles No. 122.

115 See the *Public Schools (No. 4) Bill* in *Hansard*, CLXXXV, 7 February 1867, col. 80.

116 See *Hansard*, CLXXXIX, 10 August 1867. Recorded in General Index but not shown in transcript of proceedings.

117 See *Hansard*, CXC, 20 March 1868, cols. 2052–3. For the Commons Select Committee, see Chapter 6, Note 110.

118 See Chapter 4, Note 24.

119 For the controversy over the school's new site, see Byrne, 'The removal of Shrewsbury School' and Lawson, '1882 Genesis: Exodus'.

120 Clement attended only on 19 May 1868. The other meetings were on 1 April 1868, 28 April 1868, 1 May 1868, 5 May 1868, 8 May 1868, 12 May 1868 and 22 May 1868. See *Commons Select Committee Report, 1868*.

121 See Powell to Peele, 27 April 1868, Bailiff's Bundles No. 122. Francis Sharp Powell (1827–1911) was Conservative MP for Wigan 1857–9, 1881 and 1885–1910, for Cambridge 1863–8 and for the North Div. of the West Riding of Yorkshire 1872–4. He was a member of the Commons Select Committee on the Public Schools Bill.

122 Powell to Peele, 22 May 1868, Bailiff's Bundles No. 122.

123 See, for example, Powell to Peele, 10 June 1868, Bailiff's Bundles No. 122.

124 Robert Jasper More (1836–1903) was Liberal Unionist MP for South Shropshire 1865–8 and for the Ludlow Div. of Shropshire 1885–1903.

125 See *Hansard*, CXCIII, 14 July 1868, col. 1164 and *Hansard*, CXCIII, 15 July 1868, col. 1214. Clement's amendments sought to prevent the abolition of burgess rights without the agreement of Shrewsbury Corporation and to give Shrewsbury Corporation power to appoint governors alternately with the

governing body. See *Notices of Motions for Tuesday 16th June 1868*, Bailiff's Bundles No. 122. These amendments were never raised.

126 See the *Public Schools Act, 1868*, Sections 5, 6, 13, 26.

127 *Suggestions at a Meeting of the Trustees of the Free Grammar School held on the 31st October 1868. With reference to the Public Schools Act*, Bailiff's Bundles No. 122. See also *Trustees' Minutes*, 31 October 1868.

128 The last meeting of the old governing body took place on 30 September 1871. The first meeting of the new governing body took place on 12 December 1871. See *Trustees' Minutes*, 30 September 1871 and 12 December 1871. The new constitution had been approved by the Special Commissioners on 22 April 1871. See *Public Schools Commission. Shrewsbury. A Statute for constituting a new Governing Body for Shrewsbury Free Grammar School. No. IV(10)*, Bailiff's Bundles No. 122. The new school regulations were adopted on 20 February 1874. See *Regulations for Shrewsbury School, as finally adopted and sealed by order of the Governing Body, 20th February, 1874*, Bailiff's Bundles No. 122. Copies of each school's new constitution and regulations may be found in the *General Alphabetical Index to the Bills, Reports, Estimates, Accounts and Papers, printed by order of the House of Commons and to the Papers Presented by Counsel, 1852-1899*, London, 1909.

129 The occupational background of Shrewsbury governors changed markedly with the appointment of the new governing body. During the period 1855–71, governors were drawn from a wide variety of backgrounds. 27 per cent had commercial or industrial experience. During the period 1871–80, the governors had virtually no such experience, being generally of an academic or legal background, were usually Shrewsbury boys and usually classics graduates. The original members of the new governing body were: William Henry Bateson (1812–81), Master of St John's College, Cambridge and nominated by the College; John Bather (1819–86), a member of the local gentry, nominted by the Lord Lieutenant of Shropshire; Rev. Dr James Cartmell (1810–81), Master of Christ's College, Cambridge, Chaplain to the Queen, nominated by the school staff; Rt Rev. James Fraser (1818–85), Bishop of Manchester, nominated by Oxford University; John Tomlinson Hibbert (1824–1908), barrister and MP for Oldham 1862–74, co-opted; Rev. William Gilson Humphrey (1815–86), Fellow of Trinity College, Cambridge and Rector of St Martin-in-the-Fields, co-opted; Rev. Benjamin Jowett (1817–93), Master of Balliol College, Oxford and Regius Professor of Greek, co-opted; Henry Keate (1814–73), the son of a Shrewsbury grocer, a surgeon in Shrewsbury and a member of Shrewsbury Corporation, nominated by the Corporation; Benjamin Hall Kennedy (1804–89), formerly headmaster and Regius Professor of Greek at Cambridge 1867–89, nominated by Cambridge University; John Loxdale (1799–1885), a solicitor and former Mayor of Shrewsbury, nominated by Shrewsbury Corporation; George Osborne Morgan (1826–97), barrister and distinguished scholar, MP for Denbighshire 1868–85, nominated by the Lord Chief Justice; Sir James Paget, Bt (1814–89), Fellow of the Royal Society, Fellow of the Royal College of Surgeons, senior surgeon at St Bartholomew's Hospital, London and surgeon to the Queen, nominated by the Royal Society. All were Shrewsbury boys except Cartmell, Jowett, Keate and Paget; Cartmell went to Carlisle Grammar School, Jowett to St Paul's and the schools of Keate and Paget are unrecorded, although Paget was a Shrewsbury parent. Most were distinguished scholars or lawyers and seven had first class degrees in classics. Keate resigned and died in 1873, Loxdale resigned in February 1874 and Osborne Morgan resigned in August 1874 after the governors' support for Moss in the flogging scandal. For the attendance, occupation and education of Shrewsbury governors 1871–80, see Shrosbree, 'Origins of the Clarendon Commission', Appendix XIV.

130 At Rugby, for example, the seven new governors included the previous head-master, three former masters or pupils and men from Eton, Harrow and Shrewsbury. See *Rugby School Register*, London, 1886, II, 1850–74, p. viii.

131 If not former pupils, the new governors usually had close personal connections with the school. At Shrewsbury, for example, the Rev. Thomas Bucknall Lloyd, appointed in 1880, was born at the school and was the grandson of Dr Butler, the former headmaster. See Shrosbree, 'Origins of the Clarendon Commission',

Appendix XIV.

132 See the *Clarendon Report*, II, p. 310.

133 Moss to the governors, 3 July 1866, *Trustees' Minutes*, 5 July 1866.

134 Westminster and Charterhouse were also given the power to move. Any schemes suggested had to be laid before the Special Commissioners or, subsequently, before the Queen in Council. See the *Public Schools (No. 78) Bill*, 1867, Clause 24 and the *Public Schools Act, 1868*, Section 26. See also Oldham, *A History of Shrewsbury School*, p. 131.

135 See Note 39 above.

136 See Note 119 above. See also Oldham, *A History of Shrewsbury School*, pp. 130–46.

137 See Shrosbree, 'Origins of the Clarendon Commission', Appendix VIII.

138 See Shrosbree, 'Origins of the Clarendon Commission', Appendix XII.

139 Shropshire had a higher proportion of its total area (44 per cent) occupied by gentry estates in 1873 than any other county in England, if a 'gentry estate' is defined as between 1,000 and 10,000 acres. The average for the whole of England was 29.5 per cent. Shropshire also had a higher proportion of its total area (31 per cent) occupied by the estates of the greater gentry in 1873 than any other county in England, if an estate of the 'greater gentry' is defined as one between 3,000 and 10,000 acres. Children of these great Shropshire families did not, in general, go to Shrewsbury School. For landed gentry in Shropshire, see F. M. L. Thompson, *English Landed Society in the Nineteenth Century*, London, 1963, pp. 113, 114. For the geographical distribution of parents, see Shrosbree, 'Origins of the Clarendon Commission', Appendix IX and Appendix XI.

140 See *Shrewsbury School Accounts*, 1890, Bailiff's Bundles No. 122. At this time, the school had a number of subsidiary accounts—particularly to handle the financial transactions of the move. There was, for example, a Tuition Fees Account and a Reserve Fund Account. See *Shrewsbury School Accounts*, 1855–90, Bailiff's Bundles No. 122.

141 See Chapter 5, p. 143 and Chapter 6, pp. 184–6.

142 The mathematics teachers were J. C. P. Aldous of Jesus College, Cambridge and G. H. Lock of Clare College, Cambridge. The modern languages teacher was T. A. Bentley and the writing teacher was Thomas Webster. See *Shrewsbury School, 1874*, Bailiff's Bundles No. 122. For the history appointment, which survived in spite of a subsequent decision by Moss to dispense with this specialist teaching, see Oldham, *A History of Shrewsbury School*, p. 148.

143 The first natural science teacher was W. S. Ingrams of Exeter College, Oxford. See *Shrewsbury School, 1883* and *Shrewsbury School, 1900*, Bailiff's Bundles No. 122.

144 The subjects for the modern division, although not exclusively classical, were hardly a significant curricular innovation. The subjects were Latin, mathematics, French, English (Shakespeare's *King John* and Macauley's *Essay on Lord Clive*), history and geography. This was a belated reappearance of Kennedy's 'Non-Collegiate' class, abandoned in 1865, and just twenty years late. See *Shrewsbury School, 1884*, Bailiff's Bundles No. 122. For chemistry, see *Shrewsbury School, 1885*, Bailiff's Bundles No. 122.

145 See *Shrewsbury School, 1886*, Bailiff's Bundles No. 122.

146 See the Lent Term list for 1889, *Shrewsbury School Lists 1889–1891*, Shrewsbury, 1889–91.

147 See *Report for the Year 1888*, 25 February 1889, Bailiff's Bundles No. 70 and the Michaelmas Term list for 1900, *Shrewsbury School Lists 1898–1900*, Shrewsbury, 1900. The Fellow of Owens College, afterwards Manchester University, was H. Holden MSc.

148 The prize list for 1849 is the earliest that has survived. See *The Schools*, p. 11, Shrewsbury Sch. Arch. Another copy may be found in *The Shropshire Journal*, 13 June 1849. For English, see *Shrewsbury School, 1872*, Bailiff's Bundles No. 122.

149 See *Shrewsbury School, 1880*, Bailiff's Bundles No. 122.

150 See the *Clarendon Report*, II, pp. 319–20.

151 See the *Clarendon Report*, II, p. 320. See also Oldham, *A History of Shrewsbury*

School, pp. 97, 82–3.

152 See the *Clarendon Report*, II, p. 320, quoting Kennedy's evidence. According to Kennedy, the cane was not used at all and he acknowledged that, in this respect, the monitorial system at Shrewsbury was quite different to the practice at other public schools. The headmaster regularly saw the Penal Sheet, which noted all punishments imposed by teachers and praeposters, and he alone inflicted corporal punishment with the birch for 'moral offences or serious indiscipline . . . bullying, wilful disrespect (both very rare) etc.'. See Kennedy's answer to Question 23, *Clarendon Report*, II, p. 326.

153 See Oldham, *A History of Shrewsbury School*, p. 167. Some of the worst examples of beating occurred after the Public Schools Acts, perhaps because the schools' new legal status made practices, otherwise indefensible, part of a distinctive and established public school system. See, for example, Peter Gwyn, 'The "tunding row": George Ridding and the belief in "boy government" ', in Roger Custance (ed.), *Winchester College: Sixth-Centenary Essays*, Oxford, 1982, pp. 431–77. The essay describes events at Winchester in 1872.

154 The circular may be found in Bailiff's Bundles No. 111. Cyril Argentine Alington (1872–1955) taught at Eton, was headmaster of Shrewsbury 1908–16 and headmaster of Eton 1917–33. He was the first headmaster at Shrewsbury appointed by the new governing body. See Oldham, *A History of Shrewsbury School*, pp. 201–8.

155 Richard Charles Cobb (b. 1917), who was at the school during this time and later became Professor of Modern History at Oxford University, describes beatings by boys and 'elaborate collective beatings' during his time at the school. See R. C. Cobb, *A Sense of Place*, London, 1975, p. 30.

156 *Clarendon Report*, II, p. 319.

157 See evidence given to the publc inquiry, in the *Shrewsbury Chronicle*, 31 July 1874.

158 See the *Shrewsbury Chronicle*, 31 July 1874.

159 See Notes 39, 42 and 129 above. John Loxdale was Mayor of Shrewsbury in 1840, 1858 and 1872, was an Alderman, and had been a governor of the school since 1848. Geoffrey Loxdale's grandfather and an uncle were also both former mayors of Shrewsbury. See Shrosbree, 'Origins of the Clarendon Commission', Appendix XIII. Another boy, whose name was not revealed to the inquiry, was flogged before Loxdale and given forty-nine strokes of the birth for using bad language. According to evidence at the inquiry, Moss flogged Loxdale 'till from exhaustion, he could flog no further', using two birches and, at times, two hands. See the *Shrewsbury Chronicle*, 31 July 1874.

160 Moss was the last headmaster appointed by St John's College, Cambridge so that in 1866, at a critical time in the school's history, the governors were faced with a headmaster completely out of sympathy with their opposition to the Public Schools Bills and their determination to preserve the school's local responsibilities. What Moss feared—that the school might sink 'sooner or later into a mere country grammar school'—was what the governors, in a sense, wished to achieve. For this comment, written in 1873, see Oldham, *A History of Shrewsbury School*, p. 149.

161 See *Trustees' Minutes*, 5 July 1871.

162 See Note 39 above.

163 See Note 159 above.

164 See *Trustees' Minutes*, 5 April 1867.

165 The deputation, from a town meeting a few weeks before, was led by the Mayor of Shrewsbury, Mr Pountney Smith. Apart from the Earl of Powis, the deputation included former school governors, Members of Parliament, J. R. Kenyon QC, who was Chairman of the County Quarter Sessions, the Town Clerk and other prominent people of local influence. See *Trustees' Minutes*, 9 December 1873.

166 See *Trustees' Minutes*, 20 February 1874 and 20 March 1874.

167 See Oldham, *A History of Shrewsbury School*, pp. 132–3.

168 For Keate, who resigned in 1873 and died shortly after, see Note 129 above. For the move and all the possible sites, see Lawson, '1882 Genesis: Exodus'.

6 Parliament and the Public Schools Bills

The major Public Schools Bills came before Parliament between 1865 and 1868, but did not reach the House of Commons for serious discussion until 1868. The Public Schools Act of 1868 is, in reality, an act of the House of Lords rather than an Act of Parliament, except in a formal legal sense. In its political purpose, presentation and content, it is an expression of Conservatism in the Lords that overrode the more subtle conservatism of the *Clarendon Report* and created a new kind of school, with Eton as its model, founded on public funds but available only through fees. Like a means test in reverse, these great public endowments were reserved for those who could pay, often in a perverse reversal of their founders' intentions and the pious hopes of many of their benefactors. The compliance of the Commons to these political arrangements was the result of circumstances. The settlement of Eton's future was the *quid pro quo* for the consideration of other schools and further educational change. The House of Commons too, although reformed in 1867, was still unrepresentative of the people and, in 1868, controlled by a Conservative majority. The extension of the franchise, and development of more democratic government and a more open educational system were inevitable, however; the Public Schools Act of 1868 was a pre-emptive claim to Eton and the other great schools—a defence of political and educational advantage in the face of imminent democracy.

The *Public Schools (No. 32) Bill* was presented for its first reading in the Lords by Clarendon on 13 March 1865 and for its second reading on 3 April 1865.[1] The Bill was in two parts, the first containing the general provisions of the Bill and the second containing specific proposals for each school. Merchant Taylors' School was omitted, but the other eight schools of the *Clarendon Report* were included. The Bill, although ostensibly based on the *Clarendon Report*, was of a very limited nature so that it was clear, from the beginning of legislation, that the public schools' supporters had already discouraged the government from implementing many of the Report's recommendations. The Bill was concerned only with the formation of new governing bodies and the provision of new school statutes.[2] The new governing bodies were based on the existing ones, but with other members added in varying proportions. At Eton, for example, the Bill proposed a Provost and fourteen Fellows (nine honorary and five paid) in place of the current Provost, Vice-Provost and six Fellows. All would have to be Anglicans, but they need not have been educated at Eton. The Provost would have to be a graduate of Oxford or Cambridge, and over thirty-five years of age, but need not be a clergyman. He would be nominated by the Crown, and would be expected to live at Eton during the school terms. The Provost of King's College, Cambridge was to be *ex officio* one of the honorary Fellows. Of the other eight honorary Fellows, who were unpaid and not required to live at Eton, three were to be nominated by the Crown from Oxford and Cambridge graduates, and the remaining five to be elected by the governing body. The five paid Fellows were also to be elected by the governing body and all had to be 'either distinguished for literary or scientific attainments, or have done service to the school as Head or Assistant-Masters'.[3] At least three of the paid Fellows had to be clergymen, and all had to live at the school for at least three months of each year. They were to receive £700 per year and a house.[4]

Similar changes were proposed for Winchester, although there the number of Fellows was to be increased only to eleven, of whom seven were to be honorary and four paid.[5] At Harrow, Charterhouse and Rugby, the proposed changes were simpler and merely involved an addition to the number of governors, with the provision that a quarter of each new governing body should be made up of men distinguished by their literary or scientific attainments.[6] At Westminster, Shrewsbury and St Paul's, the proposed changes were slightly more complicated but of a similar kind.[7] To these new governing bodies, all the 'Property Rights, Powers, Privileges, or Obligations' of the existing governing bodies were to be transferred, although at Westminster and St Paul's some other changes were necessary with respect to school property.[8] The times and places of their meetings and the management of school business were both to be entirely under their own control. Decisions were to be made by a majority vote of members present, with the chairman having a casting vote. There was to be a fixed quorum and the reasonable expenses of their meetings were to be met from school funds.[9] Resolutions that affected the statutes concerning their foundation were made subject to the approval of Parliament and the Queen in Council.[10] In making regulations for the general management of the school, the governors could amend or alter any existing statutes and make new statutes concerning the terms of admission and the numbers of foundation boys, the retention of any scholarships offered at the school or the universities (except scholarships established during the previous fifty years), the terms of any Church patronage, the salaries of the masters and their numbers, and the disposal of any surplus income.[11]

The only exception to this power to make independent decisions concerned the foundation boys.[12] At Eton nobody was to be given preference because of where he lived or his place of birth.[13] At Shrewsbury, the rights of burgesses were to cease in 1880 and, after that, there were to be forty free scholarships awarded by open competition.[14] At Harrow and Rugby, the right to free education for those living locally was to be abolished, except for those children born within ten years of the passing of the Act. These schools also had to provide schemes for allocating some of their money for local education, 'in such manner as may appear best, regard being had for the local Objects contemplated by the Founders of those schools and to the altered Circumstances of the present Time'.[15] There were to be some other general limitations on the powers of the governors; for example, no new school statute which affected common endowments was to be made without the consent of the other school involved and no new statutes affecting the universities were to be made without their prior knowledge.[16] New statutes were valid only after they had been approved by the Queen in Council, after having been laid before the Queen and published in the *London Gazette*. Any person could then petition the Queen against the statutes or any part of them; these petitions were to be referred to five members of the Privy Council when the petitioners could be heard by counsel. All new statutes also had to be laid before

Parliament, and either House could address the Queen against all or any part of them. If there were no petitions or objections, the Queen could approve the statutes, or any part of them that did not raise objections. Statutes which raised objections were to be referred back to the school, but could be resubmitted in an amended form. Initially, changes in school statutes had to be made before 1 January 1867, unless the Queen granted an extension of time. Once made, new statutes could be altered or amended from time to time by following the same procedures as before.[17]

In making general regulations for school management, the new governing bodies were not to be subject to any external controls. They could decide the number of boys in the school (other than foundation boys), make regulations about their ages and the conditions of entry, decide fees and charges of all kinds, decide what payments were to be made, make decisions about the church services to be attended, arrange the dates of terms and the length of holidays, decide upon the subjects of study, regulate general discipline and management, dispose of any surplus income and, subject to the school statutes, appoint the headmaster and all other masters already appointed by the existing governing body. All other masters were to be appointed by the headmaster 'at his pleasure'.[18]

Finally, there were some miscellaneous provisions. The Dean and Chapter of Westminster were, with the Ecclesiastical Commissioners, to invest the governing body with sufficient funds to maintain the school and make over to it the buildings then in use.[19] Any governing body could raise a mortgage for altering or enlarging school buildings in accordance with the recommendations of the Commission, but these financial proposals were subject to the same restrictions that applied to new school statutes.[20] The parish of Eton was no longer to be in the spiritual charge of the Provost, but was to be a separate living with an endowment of £600 each year, in the gift of the Provost and Fellows.[21] The governing bodies of St Paul's, Westminster and Charterhouse could propose schemes for the removal of the schools from their existing sites, these schemes being subject to the same restrictions as school statutes.[22] There were, finally, two clauses preserving the rights and interests of the existing governing bodies between the passing of the Act and the reconstitution of the new governing bodies.[23]

There was no reflection at all in the Bill of the great educational debates that accompanied the appointment of the Commission and the publication of the *Clarendon Report*. Nor was there any guidance given about the curriculum in general or about the importance, or otherwise, of the classics. There was no reference to the general function of the schools or of the part they could, or were expected, to play in national secondary education. There was no attempt to define the relationship of these schools with schools for younger boys, with the other endowed grammar schools or with the universities. There was no mention of any formal provision for safeguarding the interests of parents (except temporarily of the interests of parents of foundation boys), nor of making any formal provision for the representation of staff views within the school or on the governing body. Headmasters had no access to the new governing bodies except by invitation. The important innovations of the Bill were the provisions for the new appointments to the governing bodies—primarily by the Crown and the Universities of Oxford and Cambridge—the added powers given to the governors to appoint headmasters and to have general oversight over the 'Subjects of Study and the general Discipline and Management of the School' and the complete abolition within ten years to all local claims to free education or preferential treatment.[24] It was around these innovations that opposition to the Bill centred. The existing governing bodies were generally opposed to the new appointments.[25] The Universities were opposed to the loss of the power which particular colleges had previously enjoyed in the appointment of headmasters, and also to the loss of some particularly close connections between some schools and colleges through scholarships.[26] The headmasters were opposed to the powers of the new governing bodies to direct the discipline, studies and general conduct of the schools, and local parents were opposed to the loss of established educational rights.[27] As a result, there were many objections to the Bill voiced through petitions, correspondence in *The Times*, opposition in the Lords at the second reading and continued objections by counsel before the Lords Select Committee.[28]

At the first reading, petitions were presented against the Bill from, amongst others: Magdalene College, Cambridge; 'Persons educated at Eton'; New College, Oxford; the Governors and

Trustees of Shrewsbury School; the Trustees of Rugby School; the inhabitants of Harrow and Pinner; twelve Professors and eighty-one Tutors and Lecturers of the University of Oxford (comprising, Lord Derby thought, 'three-fourths of the whole educational staff of the University') and, finally, from the Wardens and Commonality of the Mercers' Company praying that 'the measure might not pass into law' but, if it did, that 'the clauses affecting their rights and interests might be expunged therefrom'.[29]

The opposition to the Bill continued during the second reading in the Lords on 3 April 1865. Of eleven peers who spoke, only three were in favour of the Bill.[30] The peers in favour of the Bill—Clarendon, Devon and Lyttelton—had all been members of the Clarendon Commission, and even Lyttelton was not wholly in favour. The Bill, he said, 'was not the Bill of the Commissioners' and 'he had never seen it until it was printed'.[31] In his view, the Bill did not go far enough in defining the powers of the headmasters, reforming the governing bodies or eliminating the remaining responsibilities of the schools for local boys. His comments showed that, like Clarendon, he wanted to reform these schools only to make them more serviceable for the 'higher classes', rather than reform all endowed schools in the national interest. He strongly opposed use of any money at Harrow or Rugby to help local education. There was, he said, 'ample provision' for the education of 'the lower classes' and he thought 'that these great schools ought to be reserved for the upper classes, for whose benefit they now existed'.[32] Lyttelton was unusual in that he wanted to introduce radical reforms into the schools in order to preserve their traditional position and conservative role as schools for the 'upper classes'. In his own views, he acted as a microcosm for the central dilemma facing the Lords. Public opinion, reinforced by the *Clarendon Report*, made some government action inevitable, but how could reform be introduced without admitting the faults of the schools—particularly Eton—or the justice of the reformers' case? How could the schools be reformed yet preserved for the higher classes? There were several possibilities for the public schools' supporters. One way was to discredit the Clarendon Commission and its Report, but this was never seriously attempted; the members of the Commission were too eminent and too respected.[33] Their inquiries had been too thorough and too well-documented. Another possibility was to delay and obstruct the Bill so that it was eventually abandoned. The turmoil of contemporary politics, the divisions within the Liberal Party, Palmerston's age and the controversial issue of Parliamentary reform all made the future of the government uncertain and the future of the Public Schools Bill even more so. A policy of procrastination tended to be adopted by the schools themselves, along with earnest attempts at reform which were designed to show that legislation was, after all, unnecessary.[34] This course of action offered hope to the schools right up to the passing of the Public Schools Act of 1868.[35] The difficulty of this approach was that such inaction left the schools' finances and government unreformed, and their supporters who wished to see them reformed for the benefit of the upper classes continued to press for legislation. The third course of action for the schools' supporters, which resulted in the *Public Schools Act, 1868* and the subsequent Acts, was to reform the schools' government and finances, but leave them otherwise undisturbed so that they could continue to offer the same kind of education to the upper classes, but within a more defensible financial and administrative framework.

The first course of action had been successful even before the presentation of the *Public Schools (No. 32) Bill* of 1865, for this Bill left the education provided at the schools to be decided by the schools themselves—by the governors in consultation with the headmasters. The first debate in the Lords on the *Clarendon Report*, in May 1864, had centred around discussion of the curriculum but, in the Bill of 1865, all educational matters were left to the schools themselves; the schools' supporters who wanted them left alone to reform themselves thus won a significant victory before any legislation was introduced. Discussion of educational matters virtually ceased after the initial debates on the *Clarendon Report* itself. Although Clarendon referred pointedly to the schools' educational failings and the Commission's responsibility to bring this information before the public, the debate on the Bill was largely concerned with the proposed new constitutions for the schools—particularly the new governing bodies and the abolition of the schools' local responsibilities.[36]

The proposed new governing bodies were criticised on a number of grounds. Firstly, it was suggested that they would have too much power to interfere in the running of the schools. The Bishop of London, for example, made this criticism of the new constitution for Eton and thought that it applied to all the governing bodies. 'In fact', he said, 'they will have nothing else to do but to interfere, and they are called upon by Act of Parliament to interfere as much as possible.'[37] This apprehension was increased by the proposals to include in their numbers Crown appointees and men eminent in science or literature. Crown appointees, it was argued, might diminish the political independence of the schools and eminent men might be tempted to promote their own academic interests too vigorously.[38] The Bishop of London quoted the headmaster of Rugby, who feared that scientists might become too influential and would be 'perpetually tempted to justify the necessity of their appointment by trying to do what the Head Master ought to do if he is fit for his post'.[39] The fact that otherwise the governors might be, like their Lordships, men educated mainly in the classics, that many headmasters clearly did not wish to reform the curriculum and that, even when they did, a reforming headmaster could be stopped by conservative governors, received no comment. Clearly, it was thought that eminent men, and scientists in particular, would have an irresistible and reprehensible tendency to impose their own academic interests upon the schools in a way that classical scholars did not. Lord Derby, for example, thought that these eminent men could contribute nothing that was not already provided by the existing governors but, if they did, it was likely to do harm because they would 'attempt to put forward that particular study in which they have obtained eminence'.[40] Concern was expressed for these scientists because, being in a minority, they would be in a difficult position if they pressed the claims of their subject.[41] There was some inconsistency here, of course, for the influence of these men could hardly be feared if they were so isolated that they needed the solicitations of Parliament. If the self-interest of a few scientists who were not yet even appointed was to be feared, what was the effect of the near-complete classical monopoly of education amongst school staff, many governing bodies and the Lords themselves? Consistency was disregarded in the Lords' attempt to preserve the schools and their curriculum intact. There was an equally obvious inconsistency in seeking to preserve the schools' individual character whilst complaining about schools being treated differently, or seeking to defend the influence of headmasters whilst apologising for their limited success in reforming their schools since the *Clarendon Report.*[42] These inconsistencies were not so much those of a single speaker, but rather the contradictions within the case put forward by peers seeking the same objective—that is, the preservation of the schools as they were, if possible, and the defeat of the Bill. The most glaring inconsistency was their concern about the influence of a handful of scientists or men of letters, probably public school men anyway, when their own education was so overwhelmingly classical. It is difficult to believe that their concern for the welfare of these eminent men, who were to be imposed upon and surrounded by classics scholars, was entirely genuine, as when Lord Houghton expressed his own concern.

> This extraneous element cannot, according to my experience of human nature, be received with anything like reverence or amity; and I cannot believe it possible that these three or four gentlemen, imported into any of these governing bodies, can act in any way save as a solvent of the governing body altogether. From the very circumstances of their professional habits and long residence and connection with one school, the heads . . . must feel themselves incumbered by the introduction of new Members, and to suppose that they will be ready to receive the advice given to them by those literary and scientific gentlemen in any spirit of goodwill, is a supposition opposed to all my experience. I fear the position of these gentlemen . . . will be extremely uncomfortable when they get into any one of these governing bodies.[43]

Such a suggestion, that the headmasters and present governors would obstruct the reforms recommended by the *Clarendon Report* even if endorsed by the wishes of Parliament, was a very strong criticism of the existing situation and a compelling argument for even more radical reform. Indeed, the argument provokes the question of whether the reforms envisaged by the Commission could be introduced at all with the existing governors and headmasters. But for Houghton, the argument led to the need for an 'Executive Commission', so that each school could negotiate its own reform. And reform, for Houghton, meant helping the schools preserve not just their own traditions and institutions, but also the political supremacy of the higher classes. It was educational improvement for the 'higher classes' rather than educational reform in the national interest.[44]

It was not surprising that the Lords should object so strongly to the inclusion of scientific expertise within the new governing bodies, for it was the promotion of science which was, of all the Commission's recommendations, the one most based on European experience and most directly related to the national interest. It was, however, the proposal which most threatened the educational superiority of the schools and therefore of the 'higher classes', based as it was on these schools and their classical traditions. The defence of the classics in Parliament was thus, by implication, a defence of Parliament and of the fitness of the men there to govern. Lord Houghton himself clearly expressed the Conservative view of political power—that its justification was not superior ability, but a superior education; that for the majority of men (apart from persons of great natural genius) 'education must be the means of making them fit to govern their fellow men'.[45] The recognition of the importance of science might raise the alarming possibility that the lower classes might be arguably better educated than the legislators in Parliament, and that such education might qualify them to govern themselves through the extension of the franchise. The political implications of educational reform therefore went far beyond the difficulties of school governors.

The debate in the Lords between reformers and conservatives, between those who wished to change the schools and those who wished to preserve them, was not a debate about ends but about means—how best to preserve the educational supriority of the 'higher', governing classes. Some difficulties were presented by the fact that none of the public schools had originally been founded for the 'higher classes', and some were intended specifically to make some provision for the poor.[46] These provisions, which usually gave the school an obligation to provide some free education for local children, were of some political importance because in many cases the local inhabitants petitioned against the Bill.[47] All the schools had some foundation boys, although the conditions for their admission varied from school to school and those at Harrow, Rugby and Shrewsbury received most attention in the debates.[48] The existence of foundation boys posed some problems for the schools. Their particular legal status meant that at some schools they tended to form a distinct group that was not easily assimilated into the life of the school. They were usually day-boys, usually poorer than the boarders and usually from a lower social class.[49] The Commission's proposal to abolish the claims of foundation boys within ten years, replacing them with scholarships, was included in the *Public Schools (No. 32) Bill*, but met with bitter opposition.

The difficulty for the Lords, believing as they generally did that these schools were for the higher classes, was what to do with the foundation boys. There was a considerable difference of opinion about what should be done. Lyttelton, for example, wanted to abolish the foundation rights which, he said, 'were obsolete, and, with the exception of vested interests, were not deserving of the consideration of Parliament'.[50] Most speakers in the Lords wanted to keep foundation rights, but only for impoverished members of the higher classes, even if their sons were stupid. Lord Derby, for example, found the selection of foundation boys by competitive examination 'highly objection-able'.[51]

The Bishop of London precisely described the kind of people who might need free education:

> It has always struck me that persons of moderate means among the upper classes—clergy, professional men, half-pay officers and others—are with regard to the education of their sons placed in a great difficulty, to which such persons are not exposed in other countries. In Germany, France, Scotland, and other countries there is a facility of education for persons of moderate means which does not exist in England, and these foundations . . . do open a means of education at moderate expense for such persons.[52]

The Archbishop of Canterbury regretted that poorer people did not use the foundation places at Harrow, but thought that they should be retained for 'persons of moderate means among the upper classes'.[53]

Another proposed solution was to preserve the foundation rights of local children, but to educate them in a separate school. This proposal was put forward by Lord Powis who argued, from the example of Shrewsbury School, that this would meet the founders' wishes to benefit local children whilst preserving 'the ancient character of the education which the upper and middle classes were desirous to secure for their children'.[54] He suggested a 'separate department for the lower class of education required'.[55] Powis, like many in the Lords, was concerned to preserve above all the 'existing character' of the public schools which he associated with higher social class and superior education.[56] The tragedy for English education was not just that the conservative ways of the schools were left entrenched, that English education was irreparably divided, or that 'commerical education' was given separate consideration: it was that the education given to most people, on which the progress, prosperity and survival of the nation depended, was deliberately given an inferior place. In Parliament loyalty to Eton, the conservative interests of the public schools and conservative political calculation were all placed before the national interest.

The difficulties of resolving the differences over foundation boys were increased, as in the case of school governors, by the great diversity of provision within the schools. The referral of the Bill to a Select Commission and the eventual appointment of an Executive Committee were advocated by many speakers.[57] Such a course enabled the opponents of the Bill to continue their opposition without the immediate need to reconcile the often contradictory nature of their objections. The lengthy procedure involved meant that there would be a considerable delay before the Bill's provisions would be implemented—even if it survived.

Another difficulty the Lords faced was that, just as the Commission had been appointed as the result of articles about Eton and had a special responsibility to investigate it, so also a major aim of the Bill was to protect and reform this school. It was thus difficult to reconcile the provisions of the Bill that were directed towards Eton with the needs and circumstances of the other schools. The Bishop of London, for example, made clear the importance of Eton by devoting most of his speech to a defence of the school and an assertion of its importance. The Bill was 'especially framed for the reform of Eton', a school whose hold 'upon the affections of the country, can never . . . be diminished'.[58] The stress which so many speakers put upon the singular importance of Eton makes it clear that the Bill was introduced only because the school could be reformed in no other way, and that the inclusion of other endowed grammar schools was a necessary, but incidental, accompaniment.[59] The legal division thus made by the *Public Schools Act, 1868* between the schools of the Act and the other endowed grammar schools of the country, a division which served the interests of the 'higher classes' represented in the Lords, was the consequence solely of the need to create a separate category for the benefit of Eton. It was the influence of Eton, and of Eton men in Parliament, that divided the public schools from all the other endowed grammar schools, and it is in this division that the present fragmentation of English secondary education has its origin.

The difficulties of legislating for both Eton and the other schools had some political significance, since they made agreement on the Bill even more difficult to achieve and added to the attractions of an Executive Commission, which many speakers supported.[60] An Executive Commission was favoured also by those who, like Derby, wanted to allow the schools to reform themselves on a voluntary basis since it would give them more time to do this and also more freedom to negotiate their own statutes and the composition of their own governing bodies. Derby thought that the schools—and specifically Eton— had already begun to reform themselves and used this as an additional argument against Parliamentary control, suggesting that the schools needed more time to implement the recommendations of the Clarendon Commission. He agreed with the Bishop of London that 'the main object of the Bill is to attack Eton' but 'they could not alter in a few months things which had been going on for 300 years'. He wanted more time for all the schools to act of their own accord on the *Clarendon Report*'s recommendations. The idea of any compulsion by legislation was objectionable to him and he thought the governing bodies should be left alone to use their own discretion.[61] Many speakers favoured an Executive Commission and it seems probable that the Bill passed the second reading in the Lords only because Clarendon eventually agreed to the possibility of an Executive Commission and to the consideration of the Bill by a Lords Select Committee.[62]

The Select Committee was appointed in May 1865. Of the sixteen members eventually appointed, most had been to the schools concerned and, of these, most had been to Eton.[63] Three members of the Clarendon Commission were included— Clarendon himself, Lord Devon and Lord Lyttelton—and Clarendon was elected Chairman.[64] The Committee met several times in May and June 1865, and concluded its meetings on

22 June when Clarendon was asked to report the amended Bill to the Lords.[65] While the Select Committee was sitting, Eton sent to Clarendon a petition, published in *The Times* on the following day, supporting the appointment of an Executive Commission. The petition admitted that Eton was opposed to the Bill but did not wish to 'thwart the objects or disparage the conclusions' of the Clarendon Commission. It objected to the proposed new governing body which, it said, would have 'no tendency to forward reform and fatal power to obstruct it'. It favoured an Executive Commission, arguing that the proposed Bill would lead to 'scanty and isolated improvements, undertaken without system and effected without zeal'.[66] This was an apt description of reform in the public schools both before and after the Clarendon Commission. The Bill, which only partially implemented the *Clarendon Report*, had met with such opposition in the Lords that the price of its survival had been referral to a Select Committee, where its opponents who had spoken against it in the debate—like Derby, Stanhope, Powis, Stratford de Redcliffe, Houghton and the Bishop of London—were in a majority and could further amend it.[67] These men wanted to maintain the classical curriculum, to preserve the independence of these schools and to reserve them as schools for the 'higher classes'. To do this, they wanted an Executive Commission to negotiate the arrangements for new governing bodies with the schools, and to remove the schools' responsibilities to local children. The reformers on the Select Committee—Clarendon, Devon and Lyttelton—were also opposed to maintaining the schools' obligations to local children and wanted to preserve them for the 'higher classes', but wanted also to reform their government, finance and curriculum so that the 'higher classes' could be better educated. Neither the reformers nor the defenders of the schools' traditional ways were concerned with national policy, with the education of the middle and lower classes, or with educational equality. Both were concerned with maintaining class advantage, and the differences between them were differences of approach rather than of aim. The Clarendon Commission and the *Public Schools (No. 32) Bill* were both the products of Whig governments and of a distinctive Whig view of aristocratic education, with its emphasis on fashionable progress, scholarship and European culture; the opponents of the Bill expressed a Tory view of

aristocratic education, largely shared by the schools, with its emphasis on the classics, on traditional ways, and on the preservation of hallowed institutions and of the influence of the Church of England. Clarendon, who introduced the Bill of 1865, and Derby, who opposed the Bill but supported the much-amended Bills of 1866 and 1867, typified respectively in their attitudes and educational background the Whig and Tory views of aristocratic education. The Public Schools Acts were in origin an expression of Whig reformist attitudes but, in effect and operation, were an expression of Conservative values which, however suitable for a gentleman's education, were likely to prove disastrous as a guide to secondary education in an industrial democracy.[68]

During the meetings of the Lords Select Committee, local people from Rugby, Harrow and Shrewsbury called many witnesses, through counsel, to support their claims that the education provided free for local children was valued—even if it was almost entirely classical.[69] The headmasters of Harrow, Rugby and Shrewsbury appeared to give evidence and many petitions against the Bill were received—mainly from local residents or university colleges closely connected with the schools.[70] The Mercers' Company appeared by counsel to ask for the complete exclusion of the school from the Bill.[71] The opponents of the Bill in the Lords achieved in the Lords Select Committee the changes they wanted: an Executive Commission was included and, although the local responsibilities of the schools were not completely abolished, an attempt to extend free education at Harrow and Rugby from ten to twenty years was heavily defeated.[72] St Paul's School was excluded from the Bill after a narrow vote—Clarendon, Granville and the Prince of Wales voting for its inclusion. The number of schools to be included in the Bill was thus finally reduced to seven: Eton, Winchester, Westminster, Charterhouse, Harrow, Rugby and Shrewsbury.[73]

When the Lords Select Committee concluded its proceedings in June 1865, there was not sufficient time left in the Parliamentary year for legislation, and so the Bill lapsed.[74] It was this Bill, however (the *Public Schools (No. 202) Bill* of 1865 as amended in the Lords Select Committee), which became unchanged the *Public Schools (No. 110) Bill* of 1866.[75] Introduced into the Lords by Clarendon in May 1866, this Bill proceeded uneventfully through the Lords, but two important amendments were attempted at the Committee Stage. The first was an attempt to maintain foundation rights for poor sons of the gentry, and the second was an attempt to nominate a scientist as one of the Special Commissioners now included in the Bill. Both amendments failed.

The first amendment was moved by Lord Ellenborough, who wanted to amend Clause 5 (which concerned the power of the governors to make school statutes) so that governors would be prevented from replacing foundation places with places awarded by competitive examination.[76] He wanted this so that governors could give preference to the sons of poor gentry rather than the sons of tradesmen. He feared that well-off tradesmen might be able to afford better tuition than the poor gentry, and thus obtain places for their sons. He was opposed to the education of tradesmen's sons at public schools because, he alleged, they were of dubious honesty and concerned only with making money. His grandfather, 'a poor clergyman with a very large family' who afterwards became a bishop, had educated all six of his sons at Charterhouse, and three of those sons later became peers. 'Had there been a competitive examination he did not believe any one of these boys would have passed.'[77] Clarendon opposed the amendment as unworkable and invidious, and so it was lost.[78]

The second amendment, to include a scientist as one of the Special Commissioners, was proposed by Lord Houghton.[79] Stratford de Redcliffe, Stanhope and Lyttelton opposed the amendment—Stratford de Redcliffe and Stanhope because they did not wish to impose the study of science upon the schools, and Lyttelton because 'he thought that seven Commissioners was the number which would be found most convenient'.[80] Clarendon supported the amendment, but it was lost. Immediately afterwards, Clarendon proposed the inclusion of Thomas Dyke Acland, a classicist, and this was agreed without a vote.[81]

Some other minor amendments were made to Clause 4, which concerned the parishes of Harrow and Pinner, and to Clause 5, which concerned the powers of the governors to regulate the number of teaching staff and to sell off Church livings. Clauses 14 and 15, which concerned candidates for foundation places at Eton and the voting rights of the Provost of Eton and of the Provost of King's College, Cambridge in the award of foundation places and scholarships, were deleted. These last two clauses, which had begun as Clauses 18 and 19 in the *Public Schools (No. 32) Bill* of 1865, were rendered obsolete by the inclusion in the Bill of the Special Commissioners, whose job it was to negotiate such details with the school's governors. These minor amendments were agreed without a division.[82]

Derby also proposed an amendment to Clause 21, which concerned powers of the Special Commissioners. As the Bill stood, the Special Commissioners could impose a reformed governing body upon a school if the existing governors failed to propose an acceptable scheme for reform. Derby wanted to remove this power so that reform of the existing governing bodies could not take place without their consent.[83] Derby's amendment, which was not debated until the third reading on 18 June 1866, was opposed by Clarendon, who accused Derby of trying to protect Eton at the risk of jeopardising the reform of the other schools and rendering the whole Bill ineffectual. 'The real foundation of the noble Earl's objection', suggested Clarendon, 'was the fear that the unhallowed hand of the Reformers should touch Eton'.[84] Derby's amendment was accepted, however, and became part of Clause 19 in the *Public Schools (No. 212) Bill*, which received its first reading in the Commons on 16 July 1866.[85]

The future of this amendment was curious, but illustrated the importance of Eton in these proceedings. The amendment was included in the *Public Schools (No. 78) Bill*, which came from the Lords in March 1867 and which received a first reading in the Commons on 15 March 1867.[86] This Bill failed to complete its second reading on 10 August 1867 and the Bill lapsed.[87] When the *Public Schools (No. 24) Bill* was reintroduced into the Commons on 5 December 1867, Clause 19 had been redrafted and Derby's restrictive and contentious amendment had disappeared.[88] Other minor amendments were merely matters of convenience or rewording, non-controversial and procedural in nature, but the omission of Derby's amendment greatly increased the powers of the Special Commissioners and reduced the independent bargaining power of the schools. Derby attached great importance to this amendment; the same government introduced both Bills and Derby was still Prime

Minister, so the omission of his amendment was significant.

Political circumstances suggest the probable reasons. Derby's health was bad and deteriorating; he resigned as Prime Minister on 24 February 1868 and died in October 1869. Throughout these months, he was concerned with the great issue of Parliamentary reform, so he and his colleagues had less time and inclination to press controversial amendments in the Public Schools Bill. Derby's amendment had proved controversial in the Lords and was likely to prove more so in the Commons so that, while it was certain to delay the Bill, it would almost certainly be deleted. The future of the government was uncertain, particularly in view of Lord Derby's health, and any government or House of Commons in the future was likely to be less sympathetic to Derby's amendment and the independence of Eton, particularly following Parliamentary reform in 1867. Delay in passing the *Public Schools (No. 24) Bill* might have meant the abandonment of the Bill and the subsequent introduction of more radical legislation. As it was, the Bill was subjected to much radical criticism in the Commons—indeed, it was only in the Commons debates of 1868 that the principles and assumptions of the Public Schools Bills received any serious examination. In the Commons, as in the Lords, the affairs of Eton received particular attention and it was evident that Eton itself now wished to promote the quick passage of the Bill.[89] The more radical Members of the Commons wanted to abandon the Bill altogether. It is clear that Derby's deletion of his amendment to Clause 19 was an attempt to improve the prospects of the Bill in the Commons, and thus to protect Eton from more radical legislation, just as his earlier amendment had been a conservative attempt to preserve Eton's independence from the provisions of the Bill. The changed political circumstances had now made it more important to secure the position of Eton within the provisions of the Bill than to risk more radical legislation from a reformed House of Commons.[90]

The *Public Schools (No. 212) Bill* did not reach the Commons until 12 July 1866 and the second reading was discharged after a short debate on 7 August 1866.[91] Even in this very brief debate, however, there were indications that Members of the Commons would subject the Public Schools Bills to radical, fundamental criticism when given the opportunity to do so.

Charles Neate, the radical Liberal MP for Oxford, 'had serious objections to the Bill, the further progress of which he should have opposed'. He wanted the Clarendon Commission schools considered along with the Taunton Commission schools and the universities, so that the whole educational system could be reformed to meet 'the wants of the present age'.[92] A. S. Ayrton, another radical Liberal MP for Tower Hamlets, wanted an inquiry into schools in London and into the 'whole educational resources of the country'. He was critical of the emphasis on classical education 'whilst we neglected that technical education which was attended with such surprising results on the Continent'.[93] Even at this early stage, the comments of Neate and Ayrton indicated that the Bill might have been different—more questioned, perhaps more radical, more concerned with national education or perhaps obstructed altogether—if it had been introduced first into the Commons rather than the Lords. Indeed, there was a hint in the government's introduction of the Bill, by George Goschen, that opposition to parts of the Bill in the Commons had already led to the deletion of the conservative amendment to Clause 19, moved by Lord Derby earlier in the Lords.[94] Goschen's view, however, was that there was insufficient time either for proper discussion in the Commons or to refer any amendments back to the Lords.[95] On 28 June 1866 Russell had resigned. Derby formed a new Conservative administration and the Bill once more lapsed through lack of Parliamentary time.[96]

In February 1867 Derby introduced the *Public Schools (No. 4) Bill*, which was virtually identical with Clarendon's previous Bill, and which passed through the Lords with hardly any change.[97] Derby was clearly anxious to get the Bill through without further amendment and possible consequent delay.[98] One important amendment which was agreed at the Report Stage was the inclusion of two new 'efficient' Members of the Commons as Special Commissioners. This amendment was first suggested by Stanhope at the second reading, perhaps as another means of reducing opposition to the Bill in the Commons.[99] The two new Commissioners were John Coleridge QC, Liberal MP for Exeter 1865–73, and Russell Gurney, Conservative MP for Southampton 1865–78 and Recorder of the City of London.[100] In the *Public Schools (No. 143) Bill* of 1866, three MPs had been named as Special Commissioners, but two had withdrawn by 1867. The original Members were Sir William Heathcote, Sir John Lefevre and Sir Thomas Acland, but only Sir John Lefevre remained. The number of MPs thus remained the same but the total number of Special Commissioners was reduced from eight to seven, for Lord Carnarvon had also withdrawn on becoming Colonial Secretary.[101] No reason was given in Parliament for the withdrawal of these members, Derby simply commenting in the Lords that 'two of the gentlemen who had been originally appointed on the Commission had desired that their names might be withdrawn from it'.[102] The Special Commissioners named in the *Public Schools (No. 78) Bill* which came to the Commons in March 1867 were thus as follows: the Archbishop of York, Lord Harrowby, Sir Edmund Walker Head Bt, Russell Gurney, Sir John Lefevre, John Coleridge and the Rev. Joseph Blakesley.[103]

One other amendment was attempted at the Report Stage when Lord Houghton attempted to include in the Special Commissioners 'some gentleman eminent for his skill in natural science'.[104] The amendment was opposed by Derby and failed, Derby commenting that the suggestion had already been discussed in the Lords and 'had not . . . been received with very great favour'.[105]

The *Public Schools (No. 78) Bill* reached the Commons in March 1867 but the House of Commons was preoccupied with other business at the time—particularly the Reform Bill—and the Public Schools Bill did not reach a second reading until August, when the Bill lapsed for lack of time.[106] In December 1867 virtually the same Bill was introduced into the Commons as the *Public Schools (No. 24) Bill*, which passed the second reading in the Commons in February 1868, after a long debate.[107] During this debate, there was fundamental criticism of the Bill—particularly by Ayrton who wanted to refer it to a Select Committee, to consider the general provision of education in London and to use 'a portion of the funds in the erection or maintenance of . . . commercial schools in the East End and in other metropolitan districts'.[108] The intention of the government was to refer the Bill to a Committee of the whole House, but this proved impossible—partly because of the pressure of other business and partly because the radical Members persuaded Walpole, who introduced the Bill for the government, that a Select Committee was the most appropriate way of proceeding and, by implication, the way most likely to minimise their opposition.[109]

The Bill passed the second reading, however, and was referred to a Commons Select Committee in March 1868.[110] This Committee did not hear evidence, but did make some amendments. Most were minor changes of detail, wording or definition. The most important change was the inclusion of Lord Salisbury and Dr Stewart Parker as Special Commissioners. Attempts by Charles Neate to remove the Archbishop of York, Sir John Lubbock, Russell Gurney and John Coleridge as Special Commissioners, failed. Further attempts by Neate, Ayrton and Darby Griffith to block the Bill by obstructing the appointment of all the Special Commissioners were heavily defeated.[111] The radical Members opposed to the Bill had won a minor tactical victory in getting it referred to a Select Committee, but were unable to sustain their objections against a conservative majority in favour of it from both parties. They had, however, ensured further delay and there was now concern from the schools' supporters that radical opposition might in this way prevent the Bill from becoming law. There was clearly concern in the Lords that the Bill might once more fail for lack of Parliamentary time. On 15 June 1868 Lord Stanhope moved an 'Address for Papers', in which he reminded the Lords of the progress of the Bill and made a strong defence both of Eton and of classical education. It is probable that he was concerned about the slow progress of the Bill through the Commons Select Committee, and that his remarks were intended for the schools' supporters in the Commons where the Bill was to be considered on the following day.[112]

The *Public Schools (No. 135) Bill*, which came back from the Commons Select Committee in June 1868 to be reconsidered at the Committee Stage, was again attacked by radical MPs.[113] Charles Neate made an immediate attempt to block the Bill once more by proposing that it should be referred back to the Select Committee on the grounds that the constitution and finances of Eton and Winchester had not been sufficiently reformed, and that more information was needed about their income. His speech was particularly critical of the past financial conduct of the Provost and Fellows of Eton, and suggested that 'this Bill has apparently been framed with the special object of excepting Eton and Winchester from the recommendations of the Commissioners'.[114] He suggested two ways in which surplus income from Eton's endowments could be used: 'the creation of a middle-class school, for which class the endowments were in the first instance chiefly, if not exclusively, designed' or the creation of 'a University in the North of England, founded upon principles similar to those of Oxford and Cambridge, with the difference that its curriculum should . . . encourage the industries of the district'.[115] Other speakers added to Neate's fundamental criticisms of the Bill. Ayrton thought it was 'a measure designed to carry out the most pernicious principle of selecting a few schools in order to apply to them very large endowments; not because they were necessary for the education of those who resorted to the schools, but merely because they tended to keep up the expensive character of the schools, and to maintain a kind of fashionable system of education for the fashionable classes'.[116] Robert Lowe complained that 'he could not remember whether this Bill had ever been discussed in the House before. If it had been it had left very little impression on anybody's mind, for he had asked the question of several who seemed to be in the same condition as himself regarding it'.[117] Darby Griffith wanted the parents of boys in the schools to have 'some voice in the management of those institutions' and argued that 'their supervision would be more effective than that of any Commissioners'.[118]

Other speakers supported the Bill, including Sir Stafford Northcote, George Goschen and W. E. Forster, who 'was afraid—such was the feeling of Members of the House who had personal associations with those schools—that any general scheme of dealing with endowed schools would have a better chance if the question of those public schools were excluded from it'.[119] Put more directly, Forster's view was that public school Members of Parliament would obstruct the reform of the country's endowed grammar schools unless the public schools were first given separate and privileged consideration. It was perhaps this factor, the awareness that public school Members were prepared to obstruct the national reform of secondary education unless the public schools were first excluded, that most explains why there were not more objections to the hurried and last-minute consideration given in the Commons to the Public Schools Bills. Neate eventually withdrew his proposal to refer the Bill back again to the Select

Committee after Spenser Walpole had given him an assurance that the endowments of Eton would be considered again in Committee, and after a plea on behalf of Eton that 'the governing body of Eton were very anxious that the Bill should pass, and that it would be very injurious . . . to subject them to any further delay'.[120]

Neate's amendments, which gave to the new governors of Eton and Winchester the unambiguous authority to regulate the payments made to the Provost and Fellows of Eton and the Warden and Fellows of Winchester, was initially opposed by the government on the grounds that the powers already existed in the Bill. Walpole agreed eventually, after some discussion, to insert a re-worded version of Neate's amendment and this became part of Section 7, Clause (7) in the *Public Schools (No. 262) Bill*, which came from the Commons in July 1868.[121] The government's compromise over Neate's amendment was prompted probably as much by a desire to smooth the passage of the Bill and avoid a referral back to the Select Committee as it was by any need or desire to clarify the powers of school governors. As it was, the discussion of the amendment gave opportunity for opponents of the Bill to attack Eton (and Winchester) once more as 'Colleges only in the sense of gathering together half-a-dozen idle, useless people, who are maintained at the public expense'.[122]

The Bill passed quickly through the Committee Stage and, although fundamental criticisms of the Bill continued, the amendments embodying these criticisms were mostly defeated. An objection to the title of the Bill by Thomas Acland on the grounds that 'other schools not included within its operations were equally entitled to the appellation of public schools' was withdrawn after Walpole pointed out that the title of the Bill 'did not imply that these were the only public schools; it simply indicated what public schools were dealt with in 1868'.[123] Ayrton asked why two of the schools included in the Clarendon Commission were not in the Bill, and bitterly criticised the Mercers' Company over their management of St Paul's School and their conduct over the reform of the school by Parliament. He criticised their extravagance, their secrecy and their disregard of Parliament, and accused them of deliberately instigating legal proceedings in Chancery in order to evade Parliamentary control. He alleged that the

Mercers' Company estates in his constituency yielded £9,500 a year, but that they were unwilling to provide any help at all for a local school for the poor.[124] He proposed the inclusion of St Paul's School, but his amendment was defeated on the grounds that this matter had already been discussed in the Select Committee and that the matter was *sub judice*.[125]

The difficulties that Ayrton faced in his attempt to raise the issue of St Paul's School at such a late stage in the legislative process, illustrate once more the extent to which fundamental, radical criticism of the Public Schools Bills was pre-empted and prevented by the introduction of the early Bills into the Lords and the Parliamentary precedents established there. Members of the Commons could not pursue these radical criticisms of the Public Schools Bills without questioning, in a most direct and profoundly disturbing way, the powers of the House of Lords and the constitutional propriety of Parliamentary procedure. The limited and peripheral part played by the Commons in the discussion of the Public Schools Bills may be seen not just as a commentary on the residual, but still formidable, powers of the Lords, but rather as the deliberate exploitation of these powers to defend the educational interests of the 'higher classes' in the knowledge that the political dominance of the Lords, and of the classes represented there, was already being questioned, challenged and undermined by Parliamentary reform.

Two other amendments were attempted at the Committee Stage in the Commons in June 1868. The power given to the governors of Harrow and Rugby, in Section 14 of the Bill, to establish a separate school for local children, was opposed, amended after some discussion and left to the discretion of the Special Commissioners.[126] The radical opponents of the Bill—like Ayrton, who was opposed to this clause because it was 'intended to restrict the advantages of the schools to the wealthier classes'—were joined by more conservative Members like Beresford-Hope, Charles Newdegate and Henry Labouchere, who wanted to preserve some public access to the public schools at Harrow and Rugby for 'the meritorious poor' and 'the sons of decayed gentlemen'.[127]

An attempt was then made to postpone discussion of Section 16 of the Bill, the section which named the Special Commissioners, on the grounds that there were there 'certain Gentlemen who were upon every Commission, and a little change was wanted'.[128] Some desultory discussion followed, in which the names of Robert Lowe and Beresford-Hope were put forward in improvised and only half-serious amendments, which were abandoned as soon as they were proposed.[129] Ayrton, however, used the discussion to attack the conservative views of the two Special Commissioners appointed by the Lords and, by implication, the Conservative bias of the Special Commissioners. The Archbishop of York was there, he supposed, 'to preserve inviolable the Church of England character of the schools'. Lord Salisbury was 'a party man of such strong Conservatism that he would not associate with the present Government on account of its Liberal tendencies'. If the government had been acting fairly, he said, they would have added the name of a Liberal peer.[130] But the proposal to postpone discussion of Section 16 was defeated.[131]

The Bill reached the Lords again in July 1868 as the *Public Schools (No. 262) Bill* and, although it passed quickly through the Lords and received the Royal Assent in July 1868 as the *Public Schools Act, 1868*, Eton was once more strongly defended and two last-minute amendments attempted.[132] When the second reading took place on 20 July 1868, Lord Derby made a long speech in which he recounted the history of the Bill and strongly defended Eton. Once more, it was clear that 'the great school at Eton' was that foremost in Derby's mind and the school for which the Bill was primarily intended. He praised the improvement at the school, taking care to point out that the new headmaster of Eton was related to him.[133]

The brief debates which took place at the Committee Stage and the Report Stage were concerned largely with two amendments. The first, by Lord Lyttelton, was an attempt to give headmasters complete authority in their schools in all matters not specifically the responsibility of the governors. The discussion centred around the legal difficulties of giving 'a statutory power to a servant liable to dismissal' and the amendment was withdrawn.[134] The second amendment attempted at the Committee Stage was a suggestion, again by Lyttelton, that the number of Special Commissioners should be increased from seven to nine and that the names of the Rev. Joseph Blakesley and Sir Roundell Palmer should be added. The amendment was carried, but the names were later removed by the Commons when they considered the Lords' amendments.[135]

Apart from minor changes—of wording or definition, for example—the *Public Schools Act, 1868* was identical to the Bill which emerged from the Lords in 1865. The Lords debate in April 1865 at the second reading of the *Public Schools (No. 32) Bill*, and the Lords Select Committee, which adopted important suggestions made in the Lords debate, made fundamental changes to the Bill as originally introduced by Clarendon. These changes were incorporated into the subsequent Bills and into the *Public Schools Act, 1868.*

The most evident change was that only seven schools were included in the later Bills—St Paul's School was excluded in view of the disputed legal basis of its endowments.[136] The second change was that the Bills no longer contained specific provision for the government of each school but instead appointed, and named, Special Commissioners who had to approve the new arrangements in negotiation with the schools.[137] This initial influence over the composition of the new governing bodies reconciled the schools' supporters in Parliament—but not the existing governing bodies generally— to the new arrangements. The reconciliation of the schools' supporters to government intervention and to the Public Schools Bills was no doubt eased by the men chosen as Special Commissioners, who were all former pupils of the schools under consideration. Five of the seven Commissioners had been to Eton, and only one member was a scientist.[138] At some stage, this reconciliation to the Public Schools Bills must also have been helped by an unofficial understanding that the men nominated as school governors under the terms of the Act would be selected predominantly from former distinguished pupils of each school, as this usually happened and can hardly have been entirely fortuitous.[139]

The claims of parents of foundation boys at Harrow, Rugby and Shrewsbury living at the time of the Act were protected. The right to free education at all the schools was, however, to disappear eventually and to be replaced by scholarships, for the new governors were empowered to make admission 'wholly or partially dependent on Proficiency in a competitive or other Examination'.[140] The effect of this was to restrict the possibility of obtaining a free education to the 'persons of moderate means among the upper classes' whose educational interests had been so carefully guarded by the Lords in 1865.[141] These people often had sufficient money to move into an area in order to obtain the free education provided by the local public school; they could therefore afford to prepare their children for a competitive examination and to meet the incidental expenses of a scholarship place. The poorer *bona fide* residents—tradesmen or tenant farmers perhaps—were generally opposed to scholarships, because they thought that their children would be excluded for financial reasons. The exclusion of the poor had begun centuries before; what the *Public Schools Act, 1868* did was to put the discouragement of the lower middle classes on a more regular and more plausible basis.[142] It confirmed the fee-paying character of the schools, and finally ended any necessary connection between the schools and the education of local children.

The Act did not in itself initiate any reform of the curriculum; the schools obtained what was virtually voluntary unspecified reform over an indefinite period. There was no immediate necessity, for example, to introduce proper science teaching, and many schools did not do so for several years.[143]

Perhaps the most important result of the Act was not so much for the public schools themselves—which tended to carry on much as before with new governors and more financial independence—but for the rest of secondary education. By beginning the reform of secondary education with an Act for seven schools which successfully claimed a higher, separate status from all other endowed schools, the Public Schools Act made a unified approach to secondary education impossible. The ideas of separate, different education for each social class, of secondary education being fee-paying, that the quality of education was essentially a function—an interdependent consequence—of social class and that the education for other, lower classes would be inevitably cheaper and of lower quality, were all given expression, by implication, in the Public Schools Acts. The *Taunton Report* and the *Endowed Schools Act, 1869*, were both to endorse these ideas and apply them throughout the remaining endowed schools. In both the *Public Schools Act, 1868* and the *Endowed Schools Act, 1869*, the acceptance of the idea that secondary education was a marketable commodity that could be self-financing through charging fees meant that all schools—even those assigned to the lower classes—

tended to gravitate towards more wealthy parents so that their income could be increased particularly at a time of increasing demand for secondary education.[144] The public schools and many other endowed grammar schools were in a favourable position to exploit this demand once the old legal restrictions had been removed by the Acts of 1868 and 1869, for they had the use of public educational capital—buildings and endowments—to support their activities in a private, fee-paying market. The need for secondary education amongst the poorer classes was not supported by sufficient money to make their demand effective, and good secondary education was usually placed beyond their reach. The advice that the poorer classes should help themselves, pay for themselves and look to the public schools as their example had a cynical ring to it.[145] Neither the poor, nor indeed the lower-middle classes, had the money to establish schools or the political influence to ensure that ancient endowments—and the national educational capital they represented—were used for all. Even the more middle-class inhabitants of Harrow, Rugby and Shrewsbury— who had joined with the schools in opposing the Public Schools Bill of 1865—found that their interests were protected less the more the Bills progressed, whilst the interests of the schools— ably and repeatedly argued in the Lords—were successfully defended at the expense of the original Bill and the recommendations of the *Clarendon Report*.[146] The schools, moreover, continued to negotiate with the Special Commissioners and, even after that, preserved their independence in educational matters.[147] In 1868, for example, a committee of Harrow residents, originally formed to oppose the Bill of 1865, protested that injustices to local boys had increased since the Bill was first published; they were concerned because the Special Commissioners had no obligation to respect their rights under the will of the school's founder.[148] The Special Commissioners could not respect the claims of local inhabitants, even had they been so inclined, for these were largely dismissed by the terms of the Act and were thus not negotiable.

Negotiations between the schools and the Special Commissioners on other matters continued for some years, however. The Public Schools Acts of 1869, 1870, 1871 and 1872 each extended the time limit by which these negotiations had to be concluded, under the terms of the Public Schools Act, 1868.

Originally, this time limit was 1 May 1869 for agreement on the new governing bodies, and 1 January 1870 for agreement on new school statutes.[149] The Public Schools Act of 1869 extended the time limit for petitions against the new governing bodies from 1 January 1869 to 1 May 1869, and also clarified the original wording of the Act of 1868 regarding Westminster School.[150] The Public Schools Act of 1870 further extended the time for negotiations—until 31 July 1871 for school governors and 31 July 1872 for school statutes—with the option to extend the latter date until 31 December 1872.[151] The Public Schools Act of 1871 extended the time for the negotiations of new governing bodies at Winchester, Charterhouse, Harrow, Rugby and Shrewsbury until 25 March 1872, and extended the time for the negotiation of statutes until 25 March 1873.[152] The Public Schools Act, 1872 finally extended the time for the negotiation of school statutes until 25 August 1873, with the proviso that the Queen in Council could extend this time further until 25 February 1874. The power of the Special Commissioners to intervene, if agreement over statutes was not reached, was extended until 25 March 1874—again with provision for further extension by the Queen in Council until 25 September 1874. This last Act also contained some legal provisions concerning the transfer of property from Rugby Charity to Rugby School.[153] These later Public Schools Acts did not, of course, change the provisions of the Act of 1868, but merely continued its implementation. That such an extension of time was necessary indicated the long, sometimes tortuous negotiations that delayed the implementation of the Act of 1868, for agreement about new governing bodies and new statutes was not finally reached until nearly two years after the Act and nearly six years after the *Clarendon Report.*[154]

Grant Duff and Clarendon himself—the men who had perhaps done most to initiate reform and promote legislation—did not feel satisfied with the Public Schools Act of 1868. As late as June 1868, Clarendon seemed unconvinced that any legislation at all would come from the *Clarendon Report*. In June 1868 he 'regretted to say that hitherto the labours of the Commission had been almost barren of results'. A Bill had been introduced, he said, but 'valuable clauses had been struck out after the Bill came from the Select Committee. It was now two years since the Bill had passed . . . If the Government had been earnest on the subject . . . there would have been no insurmountable difficulty in passing it last year'. He did not know, he said, whether the Bill would again appear in the Lords.[155] It did appear again in the Lords in July, this time successfully, but Clarendon died before even this limited Act was fully implemented.[156]

Grant Duff was still more despondent when he considered secondary education in England in 1877, nearly ten years after the Public Schools Act of 1868.

> Many of us who were not, alas! so old then as we are now, fondly imagined, when the Palmerston Government appointed the Commission to inquire into the nine great schools, in 1861, that when we ourselves had children fit to go to those schools, they would be able to obtain a really good education there. Now, however, in 1877, although doubtless many improvements have been made, it would be mere flattery to say that anything which deserves to be called a good education, for the ordinary purposes of a man of the world, is to be obtained at any one of them . . . I do not even say that a good education may not be obtained at our great schools *for some purpose or other.* I only venture to affirm that, for any purposes with which I am acquainted, the education is a very miserable one; and that I see its bad effects in the world of English politics at every turn.[157]

Notes

1 See *Hansard*, CLXXVII, 13 March 1865, col. 1533 and *Hansard*, CLXXVIII, 3 April 1865, cols. 630–68.
2 See the *Public Schools (No. 32) Bill*, 1865, in *The Times*, 20 March 1865, p. 5.
3 See the *Public Schools (No. 32) Bill*, 1865, First Schedule and *The Times*, 20 March 1865, p. 5.
4 See the *Public Schools (No. 32) Bill*, 1865, First Schedule and *The Times*, 20 March 1865, p. 5.
5 See the *Public Schools (No. 32) Bill*, 1865, Second Schedule and *The Times*, 20 March 1865, p. 5.
6 See the *Public Schools (No. 32) Bill*, 1865, Fourth, Fifth and Sixth Schedules. See also *The Times*, 20 March 1865, p. 5.
7 See the *Public Schools (No. 32) Bill*, 1865, Third, Seventh and Eighth Schedules. See also *The Times*, 20 March 1865, p. 5.
8 See the *Public Schools (No. 32) Bill*, 1865, Section 8 and *The Times*, 20 March 1865, p. 5.
9 See the *Public Schools (No. 32) Bill*, 1865, Sections 5, 6, 7. See also *The Times*, 20 March 1865, p. 5.
10 See the *Public Schools (No. 32) Bill*, 1865, Sections 9, 12, 13, 14. See also *The Times*, 20 March 1865, p. 5.
11 See Note 10 above.
12 The term 'foundation boy' was used throughout the Public Schools Bills to mean a boy at any of the schools wholly or partly entitled to a gratuitous education.
13 See the *Public Schools (No. 32) Bill*, 1865, Section 19 and *The Times*, 20 March 1865, p. 5.
14 See the *Public Schools (No. 32) Bill*, 1865, Sections 23, 24. See also *The Times*, 20 March 1865, p. 5. The unlimited rights of sons of burgesses were to cease

with the passing of the Act, except for boys already at the school at that time. However, sons of burgesses were to have first choice of forty free scholarships until 1 January 1880. For the definition of a Shrewsbury burgess, see Chapter 1, Note 24.

15 See the *Public Schools (No. 32) Bill*, 1865, Section 22 and *The Times*, 20 March 1865, p. 5.

16 See the *Public Schools (No. 32) Bill*, 1865, Sections 11(1), 11(2). See also *The Times*, 20 March 1865, p. 5.

17 See the *Public Schools (No. 32) Bill*, 1865, Sections 12, 13, 14. See also *The Times*, 20 March 1865, p. 5.

18 See the *Public Schools (No. 32) Bill*, 1865, Sections 15, 16. See also *The Times*, 20 March 1865, p. 5.

19 See the *Public Schools (No. 32) Bill*, 1865, Section 25 and *The Times*, 20 March 1865, p. 5.

20 See the *Public Schools (No. 32) Bill*, 1865, Section 26 and *The Times*, 20 March 1865, p. 5.

21 See the *Public Schools (No. 32) Bill*, 1865, Section 27 and *The Times*, 20 March 1865, p. 5.

22 See the *Public Schools (No. 32) Bill*, 1865, Section 28 and *The Times*, 20 March 1865, p. 5.

23 See the *Public Schools (No. 32) Bill*, 1865, Sections 29, 30. See also *The Times*, 20 March 1865, p. 5.

24 See the *Public Schools (No. 32) Bill*, 1865, Sections 15(6), 20–4.

25 See, for example, *To the Right Honourable the Lords Spiritual and Temporal, in Parliament Assembled: The Humble Petition of the Mayor, Aldermen, and Burgesses of the Borough of Shrewsbury in Council Assembled*, presented to the Lords Select Committee 29 May 1865, Bailiff's Bundles No. 122.

26 See, for example, a letter from W. H. Bateson, Master of St John's College, Cambridge, in *The Times*, 28 March 1865, p. 7. See also Chapter 4, Note 84 and Chapter 5, Note 129.

27 See Chapter 5, pp. 139–41.

28 See the following correspondence in *The Times*: 28 March 1865, p. 7; 31 March 1865, p. 12; 6 April 1865, p. 11; 7 April 1865, p. 5; 15 April 1865, p. 10; 18 May 1865, p. 7.

29 *Hansard*, CLXXVIII, 3 April 1865, col. 632. For all the petitions and Derby's comment, see *Hansard*, CLXXVIII, 3 April 1865, cols. 630–2.

30 The eleven peers who spoke were Derby, Clarendon, Stanhope, Devon, the Bishop of London, the Archbishop of Canterbury, Strateford de Redcliffe, Houghton, Powis, Lyttelton and Campbell. See *Hansard*, CLXXVIII, 3 April 1865, cols. 630–68.

31 Lyttelton, *Hansard*, CLXXVIII, 3 April 1865, col. 664.

32 Lyttelton, *Hansard*, CLXXVIII, 3 April 1865, col. 666.

33 The only serious attack made in Parliament upon the evidence of the *Clarendon Report* was made by Lord Malmesbury in June 1864 when the Lords were considering the Committee Stage of the *Public Schools (No. 100) Bill*, which later became the Public Schools Act, 1864. He thought the Commissioners had shown 'a certain want of discretion' in publishing damaging evidence. It was clear from his comments, and from Clarendon's reply, that he wanted discreditable evidence about Eton omitted. See *Hansard*, CLXXV, 13 June 1864, cols. 1631–4. James Howard Harris (1807–89), 3rd Earl of Malmesbury, was educated at Eton. A Conservative, he was Foreign Secretary 1852, 1858–9.

34 The argument that the schools should be left to reform themselves was often linked with the argument that legislation would hinder reforms already begun. See Eton's petition to Clarendon, in *The Times*, 18 May 1865, p. 7.

35 The future of the Public Schools Bills in Parliament always seemed uncertain, even as late as June 1868. See Clement to Peele, undated but probably 16 June 1868, Bailiff's Bundles No. 122. See also Chapter 4, Note 24.

36 See Clarendon, *Hansard*, CLXXVIII, 3 April 1865, cols. 635–6. See also *The Times*, 20 March 1865, p. 5.

37 Bishop of London, *Hansard*, CLXXVIII, 3 April 1865, col. 651. See also Chapter 4, Note 34.

38 See Stanhope, *Hansard*, CLXXVIII, 3 April 1865, col. 642.
39 Bishop of London, *Hansard*, CLXXVIII, 3 April 1865, col..651.
40 Derby, *Hansard*, CLXXVIII, 3 April 1865, col. 655. Derby was himself a governor of Charterhouse and an eminent classical scholar whose translation of Homer could be compared to that of Dryden, Pope and Cowper. See G. Saintsbury, *The Earl of Derby*, London, 1906, pp. 148–64. Enthusiasm for science was not to be expected from him, for he disliked enthusiasm of any kind and his loyalties were those of traditional Conservatism. 'His own order, the agricultural interest, and the Church were the three things to which he had always looked and did always look.' Saintsbury, *The Earl of Derby*, pp. 33–4. Educated at Eton, Derby was Prime Minister in 1852, 1858–9, 1866–8 and previously MP for Stockbridge 1820–6, for Preston 1826–30, for Windsor 1830–1 and for N. Lancashire 1832–44. See also Note 63 below.
41 Derby, *Hansard*, CLXXVIII, 3 April 1865, col. 661.
42 Stanhope argued that 'of all reforms none was so safe or so lasting as self-reform' but Derby, after reading from a letter written by the Provost of Eton and listing reforms carried out since the publication of the *Clarendon Report*, admitted that 'they could not alter in a few months things which had been going on for 300 years'. See *Hansard*, CLXXVIII, 3 April 1865, cols. 645, 653. Some defence of the headmasters was extreme; Stratford de Redcliffe, after a fulsome defence of Eton, argued that any interference by Parliament 'would tend . . . to lower the authority of the Head Master in the eyes of the boys to a very unfortunate degree'. Stratford de Redcliffe, *Hansard*, CLXXVIII, 3 April 1865, col. 660. Clarendon clearly thought that headmasters had been given enough time and praised the headmaster of Rugby who had proposed a programme of reform within three months. See Clarendon, *Hansard*, CLXXVIII, 3 April 1865, cols. 634–5.
43 Houghton, *Hansard*, CLXXVIII, 3 April 1865, col. 661. Richard Monckton Milnes (1809–85), 1st Baron Houghton, was a member of the Lords Select Committee on the Public Schools Bill.
44 See Houghton, *Hansard*, CLXXVIII, 3 April 1865, col. 662.
45 Houghton, *Hansard*, CLXXVIII, 3 April 1865, col. 662.
46 For a comment on the foundation boys at Harrow, for example, see the Archbishop of Canterbury, *Hansard*, CLXXVIII, 3 April 1865, col. 658. See also Chapter 4, Note 34.
47 For the petitions against the Bill at the second reading, see *Hansard*, CLXXVIII, 3 April 1865, cols. 630–2.
48 None of the boys at Merchant Taylors' were foundation boys, but this school was not included in the Bill nor in subsequent Bills. In comparison, all the boys at St Paul's were foundation boys. Of the 2,708 boys at the nine Clarendon Commission schools in 1861, 495 were foundation boys. See the *Clarendon Report*, I, pp. 7–11.
49 The schools' headmasters, and the peers who supported them, generally maintained that the foundation boys were accepted on equal terms by the fee-paying boys. See, for example, the Archbishop of Canterbury, *Hansard*, CLXXVIII, 3 April 1865, col. 658. The evidence given to the Lords Select Committee in May and June 1865, however, suggested that there was a social barrier against foundation boys and that some headmasters—particularly at Rugby and Harrow—actively discouraged them. Even Dr Arnold, it was alleged, had tried to 'degrade the education of that part of the school'. See Houghton's question to M. H. Bloxam, a solicitor and former pupil at Rugby, in the *Lords Select Committee Report, 1865*, 12 May 1865, p. 46. At Harrow, foundation boys were made to sign a paper 'saying that though they are upon the foundation, they are not upon the foundation'. This paper, which had to be signed by the parents of all foundation boys and which was produced in evidence, imposed considerable restrictions. See the evidence of W. Winkley, Vestry Clerk of Harrow, a bookseller and house agent, in the *Lords Select Committee Report, 1865*, 15 May 1865, pp. 133–4. For the whole evidence concerning foundation boys, see the *Lords Select Committee Report, 1865*, pp. 27–155.
50 Lyttelton, *Hansard*, CLXXVIII, 3 April 1865, col. 666.
51 Derby, *Hansard*, CLXXVIII, 3 April 1865, col. 656.

52 Bishop of London, *Hansard*, CLXXVIII, 3 April 1865, col. 652.
53 Archbishop of Canterbury, *Hansard*, CLXXVIII, 3 April 1865, col. 658.
54 Powis, *Hansard*, CLXXVIII, 3 April 1865, col. 664. Edward James Herbert (1818–91), 3rd Earl of Powis, was MP for North Shropshire 1843–8. A Conservative, he succeeded to the title after accidentally shooting his father. See Chapter 5, Note 109 and Frederick Boase, *Modern English Biography*, II, col. 1615.
55 Powis, *Hansard*, CLXXVIII, 3 April 1865, col. 664.
56 Powis, *Hansard*, CLXXVIII, 3 April 1865, col. 664.
57 The proposal of an Executive Commission was made by Derby and supported by Stanhope, the Bishop of London, the Archbishop of Canterbury, Houghton and Campbell. The proposal was opposed by Clarendon, Powis, Devon and Lyttelton. See *Hansard*, CLXXVIII, 3 April 1865, cols. 631–4, 644–8, 652, 657, 662, 664–8.
58 Bishop of London, *Hansard*, CLXXVIII, 3 April 1865, col. 651.
59 Even the supporters of Eton, who were not in general happy with the Bill of 1865, acknowledged that the Bill was before Parliament because of the importance of Eton. The proposals for an Executive Commission, which delayed and fundamentally changed the Bill, were made with particular reference to Eton. See *Hansard*, CLXXVIII, 3 April 1865, cols. 648–51, 652, 653, 657, 659–60, 667.
60 See the Bishop of London, *Hansard*, CLXXVIII, 3 April 1865, col. 648.
61 Derby, *Hansard*, CLXXVIII, 3 April 1865, cols. 653, 656.
62 See *Hansard*, CLXXVIII, 3 April 1865, cols. 667–8 and *Hansard*, CLXXVIII, 2 May 1865, cols. 1304–5.
63 For the appointment of the Lords Select Committee, see *Hansard*, CLXXVIII, 2 May 1865, cols. 1304–5. The members of the Lords Select Committee were: Albert Edward, Prince of Wales (1841–1910); George Leveson-Gower (1815–91), 2nd Earl Granville; John Winston Spencer Churchill (1822–83), 7th Duke of Marlborough; Edward George Geoffrey Smith Stanley (1799–1869), 14th Earl of Derby; William Reginald Courtenay (1807–88), 11th Earl of Devon; Philip Henry Stanhope (1805–75), 5th Earl Stanhope; George Frederick William Villiers (1800–70), 4th Earl of Clarendon; Henry Howard Molyneux Herbert (1831–90), 4th Earl of Carnarvon; Edward James Herbert (1818–91), 3rd Earl of Powis; Dudley Ryder (1798–1882), 2nd Earl of Harrowby; Stratford Canning (1786–1880), 1st Viscount Stratford de Redcliffe; Charles Shaw-Lefevre (1794–1888), 1st Viscount Eversley; Archibald Campbell Tait (1811–82), Bishop of London; George William Lyttelton (1817–76), 4th Baron Lyttelton; Robert Monckton Milnes (1809–85), 1st Baron Houghton; John Wrottesley (1798–1867), 2nd Baron Wrottesley. The name of Lord Wrottesley, an eminent scientist and former President of the Royal Society, was added later. See *Hansard*, CLXXVIII, 5 May 1865, col. 1524. Of the sixteen members, seven had been to Eton, two to Westminster, one to Winchester, one to Christ's Hospital, one to Edinburgh Academy and four were educated privately. All were eminent men, but only Wrottesley was an eminent scientist. For biographical details, see C. J. Shrosbree, 'The origins and influence of the Clarendon Commission (1861–1864), with special reference to Shrewsbury School', PhD thesis, Birmingham University, 1985, Appendix IV.
64 See 'Order of Reference', *Lords Select Committee Report, 1865*, 5 May 1865, p. v.
65 See 'Order of Reference', *Lords Select Committee Report, 1865*, pp. v–xii.
66 The Petition was sent to Clarendon on 17 May 1865 and published in *The Times*, 18 May 1865, p. 7. Eton was clearly doing some energetic lobbying, for Derby later referred to a letter from the Provost which stressed the willingness of the school to reform. The Archbishop of Canterbury also referred to letters to him from Eton and Harrow. See *Hansard*, CLXXVIII, 3 April 1865, cols. 653, 657. Lord Campbell ended his speech against the Bill by suggesting that Parliament should wait for further guidance from Eton before proceeding. See *Hansard*, CLXXVIII, 3 April 1865, col. 667. For the petition from the 'inhabitants of Harrow and Pinner', from which the school disassociated itself, see *The Times*, 6 April 1865, p. 11.

67 The Prince of Wales proved an ally—attending for a day of important votes on 16 June 1865 and voting with Clarendon on seven of the nine divisions, including the vote to keep St Paul's School in the Bill which Clarendon lost. See the *Lords Select Committee Report, 1865*, pp. ix–xi.

68 For Whig aristocratic attitudes, see Lord David Cecil, *Melbourne*, London, 1976, pp. 1–10. For a more analytical examination of Whig and Tory attitudes, from which educational implications may be drawn, see S. H. Beer, *Modern British Politics*, London, 1969, Chapter 1, esp. pp. 3–15.

69 See the *Lords Select Committee Report, 1865*, pp. 27–54, 64–5, 76–134, 269–70.

70 For the evidence of the headmasters, see the *Lords Select Committee Report, 1865*, pp. 139–61, 166–88, 254–69. For the petitions, see 'Order of Reference', *Lords Select Committee Report, 1865*, pp. iv–viii.

71 See the *Lords Select Committee Report, 1865*, 15 May 1865, p. 75.

72 The motion for the introduction of an Executive Commission was introduced by Stanhope on 12 June 1865, 'that there shall be no change in the present governing bodies . . . but that there shall be an Executive Commission for a limited time', but Clarendon had clauses already prepared. Stanhope withdrew his motion and Clarendon's clauses became Clauses 9, 10 and 11 of the *Public Schools (No. 110) Bill* of 1866. Stanhope's amendment would have precluded any change in the schools' governing bodies, leaving the Executive Commission to supervise the other reforms recommended by the *Clarendon Report*. Since the Bill envisaged the reform of the governing bodies as a necessary prelude to the introduction of the other reforms, Stanhope's amendment would have reduced the Executive Commission to an advisory body, left the schools essentially unchanged with the headmasters in effective control of the curriculum. See 'Order of Reference', *Lords Select Committee Report, 1865*, p. viii.

73 See Note 67 above.

74 The Lords Select Committee concluded its proceedings on 22 June 1865. See 'Order of Reference', *Lords Select Committee Report, 1865*, p. xii.

75 See Clarendon, *Hansard*, CLXXXIII, 29 May 1866, cols. 1409–10.

76 Edward Law (1790–1871), 2nd Baron Ellenborough, was Conservative MP for St Michael's, Cornwall 1813–18. He was Lord Privy Seal 1828–9 and later Governor-General of India 1841–4.

77 Ellenborough, *Hansard*, CLXXXIII, 5 June 1866, col. 1926. For his comments on tradesmen, examinations and the sons of gentlemen, see *Hansard*, CLXXXIII, 5 June 1866, cols. 1924–6. His earlier career in India had been touched by the ridiculous when, in Ferozepur, he supervised the painting of ceremonial elephants and triumphantly returned to Agra sacred Hindu temple gates which were fakes. He was recalled when his actions, intended to impress the native population, proved inept. See *Dict. Nat. Biog.*, XI, pp. 662–8.

78 See *Hansard*, CLXXXIII, 5 June 1866, cols. 1924–8.

79 See Houghton, *Hansard*, CLXXXIII, 5 June 1866, col. 1929.

80 Lyttelton, *Hansard*, CLXXXIII, 5 June 1866, col. 1931.

81 See *Hansard*, CLXXXIII, 5 June 1866, cols. 1930–2. Sir Thomas Dyke Acland (1809–98) was Liberal MP for West Somerset 1837–47, for North Devon 1865–85 and for the Wellington Div. of Somerset 1885–6. His name was later withdrawn. See Notes 102 and 103 below.

82 See *Hansard*, CLXXXIII, 5 June 1866, cols. 1924, 1928–9. The amendments to Clauses 4 and 5 were incorporated in the Bill at the Report Stage on 14 June 1866, proposed by Clarendon and Powis respectively. For details of these amendments, see *Public Schools Bill (H.L.) Amendments to be Proposed on Report by the Earl of Clarendon and the Earl of Powis. 11th June 1866. (110c)*. For the Report Stage, see *Hansard*, CLXXXIV, 14 June 1866, col. 359.

83 See Derby, *Hansard*, CLXXXIII, 5 June 1866, cols. 1932–3.

84 Clarendon, *Hansard*, CLXXXIV, 18 June 1866, cols. 527–8.

85 See *Hansard*, CLXXXIV, 18 June 1866, cols. 526–9 and *Hansard*, CLXXXIV, 16 July 1866, col. 820.

86 See *Hansard*, CLXXXV, 15 March 1867, col. 1914.

87 See *Hansard*, CLXXXIX, 10 August 1867. Recorded in General Index but not

shown in transcript of proceedings.

88 See *Hansard*, CXC, 5 December 1867, cols. 634–5.

89 See *Hansard*, CXCII, 16 June 1868, col. 1648.

90 For Clause 19, see the *Public Schools (No. 78) Bill* and the *Public Schools (No. 24) Bill*. For Derby's involvement with Parliamentary reform and his health at the time, see Saintsbury, *The Earl of Derby*, pp. 165–95.

91 See *Hansard*, CLXXXIV, 16 July 1866, col. 820 and *Hansard*, CLXXXIV, 7 August 1866, cols. 2149–51.

92 Neate, *Hansard*, CLXXXIV, 7 August 1866, cols. 2150–51. Charles Neate (1806–79) was Liberal MP for Oxford in 1857 and 1863–8. Educated in Paris, he was a former Professor of Political Economy at Oxford. He was a member of the Commons Select Committee on the Public Schools Bill.

93 Ayrton, *Hansard*, CLXXXIV, 7 August 1866, col. 2151. Acton Smee Ayrton (1816–86) was Liberal MP for Tower Hamlets 1857–74. He was a member of the Commons Select Committee on the Public Schools Bill.

94 See Goschen, *Hansard*, CLXXXIV, 7 August 1866, cols. 2149–50. George Joachim Goschen (1831–1907) was Liberal MP for the City of London 1863–80, for Ripon 1880–5 and for Edinburgh 1885–6. He was a member of the Commons Select Committee on the Public Schools Bill.

95 See Goschen, *Hansard*, CLXXXIV, 7 August 1866, cols. 2149–50.

96 See Note 91 above.

97 For the first reading, see *Hansard*, CLXXXV, 7 February 1867, col. 80. See also *Hansard*, CLXXXV, 14 February 1867, cols. 333–4; *Hansard*, CLXXXV, 26 February 1867, cols. 1002–3; *Hansard*, CLXXXV, 7 March 1867, col. 1428 and *Hansard*, CLXXXV, 8 March 1867, cols. 1546–7. The Bill was brought to the Commons as the *Public Schools (No. 78) Bill*. See *Hansard*, CLXXXV, 15 March 1867, col. 1914.

98 See Derby, *Hansard*, CLXXXV, 26 February 1867, col. 1003.

99 See *Hansard*, CLXXXV, 14 February 1867, col. 333.

100 See Note 103 below.

101 Henry Howard Molyneux Herbert (1831–90), 4th Earl of Carnarvon, was Conservative Under-Secretary for the Colonies 1858–9 and Colonial Secretary 1866–7 and 1874–8.

102 Derby, *Hansard*, CLXXXV, 7 March 1867, col. 1428.

103 The names of the Special Commissioners continued to be liable to change until the final passing of the Act, Sir Roundell Palmer and the Rev. Joseph Blakesley being removed by a Commons amendment in July 1868. See *Hansard*, CXCIII, 28 July 1868, cols. 1903–8. There were seven Special Commissioners in the Act: the Rev. William Thomson (1819–90), Archbishop of York 1863–90; Robert Arthur Talbot Gascoigne-Cecil (1830–1903), 3rd Marquess of Salisbury; Rt Hon. Russell Gurney (1804–78), a barrister, Recorder of London 1856–78 and MP for Southampton 1865–78; Sir John Lubbock Bt (1834–1913), a distinguished banker and scientist, later an MP and Chairman of the Public Accounts Committee; Sir John George Shaw Lefevre (1831–1928), a barrister and MP for Reading 1863–85, later Baron Eversley; John Duke Coleridge (1820–94), a barrister and MP for Exeter 1865–73, later Lord Chief Justice; Charles Stewart Parker (1829–1910), Public Examiner in Classics at Oxford in 1868, MP for Perthshire 1868–74 and for Perth 1878–92. All had distinguished careers, Lord Salisbury becoming Foreign Secretary 1878–80, 1885–6, 1887–92 and Prime Minister 1885–6 and 1886–92. Of the seven members, five had been to Eton, one to Harrow and one to Shrewsbury. One member, Sir John Lubbock, was an eminent scientist. Sir Edmund Walker Head (1805–68), former Governor-General of Canada, died in January 1868. See also Note 105 below.

104 Houghton, *Hansard*, CLXXXV, 7 March 1867, col. 1428.

105 Derby, *Hansard*, CLXXXV, 7 March 1867, col. 1428. In the changes in the Special Commissioners that followed, a scientist was included. See Shrosbree, 'Origins of the Clarendon Commission', Appendix VII.

106 For the first reading in the Commons, see *Hansard*, CLXXXV, 15 March 1867, col. 1914. For the second reading, see Note 87 above.

107 See *Hansard*, CXC, 5 December 1867, cols. 634–5 and *Hansard*, CXC, 14 February 1868, cols. 742–75.

108 Walpole, summarising Ayrton's views, in *Hansard*, CXC, 14 February 1868, col. 751.

109 See Walpole, *Hansard*, CXC, 20 March 1868, cols. 750–2, 1982, 2052–3.

110 See *Hansard*, CXC, 20 March 1868, cols. 2052–3. The members of the Committee, with their constituencies and Parties, were as follows: Acton Smee Ayrton (1816–86), Radical Liberal, Tower Hamlets 1857–74; Richard Benyon (1811–97), Conservative, Berkshire 1860–76; Edward Cardwell (1813–86), Liberal-Conservative, Oxford City 1857–74; George Augustus Frederick Cavendish-Bentinck (1821–91), Conservative, Whitehaven 1865–91; William James Clement (1802–70), Liberal, Shrewsbury 1865–70; Mountstuart Elphinstone Grant Duff (1829–1906), Liberal, Elgin 1857–81; Viscount Enfield (1830–98), Liberal, Middlesex 1857–74; William Edward Forster (1818–86), Liberal, Bradford 1851–86; George Joachim Goschen (1831–1907), Liberal-Unionist, City of London 1863–80; Ralph Neville Grenville (1817–86), Conservative, East Somerset 1865–8 and Middle Div. of Somerset 1868–78; Christopher Darby Griffith (1804–85), Liberal-Conservative, Devizes 1857–68; Sir William Heathcote (1801–81), Conservative, University of Oxford 1854–68; Edward Howes (1813–71), Conservative, Norfolk E. 1859–68 and Norfolk S. 1868–71; Robert John Mowbray (1815–99), Conservative, Durham 1853–68 and University of Oxford 1868–99; Charles Neate (1806–79), Liberal, Oxford City 1863–8; Sir Stafford Henry Northcote (1818–87), Conservative, Stamford 1858–68 and North Devon 1868–85; Francis Sharp Powell (1827–1911), Conservative, University of Cambridge 1863–8; William Henry Stone (1834–96), Liberal, Portsmouth 1865–74; Spenser Horatio Walpole (1806–98), Conservative, University of Cambridge 1856–82. Of the nineteen members of the Committee, thirteen had been to the public schools of the Clarendon Commission: five to Eton, two to Westminster, one to Winchester, one to Rugby, one to Harrow, one to Shrewsbury, one to Charterhouse and one to St Paul's. Of the other six members, four were educated privately, one at the College Bourbon in Paris and one at Wigan Grammar School, at Uppingham and at Sedbergh Grammar School. Most were classics graduates and lawyers, there was one surgeon but no scientist. For biographical details, see Shrosbree, 'Origins of the Clarendon Commission', Appendix V.

111 See *Commons Select Committee Report, 1868*, 22 May 1868, p. xiv.

112 See *Hansard*, CXCII, 15 June 1868, cols. 1538–53.

113 For the Committee Stage, see *Hansard*, CXCII, 16 June 1868, cols. 1631–57; *Hansard*, CXCII, 23 June 1868, cols. 1924–42; *Hansard*, CXCIII, 7 July 1868, cols. 812–27. For the Report Stage, see *Hansard*, CXCIII, 14 July 1868, col. 1164. For the third reading, see *Hansard*, CXCIII, 15 July 1868, col. 1214.

114 Neate, *Hansard*, CXCII, 16 June 1868, col. 1634.

115 See Neate, *Hansard*, CXCII, 16 June 1868, col. 1635.

116 Ayrton, *Hansard*, CXCII, 16 June 1868, col. 1641.

117 Lowe, *Hansard*, CXCII, 16 June 1868, col. 1642. Robert Lowe (1811–92) was Liberal MP for Kidderminster 1852–9, for Calne 1859–68 and for London University 1868–80. He was Chancellor of the Exchequer 1868–73 and Home Secretary 1873–4.

118 Griffith, *Hansard*, CXCII, 16 June 1868, col. 1648.

119 Forster, *Hansard*, CXCII, 16 June 1868, col. 1647. Forster was Vice-President of the Committee of the Council on Education 1868–74 and a member of the Commons Select Committee on Public Schools Bill. See Note 110 above.

120 See *Hansard*, CXCII, 16 June 1868, cols. 1648, 1649.

121 See *Hansard*, CXCII, 23 June 1868, cols. 1930–1.

122 Ayrton, *Hansard*, CXCII, 23 June 1868, col. 1931.

123 See *Hansard*, CXCII, 16 June 1868, cols. 1649–50.

124 See Ayrton, *Hansard*, CXCII, 16 June 1868, col. 1651.

125 For Ayrton's speech, see *Hansard*, CXCII, 16 June 1868, cols. 1650–1. For the amendment and its defeat, see *Hansard*, CXCII, 16 June 1868, cols. 1656–7.

126 See *Hansard*, CXCII, 23 June 1868, cols. 1933–9.

127 Ayrton, *Hansard*, CXCII, 23 June 1868, col. 1937 and Beresford-Hope, *Hansard*, CXCII, 23 June 1868, col. 1936. Alexander James Beresford-Hope (1820–87) was Liberal-Conservative MP for Maidstone 1841–52 and 1857–9, for Stoke

1865-8 and for Cambridge University 1868-87. Henry Labouchere (1798-1869) was Whig-Liberal MP for Michael Borough 1826-30 and for Taunton 1830-69. Charles Newdigate Newdegate (1816-87) was Conservative MP for N. Warwickshire 1843-85.

128 Gaselee, *Hansard*, CXCII, 23 June 1868, col. 1939. Stephen Gaselee (1807-83) was Liberal MP for Portsmouth 1865-8.

129 See *Hansard*, CXCII, 23 June 1868, cols. 1939-42.

130 Ayrton, *Hansard*, CXCII, 23 June 1868, cols. 1940-1.

131 See Note 129 above.

132 The *Public Schools (No. 262) Bill* was given a first reading in the Lords on 16 July 1868. See *Hansard*, CXCIII, 16 July 1868, col. 1125. For the Royal Assent, see *Hansard*, 31 July 1868, col. 1936.

133 Derby, *Hansard*, CXCIII, 20 July 1868, col. 1462.

134 See *Hansard*, CXCIII, 23 July 1868, cols. 1654-8.

135 See *Hansard*, CXCIII, 23 July 1868, cols. 1658-61. See also Note 103 above and Chapter 4, pp. 108-10.

136 See Chapter 4, pp. 118-20 and Note 67 above.

137 See Note 103 above.

138 See Note 103 above.

139 See Chapter 5, Notes 129, 130, 131.

140 *Public Schools Act, 1868*, Section 6(1).

141 See Note 53 above.

142 The combined effect of scholarship examinations and the continuing classical curriculum was to make the public schools less accessible to poorer parents. Success in the entrance examinations depended on fees paid for preparatory tuition so that an appearance of entry on merit was in fact linked to social class and the ability to pay.

143 For Shrewsbury School, see Chapter 5, pp. 160-1.

144 See F. E. Balls, 'The origins of the Endowed Schools Act 1869 and its operation in England from 1869 to 1895', PhD thesis, Cambridge University, 1964, p. 195.

145 See, for example Lyttelton's comments at a meeting to support Canon Woodard's schools, reported in *The Times*, 11 April 1864, quoted in Balls, 'Origins of the Endowed Schools Act', pp. 193-4.

146 The foundation rights of local people in Harrow, Rugby and Shrewsbury, who were resident at the time of the passing of the *Public Schools Act, 1868*, were protected for their lifetime. Apart from this limitation, which must have undermined local opposition somewhat, the new governing bodies had freedom to alter or remove the provisions for foundation boys. See the *Public Schools Act, 1868*, Sections 8 and 14.

147 For Shrewsbury School, see Chapter 5, pp. 160-1.

148 See *The Times*, 10 February 1868, p. 11.

149 See the *Public Schools Act, 1868*, Sections 5 and 6.

150 See the *Public Schools Act, 1869*, Sections 1-3.

151 See the *Public Schools Act, 1870*, Sections 2 and 3.

152 See the *Public Schools Act, 1871*, Sections 2 and 3.

153 See the *Public Schools Act, 1872*, Sections 2, 3 and 5.

154 The schools concluded negotiations with the Special Commissioners about new governing bodies and the details of new school statutes on the following dates: Westminster in November 1869; Eton in February 1870; Charterhouse in February 1870; Rugby, Shrewsbury and Winchester in March 1870; Harrow in July 1870. For a general survey of the school's new constitutions, see *The Times*, 27 June 1870, p. 14.

155 Clarendon, *Hansard*, CXCII, 15 June 1868, cols. 1546-7.

156 Clarendon died on 27 June 1870. See *The Times*, 27 June 1870, p. 11.

157 Grant Duff, 'A plea for a rational education, 1877', in Rt Hon. Mountstuart E. Grant Duff, *Some Brief Comments on Passing Events made between February 4th 1858 and October 5th 1881*, Madras, 1884, pp. 261-2.

Conclusion

The Clarendon Commission was a response to public and Parliamentary demands for the reform of public education, which also resulted in the Newcastle Commission and the Taunton Commission. In a more general sense, the Clarendon Commission and the subsequent legislation form part of the movement for reform apparent in almost all aspects of English life in the nineteenth century. The Commission was appointed in 1861 partly because of widespread public criticism of the public schools, partly because of contemporary developments in Europe and partly because British politics at that time brought Clarendon and Granville, who were aware of European developments and advocated educational reform, into positions of influence in education.

Public criticism of these schools could not be ignored for, at a time of agitation for Parliamentary reform, their failings seemed to reflect on the competence and honesty of the 'higher classes' who had made them peculiarly their own. The schools' faults were widely known: the growing circulation of the provincial press, the high and increasing literacy rate and the temporary but formidable influence of the periodicals made for much public discussion and a well-informed middle-class electorate. Publicity was particularly damaging for Eton, where large-scale financial irregularities were disclosed at a time when government subsidies to education, particularly for the primary education of the poor, were opposed in Parliament on grounds of both cost and principle.

In Europe, this period saw the establishment of national systems of education in many countries, including France, Holland, Prussia and Belgium. Reformers like Grant Duff associated this educational provision with social, economic and military progress. A similar conclusion was drawn from comparison with the USA. The reform of all English schools, and particularly of endowed schools, was presented as a national necessity. The public schools were defended partly on the grounds that the classics provided a valuable education, and partly on the grounds that the schools produced English gentlemen whose value to England lay in their character rather than their knowledge. Moreover, the European emphasis on science, on national languages and literature and on more modern subjects generally, had radical political overtones in England, as it was associated with economic and social change, with the education of the lower middle and working classes, with European radicalism and with political equality. To many educated in the classical tradition, the more modern subjects were also associated with inferior schools and poor academic standards. To most of those educated in the classics, and to most of these men in Parliament, the study of the classics was associated with a gentleman's education, with scholarship and with conservative attitudes.

The circumstances in 1861 and, in particular, the embarrassing nature of the criticisms of Eton, made some government response inevitable. For this reason, the government could not meet Grant Duff's requirement that Eton be included in an inquiry into all endowed schools. The Clarendon Commission therefore investigated Eton along with other schools sufficiently well known to offer some comparability with Eton, and sufficient in number to provide enough work to justify a Royal Commission. The selection of these schools was in law quite arbitrary; they were all, including Eton, simply well known and relatively successful endowed grammar schools.

The selection of these schools for separate consideration had far-reaching consequences for English education because the resultant Public Schools Acts endowed them with a separate legal identity, recognising and enhancing their claim to be an élite group, whilst separating them from other endowed schools and from the provision of public secondary education. The failure of the Public Schools Acts to introduce any significant curricular reforms into the schools, while removing any local reforming influence over the schools' curriculum, as at Shrewsbury, meant that they maintained the association of the classical tradition in education with higher prestige, more money and better facilities. The appointment of the Clarendon Commission to give separate consideration to nine endowed schools and the Public Schools Acts which followed created a hierarchy in secondary education so that other schools were compelled to imitate them in the hope that they would acquire some parity of esteem through imitation and association. The formation of the Headmasters' Conference in 1869 was the most immediate consequence. Granville and Clarendon had hoped that the curricular reforms suggested in the *Clarendon Report* would influence all secondary schools through the public schools' example, but conservative support in Parliament for the schools' classical curriculum—particularly in the Lords—limited the scope of the Public Schools Bills essentially to matters of finance and school government. The Acts thus immediately increased the influence of the public schools in English education whilst leaving them entrenched in both educational conservatism and the classical tradition.

Parliament, and particularly the House of Lords, while it did not approve of curricular reform, did agree with three other assumptions of the Clarendon Commission about education. These were that education ought to be appropriate to social class, that public schools ought to be kept for the 'higher classes' and that finance for secondary education above the most rudimentary level ought to come from parents rather than from public money. These assumptions, and the social and curricular hierarchy that they implied, also had important consequences for English secondary education. Through the example of the public schools, the classics and more scholarly subjects became associated with academic excellence and high social status whilst more scientific, technical and vocational subjects came to be associated with inferior education and low social status. The assumptions of the Clarendon Commission about education and social class were accepted by the Taunton Commission and further implemented by the Endowed Schools Act of 1869.[1]

The more modern subjects, which Grant Duff, Granville and Clarendon had seen studied in Europe and which seemed to them to be crucial to national prosperity, remained little regarded in the public schools. The origins of the secondary modern school may perhaps be found in Kennedy's 'Non-Collegiate' class, where academic failure was associated with particular subjects and with social class. The Clarendon Commission's association of secondary education with fees meant that the government's provision of secondary education was delayed. When it was provided, it tended to follow the Clarendon

Commission's assumptions about the curriculum and social class, for it was placed in the hands of Civil Servants who were often anxious to perpetuate their own public school attitudes. Morant, it was said, 'converted English secondary schools into imitations of Winchester',[2] and many of the much-criticised characteristics of English secondary education—houses, prefects, uniforms, corporal punishment, the power of headmasters, the limited influence of parents, the concentration on boys and a predilection for single-sex schools, as well as the lingering association of subjects with social class and the divide between the 'public schools' and other secondary schools, may be traced back to the Clarendon Commission and the Public Schools Acts.

Political circumstances ensured that the Public Schools Acts should reform the government and finances of the schools, but not the curriculum, as the schools had many supporters and former pupils in Parliament, particularly in the Lords, and in the Select Committees that considered the Public Schools Bills. These men did not always agree about the details of reform but did, in general, want to keep the public schools for their own children and for other children of the 'higher classes'. They wished to preserve classical education, to abandon the schools' obligations to foundation boys, to keep the schools as independent as possible of government control and to ensure that the new governing bodies were sympathetic to the schools' continuance on these terms. The Bills of 1865 failed because they included direct Parliamentary direction of each school and new governing bodies which were based, in the first instance, on the old.[3] In opposing the Public Schools Bills of 1865, the supporters of the schools were aided by the petitions of local people who were opposed to the abolition of the schools' local obligations. The reconstruction of the Bill in 1866, and the subsequent legislation, did little to preserve these local obligations, but did introduce new governors appointed largely by outside bodies, and Special Commissioners to negotiate with each school separately.[4] The local petitions were thus used to delay the Bill whilst the schools' supporters in Parliament used the delay to introduce other amendments which strengthened their national character and educational independence. This preservation of status and traditional curriculum was aided by the return to power of a Conservative government in June 1866, and by the reintroduction of the Public Schools

Bills into the Lords on three separate occasions before there was any serious discussion on them in the Commons.[5] This was probably done deliberately to prevent, as far as possible, any fundamental challenge in the Commons to the Lords' assumptions about the public schools and their place in English education. The main supporters of the public schools and of the traditional classical curriculum were in the Lords; when the Bill eventually came to the Commons in 1868,[6] there remained no possibility of challenging its main provisions. These had been estalished in the Lords Select Committee of 1865,[7] the Commons Select Committee in 1868, itself with a majority of public school supporters,[8] attended only to detail. The Commons initiative of 1861, for the provision of English secondary education through the reform of all endowed schools, was lost in the protracted Lords defence of the public schools as distinct, separate schools which should provide a classical education for gentlemen.

The Clarendon Commission and the Public Schools Acts conferred a separate, superior status on the public schools, reformed school government and finance, but left the schools' classical curriculum largely undisturbed for many years. The evidence of Shrewsbury School suggests that the schools prospered and grew as a result of the Clarendon Commission and the subsequent legislation. The effects on English secondary education were, however, that curricular reform was delayed throughout all English secondary schools, that secondary education was seen and organised in terms of social class and that scientific, technical and other more modern, more vocational subjects continued to be associated with inferior provision, lower academic standards and lower social status. The division of English secondary education into 'the two nations' of public schools and state schools had its origin, certainly as regards legislation and administration, in the Clarendon Commission for, in selecting the schools for the Clarendon Commission to consider, Palmerston's government made an arbitrary, hurried but irrevocable distinction between the nine endowed grammar schools of the Clarendon Commission and the 782 other endowed grammar schools of the Taunton Commission.[9] This distinction, made for administrative convenience and arising from the political necessity of responding quickly to complaints about Eton, led to the creation of a separate legal category for these schools where none had existed before; 'some' public schools of the Clarendon Commission became 'the' public schools of the Public Schools Acts.

From the Public Schools Acts, the Endowed Schools Act of 1869 and the formation of the Headmasters' Conference, through the Bryce Commission of 1895 and the Board of Education Act of 1899, the Education Act of 1902 and the early period of genuine public secondary education, the influence of public school men at the Board of Education in the years before 1939 and the influence of public school attitudes in secondary education after 1945, the public schools and the public school system 'restricted and devastated' the development of English secondary education.[10]

This was hardly surprising, for the comments expressed in Parliament about the Public Schools Bills made clear that the purpose of legislation was to preserve inequality and class advantage. Private affluence, rather than personal need or national policy, was to provide the key to continuing public subsidy within the public school system. The money of the poor, through taxation and public subsidy, was (and is) used to finance inequality and to put state education at a permanent disadvantage. The pretence that public school education was open to all may be seen at its most cynical in the comment of the Provost of Eton in 1940—that 'Eton had 70 foundation places open to the poor; they had only to learn Latin and Greek'.[11]

The continuing political purpose of the public schools may be seen in the influence of public school men during the formative years of English state education, and the attempts that were made to impose public school attitudes upon secondary education. This was most evident in the grammar schools which became (and remain) a supportive, subordinate system which plausibly echoes public school political attitudes— that good secondary education is for the few, that the few have to be carefully selected and educated apart, and that selection itself is both morally defensible and politically desirable.[12] There have always, of course, been parents who want the best for their children—as they see it—and this is perfectly proper. What is not defensible, however, and what the public school system is built on, is the use of public subsidy, ancient endowments and the public capital of great historic schools to support private education—with its attendant injustice and inequalities and its illusion of excellence so cynically contrived that it would be transparent were its political purpose not so obvious and so fundamental to the public school system from the time of its origin in the Public Schools Acts.

The use of private money to supplement and then undermine public education in the 1980s is not new Conservative radicalism, but merely an extension of the conservative class interest inherent in English education from the time of the Public Schools Acts. The Public Schools Acts, like private funding today, provided social and educational discrimination for political purposes, divided and impoverished public education and created an illusion of competition in which excellence was socially determined and in which both the needs of the poor and the requirements of national secondary education were forced to the margin by the inexorable combination of private parental interests and private finance. As in the Public Schools Acts, private money is today used to gain access to enhanced public funding, and those who can afford to pay most have the greatest interest in perpetuating the system for private finance can confer political, educational and social advantage out of all proportion to ability.

As an early example of privatisation, the Public Schools Acts are not encouraging; they did not achieve significant curricular reform, they did not begin to create the basis of an open system of secondary education appropriate for a democratic, industrial society and, in practice, hindered the creation of an effective secondary education system by relating schools directly to social class and expecting parents to pay. The Public Schools Acts thus became an effective means of transferring public endowments, and the great educational assets of buildings and historic sites, from the community to private use. The schools became independent, not in the sense of being free from public subsidy or public funding, but in the sense of being free from the responsibilities imposed on state schools by economic circumstances and national priorities. Competition and the pursuit of excellence have thus taken place in wholly artificial circumstances in which the public schools, sometimes subsidised by the state two or three times over—by the original endowments, tax concessions and now, for example, by the Assisted Places scheme—have none of the national burdens that are taken on as a matter of course, quite properly by state schools. It is the state schools which take on the burden of public policy from one source of public funding; it is the public schools which escape these burdens and responsibilities, in spite of massive public funding and an additional income from fees.

In this the Public Schools Acts have been successful, for their stated political purpose was to set the public schools apart and to limit their advantages and endowments to one class. That one class has widened, as the public school system has expanded, but the private and political interest in fee-paying education remains. At a personal level, it enables parents to use public money for private, exclusive advantage. At a school level, it enables the public school system to gather public subsidies whilst serving the private interests of parents, remaining independent of any need to serve either the local community or national educational policy. The challenge of making an effective response to many desperate educational needs from limited resources is an everyday experience for state schools, but one that largely passes by the public schools, sheltered as they are by public subsidy from public responsibility. The educational problems of poverty, deprivation, unemployment, cultural change, vocational training, ethnic tensions and professional uncertainties all press in upon state schools. At a political level, the public school system remains a consequence, and almost a caricature, of Conservative views. Public assets and public funding are adapted to serve private interests. Public assets are bought or monopolised by those who can afford to pay. Public services are both impoverished and placed in competition with private agencies which do not have the burdens of public responsibility, even though they may benefit from considerable public subsidy. Public subsidy is not only divorced from public responsibility but used to fund the pursuit of private interest and social inequality. The alleged pursuit of excellence, by which this is justified, is so structured by social and financial constraints that it becomes a reflection of social and financial status. Private educational advantage, and the social and political myths that surround it, becomes self-perpetuating and public education further impoverished. The history of secondary education in England since the Public Schools Acts must raise doubts about whether free, public, democratic education can survive erosion by class attitudes, financial inequalities and the neglect of public service in favour of private interest.

Notes

1 The Taunton Commission did not attempt an exact definition of 'middle class' but 'they did recommend three grades of school to meet the needs of different groups within the middle class. There were to be first grade schools for professional and independent gentlemen, able to keep their children at school until 18 or 19; second grade schools for the "larger shopkeepers, rising men of business, and the larger tenant farmers" able to send their children to school until 16; and third grade schools for "the smaller tenant farmers, the small tradesmen, the superior artisans" where the leaving age would be 14'. F. E. Balls, 'The origins of the Endowed Schools Act 1869 and its operation in England from 1869 to 1895', PhD thesis, Cambridge University, 1964, pp. 3–4, quoting the *Taunton Report*, XXVIII (Vol. I), pp. 16–20.

2 T. W. Bamford, *The Rise of the Public Schools: A Study of Boys' Public Boarding Schools in England and Wales from 1837 to the Present Day*, London, 1967, p. 260. Sir Robert Laurie Morant (1863–1920) became educational advisor to the King of Siam in 1889 after attending Winchester and New College, Oxford. He became an assistant director with the Board of Education in 1895 and helped to prepare the Education Act of 1902. He became permanent Secretary to the Board of Education 1903–11, Chairman of the National Health Insurance Commission 1911–19 and Secretary to the Ministry of Health 1919–20. See *The Concise Dictionary of National Biography*, Oxford, 1961, II, p. 310.

3 See the *Public Schools (No. 32) Bill* of 1865.

4 See the *Public Schools Act, 1868*, Sections 15–19.

5 See *Hansard*, CLXXVII, 13 March 1865, col. 1533; *Hansard*, CLXXXIII, 11 May 1866, col. 743; *Hansard*, CLXXXV, 7 February 1867, col. 80. The Commons did not complete the second reading until February 1868. See *Hansard*, CXC, 14 February 1868, cols. 742–75.

6 Apart from the *Public Schools Act, 1864*, which was largely a formality, the Public Schools Bills came to the Commons in 1866 and 1867, but so briefly that proper debate was impossible. See Chapter 6, Notes 91 and 106.

7 See the *Lords Select Committee Report, 1865*.

8 See Chapter 6, Note 110.

9 For the endowed schools considered by the Taunton Commission, see Balls, 'Origins of the Endowed Schools Act', p. 1.

10 Brian Simon, *The Politics of Educational Reform 1920–1940, Studies in the History of Education*, London, 1974, pp. 331, 270–96. See also, Brian Simon and Ian Bradley (eds), *The Victorian Public School: Studies in the Development of an Educational Institution*, London, 1975, pp. 16–17.

11 Cited in Simon, *Politics of Educational Reform*, p. 278.

12 See Simon, *Politics of Educational Reform*, pp. 292–3, 323–33.

Sources

The editions listed are not necessarily the earliest, but are those referred to in the text.

A. UNPUBLISHED MATERIAL

1. Correspondence, minutes and evidence of the Clarendon Commission in the Public Record Office, particularly the following:

HO73/57/2 Commissioners' personal files
HO73/57/3 Private minutes books, 2 vols
HO73/58/1 Eton
HO73/58/2 Winchester
HO73/58/3 Westminster
HO73/58/4 Charterhouse
HO73/58/5 St Paul's
HO73/58/5/4
  Answers to Questions Relating to the Nature and Application of the Endowments, Funds and Revenues of St. Paul's School
  The Attorney-General and Baron de Rothschild v The Mercers' Company. Amended Information and Bill of Complaint. Filed 19th May 1860. Amended 10th April 1861
HO73/58/6 Merchant Taylors'
HO73/58/7 Harrow
HO73/58/8 Rugby
HO73/58/9 Shrewsbury
HO73/58/10 City of London School
HO73/58/11 Marlborough and Cheltenham
HO73/58/12 Wellington
HO73/59/16 Dr Carpenter: correspondence
HO73/59/18 Prof. Faraday: correspondence
HO73/59/19 Dr Hooker: correspondence
HO73/59/21 Sir Charles Lyell: correspondence
HO73/59/22 Max Müller: correspondence
HO73/59/23 Prof. Owen: correspondence

2. Correspondence and school records in the Shrewsbury School Archives, particularly the following:

Bailiff's Bundles No. 70
  Miscellaneous correspondence
Bailiff's Bundles No. 122
  Notes on Public Education: A Paper read by Dr. Kennedy at the meeting of the National Association for the Promotion of Social Science in York, September 1864
  Correspondence concerning the Public Schools Bills 1865–8
  Correspondence with the Special Commissioners concerning the constitution of the new governing body and new school statutes 1868–73
  Annotated Public Schools Bills and miscellaneous Parliamentary papers
  To the Right Honourable the Lords Spiritual and Temporal, in Parliament

> *Assembled: The Humble Petition of the Mayor, Aldermen, and Burgesses of the Borough of Shrewsbury in Council Assembled*, Petition presented to the Lords Select Committee on 29 May 1865
>
> *Petition of the Inhabitants of Rugby and the Neighbourhood*, March 1867
>
> *Suggestions at a Meeting of the Trustees of the Free Grammar School held on the 31st October 1868. With reference to the Public Schools Act*
>
> *Draft Statutes for Constituting a New Governing Body for Shrewsbury School, February 1869*
>
> *Draft Statutes for Constituting a New Governing Body for Shrewsbury School, with letter from Mr D'Courcy Peele, March 1869*
>
> *Draft Statutes for Constituting a New Governing Body for Shrewsbury School, November 1869*
>
> *Draft Statutes for Constituting a New Governing Body for Shrewsbury School, April 1871*
>
> *Draft Regulations for Shrewsbury School, November 1873*
>
> *Public Schools Commission. Shrewsbury. A Statute for constituting a new Governing Body for Shrewsbury Free Grammar School. No. IV(10)*
>
> *Regulations for Shrewsbury School, as finally adopted and sealed by order of the Governing Body, 20th February 1874*
>
> *Shrewsbury School Accounts 1855–90* (Accounts for 1862, 1866, 1868, 1869 and 1870 missing)
>
> *Shrewsbury School*, 1854–87 (Prize lists for each year)
>
> Shrewsbury School Examiners' Reports 1863, 1865, 1867, 1868, 1869
>
> *Shrewsbury School Fees Accounts* 1880, 1884, 1886, 1896

Bailiff's Bundles No. 111

> Kennedy, Benjamin Hall, *Proposition to establish a class for Physical Science and Linear Drawing*. Undated
>
> Kennedy, Benjamin Hall, *Outline of the Discipline of Shrewsbury School* (1849)
>
> *Shrewsbury School 1800–1851* (A leaflet published by the school on its tercentenary and collected in *Paget's Scrap Book* (qv)
>
> *Shrewsbury School 1882–1887* (A collection of articles and documents associated with the school). Undated. Editor unknown
>
> *Shrewsbury School Register 1866–90*
>
> *Shrewsbury School Trustees' Minutes 1792–1882*
>
> *The Schools* (A collection of newspaper cuttings concerning Shrewsbury School, collected by J. Humphreys and presented to the school by H. Adnitt in 1904)
>
> MS 339. *Paget's Scrap Book* (A collection of school drawings and memorabilia *c.* 1848 collected by Alfred Tolver Paget who taught at the school 1840–55)

3. The Clarendon Papers in the Bodleian Library as listed in *List of Papers of the Earls of Clarendon deposited by George Herbert Hyde Villiers, 6th Earl of Clarendon in the Bodleian Library, Oxford*, Bodleian Library, Oxford, 1959, particularly the following:

MSS Clar. Dep. c. 496(6) Correspondence from Cowley to Clarendon 1868–9

MSS Clar. Dep. c. 496(8) Delane and Henry Reeve to Clarendon 1868–70

MSS Clar. Dep. c. 525(9e) Correspondence from Henry Reeve

MSS Clar. Dep. c. 531 Sir George Cornewall Lewis to Clarendon 1858–63

MSS Clar. Dep. c. 533 Clarendon to Sir George Cornewall Lewis 1856–63

MSS Clar. Dep. c. 534 Clarendon to Henry Reeve 1853–69

MSS Clar. Dep. c. 535(3) Clarendon to Henry Reeve 1853–69

MSS Clar. Dep. c. 535(4) Clarendon to Henry Reeve 1853–69

MSS Clar. Dep. c. 536 Cowley to Clarendon 1858–66

MSS Clar. Dep. c. 560 Hayward Joyce to Clarendon (re. John Lyon's school, Harrow, of which Clarendon was a governor). December 1868

MSS Clar. Dep. c. 560 Clarendon, Lady, *Journal of the Fourth Countess of Clarendon* (unpublished)

4. Birmingham University Library

Vaughan, Charles John, *A Letter to the Viscount Palmerston Etc.* (A bound collection of correspondence and pamphlets about Harrow School, especially the monitorial system, 1853–4)

B. OFFICIAL PUBLICATIONS

Abbreviated titles of bills, petitions and commissions, following *Hansard*, are used throughout in the text and the full titles given here. The short titles of Acts of Parliament are used throughout the text. Reference is made throughout to original documents; reprinted copies, cited in secondary works, are listed separately.

1. Parliamentary papers

(a) Reports of Royal Commissions and Select Committees

Report of Her Majesty's Commissioners appointed to inquire into the State, Discipline, Studies and Revenues of the University and Colleges of Cambridge, London, 1852

Report of Her Majesty's Commissioners appointed to inquire into the State, Discipline, Studies and Revenues of the University and Colleges of Oxford, London, 1852

Report of Commissioners on the Arrangements in the Inns of Court and of Chancery, for promoting the Study of the Law and Jurisprudence; Evidence, Appendices and Index, London, 1855

Report of the Royal Commission on the State of Popular Education in England (and Wales), London, 1861

Report of Her Majesty's Commission Appointed to Inquire into the Revenues and Management of Certain Colleges and Schools, and the Studies Pursued and Instruction Given Therein, London, 1864

'Report from the Select Committee of the House of Lords on the Public Schools Bill (H.L.); together with the Proceedings of the Committee, Minutes of Evidence, Appendix and Index. Brought from the H. of L. 4th July 1865 and ordered by the House of Commons to be printed, 5th July 1865', *Reports from Committees 7th February–6th July 1865*, X

Report from the Select Committee on [sic] Public Schools Bill with the Proceedings of the Committee. Ordered by the House of Commons to be Printed, 22nd May 1868

Report from the Select Committee on Scientific Instruction together with the Proceedings of the Committee, Minutes of Evidence and Appendix. Ordered by the House of Commons to be Printed, 15 July 1868

Report of the Royal Commission on Schools not comprised within Her Majesty's two recent Commissions on Popular Education and Public Schools, London, 1868

(b) Bills and Acts of Parliament

A Bill to Abolish Punishment by Whipping for Offences Committed by Criminal Prisoners, and to Amend so much of an Act for the More Speedy Trial and Punishment of Juvenile Offenders as Relates to the Whipping of Offenders (No. 3) Bill. 1862. Presented by the House of Commons. Ordered by the House of Commons to be printed 12th March 1862 (Cited in *Hansard* as the *Whipping (No. 2) Bill*)

A Bill to Provide for the Abolition of Certain Tests in Connection with Academical Degrees in the University of Oxford (No. 18) Bill. 1864. Introduced by Mr Dodson. Ordered by the House of Commons to be printed, 12th February 1864

Public Schools (No. 168) Bill. 1864. Ordered by the House of Commons to be printed 23rd June 1864

Public Schools (No. 32) Bill. 1865. Presented by the Earl of Clarendon. Ordered by the House of Lords to be printed, 13th March 1865

Public Schools (No. 110) Bill. 1866. Presented by the Earl of Clarendon. Ordered by the House of Lords to be printed, 11th May 1866

Public Schools (No. 212) Bill. 1866. Ordered by the House of Commons to be printed, 16th July 1866

Public Schools (No. 4) Bill. 1867. Presented by the Earl of Derby. Ordered by the

House of Lords to be printed, 7th February 1867
Public Schools (No. 78) Bill. 1867. Ordered by the House of Commons to be printed, 15th March, 1867
Public Schools (No. 24) Bill. 1868. Prepared and brought in by Mr Walpole, Sir Stafford Northcote and Mr Secretary Gathorne Hardy. Ordered by the House of Commons to be printed, 5th December 1867
Public Schools (No. 47) Bill. 1868. As amended in Committee. Ordered by the House of Commons to be printed, 5th March 1868
Public Schools (No. 135) Bill. 1868. As amended in Committee and by the Select Committee. Prepared and brought in by Mr Walpole, Sir Stafford Northcote and Mr Secretary Gathorne Hardy. Ordered by the House of Commons to be printed, 22nd May 1868
Public Schools (No. 262) Bill. 1868. Brought from the House of Commons and ordered to be printed, 16th July 1868
Lords' Amendments to the Public Schools (No. 254) Bill. 1868. Ordered by the House of Commons to be printed, 27th July 1868
Public Schools (No. 217) Bill. 1869. Prepared and brought in by Mr Secretary Bruce and Mr Solicitor General. Ordered by the House of Commons to be printed, 14th July 1869
Public Schools (No. 200) Bill. 1870. Prepared and brought in by Mr Secretary Bruce and Mr Knatchbull-Hugessen. Ordered by the House of Commons to be printed, 6th July 1870
Public Schools (No. 204) Bill. 1871. Prepared and brought in by Mr Secretary Bruce and Mr William Edward Forster. Ordered by the House of Commons to be printed, 16th June 1871
Public Schools (No. 27) Bill. Brought from the House of Lords 23rd July 1872. Ordered by the House of Commons to be printed, 24th July 1872
The Amalgamation of the City of London Police with the Metropolitan Police (No. 89) Bill. 1863. Introduced by Mr Bruce. Ordered by the House of Commons to be printed, 22nd April 1863
Abolition of Flogging in the Army Act, 1881
An Act for the Better Government and Regulation of the Free Grammar School of King Edward the Sixth, at Shrewsbury, in the County of Salop, 1798
Charitable Trusts Act, 1853
Public Schools Act, 1864
Public Schools Act, 1868
Endowed Schools Act, 1869
Public Schools Act, 1869
Public Schools Act, 1870
Public Schools Act, 1871
Public Schools Act, 1872
Public Schools Act, 1873

(c) Miscellaneous papers

'A Statute for determining and establishing the constitution of the new Governing Body of Shrewsbury Free Grammar School made by the Public Schools Commissioners'. 'A Scheme made by the Governing Body of Shrewsbury, pursuant to the "The Public Schools (Shrewsbury and Harrow Schools Property) Act, 1873" and 'Regulations made by the Governing Body of Shrewsbury' in Copy of Statutes, Schemes and Regulations made under the Public Schools Acts by the Public Schools Commissioners, September 1874. Ordered by the House of Commons to be printed, 10th March 1876
'Cambridge University Commission Report', *Parliamentary Papers*, 1852–1853, XLIV
General Alphabetical Index to the Bills, Reports, Estimates, Accounts and Papers printed by order of the House of Commons and to the Papers Presented by Counsel, 1852–1899, London, 1909
Hansard's Parliamentary Debates, 3rd Series
Letters Patent of King Edward VI, referring to Shrewsbury School and cited in the *Clarendon Report*, reprinted in *Calendar of the Patent Rolls. Edward VI*, VI,

1550–3, Public Record Office, London, 1926, p. 387

Minutes of the Committee of the Council on Education, 1840–1841, Appendix III

Notices of Motions for Tuesday 16th June 1868

'Ordinances in relation to Pembroke, Winchester, New and Balliol Colleges', *Parliamentary Papers, 1857*, XXXII

'Oxford University Commission Report', *Parliamentary Papers, 1852*, XXII

Petition of Cultivators of Natural Science, Praying that they May Be Heard by Themselves or their Counsel in Favour of the Introduction into the 'Public Schools Bill' of Clauses Providing for Increased Instruction in Natural Science. (Presented to the Lords 2 May 1865 but not referred to the Lords Select Committee. Petition has not survived)

Petition to Noblemen and Gentlemen Educated at Eton against the Public Schools Bill Praying 'That the Last Mentioned Bill May Not Pass into Law without Amending so much of the same as relates to Eton College, and that an Executive Commission may be Appointed with Power to Amend the Statutes and Regulate the Revenues of Eton College' (Petition has not survived)

Public Schools Bill: Amendment to be Moved by the Lord Lyttelton, (262a). 17th July 1868

Public Schools Bill (H.L.) Amendments to be Proposed on Report by the Earl of Clarendon and the Earl of Powis. 11th June 1866 (110c)

Report of the Poor Law Commissioners, 1841

'Special Reports of Mr. George Wallis and Mr. Joseph Whitworth', *Parliamentary Papers, 1854*, XXXVI

'Statutes in Respect of Emmanuel, Magdalene, St. John's, Trinity, and King's Colleges and of the College of King Henry the Sixth at Eton', *Parliamentary Papers, 1861*, XLVIII

'The Petition of the Bristol Election (For Declaring One of the Seats Vacant for Issue of a New Writ), Delivered 14th March 1868', *Appendices to the Reports of the Committees on Public Petitions 1867–1868*

2. Other official publications

List of the Examples, Etc., which may be obtained from the Department by National and other Public Schools at half the prime cost (No. 30. May 1853). Department of Science and Art, Marlborough House, Pall Mall, London

Report and Evidence upon the Recommendations of Her Majesty's Commissioners for inquiring into the State of the University of Oxford, Presented to the Heads of Houses and Proctors, December 1st 1853, Oxford, 1853

Report of the Proceedings Respecting Rugby School before the Rt. Hon. Lord Langdale, Master of the Rolls, with His Lordship's Judgement Thereon, Rugby, 1839

The English Reports, 32, Chancery XII

The English Reports, 37, Chancery XVII

The English Reports, 54, Rolls Court VII

C. NEWSPAPERS AND PERIODICALS

1. Newspapers

Eddowes's Shrewsbury Journal, 1851–65

Morning Star, 7 June 1859

Shrewsbury Chronicle, 1861–74

The Shropshire Journal, 13 June 1849

The Times, 1860–79

2. Periodicals

All the Year Round, 1859–1905

Blackwood's Magazine, 1860–5

Chamber's Journal, 1864

Contemporary Review, 1866

Cornhill Magazine, 1861
Edinburgh Review, 1810–70
Eton College Chronicle, No. 101, 21 May 1868 (sometimes referred to as the *Eton College Magazine* or the *Eton Chronicle* in contemporary references)
Fortnightly Review, 1865–79
Fraser's Magazine, 1861–9
Home and Foreign Review, 1862
North British Review, 1844–71
Quarterly Review, 1860–70
Saturday Review, 1858–61
The Economist, 1860–77
The Spectator, 17 December 1853
Westminster Review, 1862–71

D. WORKS OF REFERENCE

Auden, J. E. (ed.), *Shrewsbury School Register 1798–1898*, Oswestry, 1898
    (ed.), *Shrewsbury School Register 1743–1908*, Oswestry, 1909
    (ed.), *Shrewsbury School Registers, I, 1798–1908*, Shrewsbury, 1928
Barker, G. F. Russell & Stenning, Alan H. (eds), *The Record of Old Westminsters: A Biographical List of all those who are known to have been educated at Westminster School from the Earliest Times to 1927*, London, 1928, 2 vols
Boase, Frederick, *Modern English Biography*, London, 1965, 6 vols
British Parliamentary Papers, Shannon, 1968–72
Burke's Landed Gentry, London, 1969, 2 vols
Concise Dictionary of National Biography, London, 1953, 3 vols
Daughlish, M. G. & Stephenson, R. K. (eds), *The Harrow School Register*, London, 1911
Doubleday, H. A., Warrand, Duncan & Walden, Lord Howard de, *et. al.*, *The Complete Peerage*, London, 1926, 13 vols
Foster, Joseph (ed.), *Alumni Oxonienses: The Members of the University of Oxford 1715–1886*, London, 1888, 2 vols
    (ed.), *Alumni Oxonionses: The Members of the University of Oxford 1715–1886*, London, 1891, 4 vols
Gardiner, Robert Barlow (ed.), *The Admission Register of St. Paul's School from 1748–1876*, London, 1884
Hart, Mrs. E. P. (ed.), *Merchant Taylors' School Register 1561–1934*, London, 1936, 2 vols
Houghton, W. E. (ed.), *The Wellesley Index to Victorian Periodicals 1824–1900*, London, 1966, 3 vols
Lee, Sir Sidney (ed.), *Dictionary of National Biography Supplement*, London, 1912, 2 vols
    (ed.), *Dictionary of National Biography Supplement 1901–1911*, London, 1927
Morris, J. (ed.), *The Provosts and Bailiffs of Shrewsbury*, undated, Shrewsbury Local Studies Library
Parish, W. D. (ed.), *List of Carthusians 1800–1879*, Lewes, 1879
Rugby School Register with Annotations and Alphabetical Index, I, 1675–1849, London, 1881
Rugby School Register with Annotations and Alphabetical Index, II, 1850–74, London, 1886
Shrewsbury School Lists and Prize Poems 1831–1848, London, undated
Stapylton, H. E. C. (ed.), *Eton School Lists from 1791 to 1850*, London, 1863
    (ed.), *Second Series of Eton School Lists 1853–1892*, Eton, 1900
Stenton, M. & Lees, S., *Who's Who of British Members of Parliament*, Sussex, 1978, 2 vols
Stephen, Leslie & Lee, Sidney (eds), *Dictionary of National Biography*, London, 1885–1900, 63 vols
    (eds), *Dictionary of National Biography*, London, 1908, 22 vols
    (eds), *Dictionary of National Biography*, London, 1928, 22 vols
The Concise Dictionary of National Biography, Oxford, 1961, 2 vols
The Historical Register of the University of Oxford, being a Supplement to the

Oxford University Calendar with an Alphabetical Record of the University Honours and Distinctions Completed to the End of Trinity Term 1900, Oxford, 1900

Townsend, P. (ed.), *Burke's Peerage, Baronetage and Knightage*, London, 1970

Venn, J. A. (ed.), *Alumni Cantabrigienses*, Part II, 1752–1900, Cambridge, 1947, 6 vols

Wainewright, J. B. (ed.), *Winchester College 1836–1906: A Register*, Winchester, 1907

Who's Who 1984, London, 1984

Wolff, M., North, J. S. & Deering, D. (eds), *The Waterloo Directory of Victorian Periodicals* 1824–1900, Phase I, Laurier University, 1976

E. CONTEMPORARY WORKS

1. Books

Arnold, Matthew, *The Popular Education of France, with Notices of that of Holland and Switzerland*, London, 1861
    A French Eton: a Middle Class Education and the State, London, 1864
    Schools and Universities on the Continent, London, 1868
    Higher Schools and Universities in Germany, London, 1874

Burke, Edmund, *Writings and Speeches of Edmund Burke*, Boston, 1901, 12 vols

Butler, Samuel, *An Atlas of Ancient Geography*, London, 1842
    The Life and Letters of Samuel Butler, London, 1890

Chambers, T. G., *The Royal College of Chemistry, the Royal School of Mines and the Royal College of Science*, London, 1896

Coleridge, Sir John, *Public School Education*, London, 1860

Creasy, E. S., *Some Account of the Foundation of Eton College, and of the Past and Present Condition of the School*, London, 1848

Darwin, Charles, *On the Origins of Species by Means of Natural Selection, or the Preservation of Favoured Races in the Struggle for Life*, London, 1859

Darwin, Sir Francis (ed.), *The Life and Letters of Charles Darwin*, London, 1887, 3 vols

Davies, Robert E., *Some Account of the Royal Free Grammar School of Edward VI in Shrewsbury*, Shrewsbury, 1869

Derby, Lord (trans.), *Iliad*, London, 1864

Dickens, Charles, *A Tale of Two Cities*, London, 1859

Duff, Mountstuart E. Grant, *Studies in European Politics*, Edinburgh, 1866
    Inaugural Address Delivered to the University of Aberdeen on his Installation as Rector, 22nd March 1867, Edinburgh, 1867
    Some Brief Comments on Passing Events made between February 4th 1858 and October 5th 1881, Madras, 1884
    Notes from a Diary 1851–1872, London, 1897, 2 vols
    Out of the Past: Some Biographical Essays, London, 1903, 2 vols

Edgeworth, R. L., *Essays on Professional Education*, London, 1809

Eliot, George, *Adam Bede*, London, 1859

Farrar, F. W. (ed.), *Essays on a Liberal Education*, London, 1867

Fisher, G. W., *Annals of Shrewsbury School*, London, 1899

Fitzgerald, Edward (trans.), *The Rubaiyat of Omar Khayyam*, London, 1859

Fraser, Rt Rev. James, *The Spirit of a Public School: A Sermon Preached at the Public Opening of the New Buildings of Shrewsbury School, on July 28th 1882*, London, 1885

Gower, Hon. F. Leveson (ed.), *Letters of Harriet, Countess Granville 1810–1845*, London, 1894, 2 vols

Gronow, Captain, *Captain Gronow's Recollections and Anecdotes of the Camp, the Court and the Clubs at the Close of the Last War with France*, London, 1864

Hatchard, John (attrib.), *Remarks on the System of Education in the Public Schools*, London, 1809

Heywood, James (ed.), *The Recommendations of the Oxford University Commissioners with Selections from their Report*, London, 1853

Johnson, W., *Eton Reform*, London, 1861

Kennedy, Benjamin Hall, *Letter to the Mayor and Town Council of Shrewsbury*, Shrewsbury, 1848
  Shrewsbury School: A Letter to His Grace the Archbishop of York on the Public Character of Shrewsbury School, as Affected by the Public Schools Bill, Cambridge, 1865
  Public School Latin Grammar, London, 1871
Kinglake, A. W., *Invasion of the Crimea*, London, 1863–1887, 8 vols
Keunen, Abraham, *Historisch-Kritisch Onderzoek*, Leyden, 1861–1865, 3 vols
Leach, Arthur F., *A History of Winchester College*, London, 1899
Lyell, Sir Charles, *Principles of Geology*, London, 1830–1833, 3 vols
Lyte, H. C. M., *A History of Eton College 1440–1910*, London, 1911
Macauley, Thomas Babington, *Essay on Lord Clive*, in *Essays*, London, 1843
Martin, Sir Theodore, *The Life of His Royal Highness the Prince Consort*, London, 1875–1880, 5 vols
Matteucci, Carlo, *Raccolta di Scritti varii intorno all' intruzione publica*, Prato, 1867, 2 vols
Mill, John Stuart, *Essay on Liberty*, London, 1859
Moss, Mrs, *Moss of Shrewsbury: A Memoire 1841–1917*, London, 1932
Newton, Sir Isaac, *Philosophiae Naturalis Principia Methematica*, ed. Lord Kelvin and H. Blackburne, Glasgow, 1871
Oxford and Asquith, Earl of, *Fifty Years of Parliament*, London, 1926, 2 vols
Parkin, G. R., *Edward Thring*, London, 1898, 2 vols
Reid, Thomas W., *Life of the Rt. Hon. W. E. Forster*, London, 1888, 2 vols
  Memoirs and Correspondence of Lyon Playfair, First Lord Playfair of St. Andrews, London, 1899
Rouse, W. H. D., *A History of Rugby School*, London, 1898
Scott, Sir Walter, *The Talisman*, in *The Tales of the Crusaders*, London, 1825
Spencer, Herbert, *Education: Intellectual, Moral, Physical*, London, 1861
Stanley, A. P., *The Life and Correspondence of Thomas Arnold D.D.*, London, 1844, 2 vols
Tennyson, Alfred, *In Memoriam*, London, 1850
  Idylls of the King, London, 1859
Thackeray, William Makepeace, *The Virginians*, London, 1859
The Book of Rugby School: Its History and Daily Life, Rugby, 1856
Vincent, W., *A Defence of Public Education*, London, 1801
Wallis, George & Whitworth, Joseph, *The Industry of the United States in Machinery Manufactures, and Useful and Ornamental Arts*, London, 1854
Wilson, J. M., *A Letter to the Master and Seniors of St. John's College, Cambridge, on the Subject of the Natural and Physical Sciences, in Relation to School and College*, London, 1867

2. Articles

Acton, Lord (attrib.), 'Nationality', *Home and Foreign Review*, July 1862, pp. 1–25.
Arnold, Matthew, 'A French Eton (Part I)', *Macmillan's Magazine*, 8, October 1863, pp. 353–62
  'A French Eton (Part II)', *Macmillan's Magazine*, 9, February 1864, pp. 343–55
  'A French Eton (Part III)', *Macmillan's Magazine*, 10, May 1864, pp. 83–96
Beale, Dorothea (attrib.–signed *A. Utopian*), 'On the education of girls', *Fraser's Magazine*, 74, October 1866, pp. 509–24
Bradley, G. G., 'The hostel system in public schools', *Macmillan's Magazine*, 21, March 1870, pp. 405–12
Browning, Oscar, 'Mr. Matthew Arnold's "Report on French education"', *Quarterly Review*, 125, October 1868, pp. 473–90
Bryce, James, 'The worth of educational endowments', *Macmillan's Magazine*, 19, April 1869, pp. 517–24
Burrows, Montagu, 'Female education', *Quarterly Review*, 126, April 1869, pp. 448–79
Cecil, Robert (attrib.), 'Competitive examinations', *Quarterly Review*, 108, October 1860, pp. 569–605
Cheney, R. H., 'Public school education', *Quarterly Review*, 108, October 1860, pp. 387–424

'Education of the poor', *Quarterly Review*, 110, October 1861, pp. 485–516

'Public schools', *Quarterly Review*, 116, July 1864, pp. 176–211

Clough, Anne J., 'Hints on the organization of girls' schools', *Macmillan's Magazine*, 14, October 1866, pp. 435–9

Collins, Lucas W., 'School and college life; Its romance and reality', *Blackwood's Magazine*, 89, February 1861, pp. 131–48

'A Visit to Rugby', *Blackwood's Magazine*, 91, May 1862, pp. 537–81

'Harrow School', *Blackwood's Magazine*, 94, October 1863, pp. 457–81

'Winchester College and Commoners', *Blackwood's Magazine*, 95, January 1864, pp. 66–92

'The Public Schools Report (No. I): Eton', *Blackwood's Magazine*, 95, June 1864, pp. 707–31

'The Public Schools Report (No. II): Harrow and Rugby', *Blackwood's Magazine*, 96, August 1864, pp. 219–40

'The Public Schools Report (No. III): the London Schools', *Blackwood's Magazine*, 96, October 1864, pp. 449–71

'The Public Schools Report (No. IV): Winchester and Shrewsbury', *Blackwood's Magazine*, 96, December 1864, pp. 696–718

'Etoniana, ancient and modern (Part I)', *Blackwood's Magazine*, 97, February 1865, pp. 209–28

'Etoniana, ancient and modern (Part II)', *Blackwood's Magazine*, 97, March 1865, pp. 356–73

'Etoniana, ancient and modern (Part III)', *Blackwood's Magazine*, 97, April 1865, pp. 471–88

Davies, James, 'Female education', *Quarterly Review*, 119, April 1866, pp. 499–515

Duff, Mountstuart E. Grant, 'A plea for a rational education', *Fortnightly Review*, 28 August 1877, pp. 170–94

'Endowed schools', *Westminster Review*, 77, April 1862, pp. 340–57

'Eton', *Macmillan's Magazine*, 15, March 1867, pp. 353–65

Farrar, F. W., 'Public school education: Lectures delivered at the Royal Institution', *Fortnightly Review*, 9, March 1868, pp. 233–49

Fawcett, Millicent Garrett, 'The education of women of the middle and upper classes', *Macmillan's Magazine*, 17, April 1868, pp. 511–17

Fitch, J. G., 'Educational endowments', *Fraser's Magazine*, 79, January 1869, pp. 1–15

Foster, Michael, 'Science in schools', *Quarterly Review*, 123, October 1867, pp. 464–90

Fowler, Thomas, 'Shall we continue to teach Latin and Greek?', *Fortnightly Review*, 9, January 1868, pp. 95–105

Heitland, W. E., 'Dr. Kennedy at Shrewsbury', *Eagle* (the journal of St John's College, Cambridge), XV, 89, June 1889, pp. 3–15

Helps. Arthur, 'Lord Clarendon: In memoriam', *Macmillan's Magazine*, 22, August 1870, pp. 292–6

Higgins, M. J., 'Paterfamilias to the Editor of the "Cornhill Magazine" ', *Cornhill Magazine*, 1, May 1860, pp. 608–15

'A second letter to the Editor of the "Cornhill Magazine" from Paterfamilias', *Cornhill Magazine*, 2, December 1860, pp. 641–9

'A third letter from Paterfamilias to the Editor of the "Cornhill Magazine" ', *Cornhill Magazine*, 3, March 1861, pp. 257–69

(attrib.), 'Eton College', *Edinburgh Review*, 113, April 1861, pp. 387–426

(attrib.), editorial comment signed 'Ed. C. M.' in reply to G. W. Littelton's letter (qv) in the same issue, *Cornhill Magazine*, 10, July 1864, pp. 639–40

'On some points on the Eton report', *Cornhill Magazine*, 10, July 1864, pp. 113–28

Jelf, W. E., 'Eton reform', *Contemporary Review*, 3, December 1866, pp. 556–70

Lewis, Sir George, 'Parliamentary opposition', *Edinburgh Review*, 101, January 1855, pp. 1–22

Lyttelton, G. W., A letter concerning the Clarendon Report, in *Cornhill Magazine*, 10, July 1864, p. 639

Lytton, Robert, 'Liberal education in England', *Edinburgh Review*, 127, January 1868, pp. 131–65

Maclaren, Archibald, 'Girls schools', *Macmillan's Magazine*, 10, September 1864, pp. 409–16
  'Private schools for boys: their management', *Macmillan's Magazine*, 9, March 1864, pp. 384–92
Markby, Thomas, 'Public schools (Part I)', *Contemporary Review*, 4, February 1867, pp. 149–75
  'Public schools (Part II)', *Contemporary Review*, 4, March 1867, pp. 397–410
Martineau, Harriet, 'Middle-class education in England: girls', *Cornhill Magazine*, 10, November 1864, pp. 549–68
Mill, J. S., 'Endowments', *Fortnightly Review*, 11, April 1869, pp. 377–90
Mozley, J. B., 'The education of the people', *Quarterly Review*, 128, April 1870, pp. 473–506
Neate, Charles, 'Endowments', *Macmillan's Magazine*, 22, September 1870, pp. 387–93
'Public schools', *Fraser's Magazine*, 63, April 1863, pp. 434–40
'Public school education', *Fraser's Magazine*, 77, March 1868, pp. 301–19
'Public schools: Report of the Commission (No. I)', *Fraser's Magazine*, 69, June 1864, pp. 655–69
'Public schools: Report of the Commission (No. II)', *Fraser's Magazine*, 70, September 1864, pp. 319–30
'Public school teaching', *Westminster Review*, 95, April 1871, pp. 383–404
Reeve, Henry, 'Popular education in England', *Edinburgh Review*, 114, July 1861, pp. 1–38
Reynolds, S. H., 'Public schools in England', *Westminster Review*, 82, July 1864, pp. 1–24
Russell, John Scott, 'Technical education a national want', *Macmillan's Magazine*, 17, April 1868, pp. 447–59
'Salopienses flagellati', *Punch*, 8 August 1874, p. 62
Sellar, Alexander Craig (attrib.–signed A. C. S.), 'School and university system in Scotland', *Fraser's Magazine*, 78, September 1868, pp. 333–52
Sidgwick, Henry (attrib.), 'Eton', *Macmillan's Magazine*, 3, February 1861, pp. 292–300
Smith, Goldwin, 'Public schools', *Edinburgh Review*, 120, July 1864, pp. 147–88
Smith, Sidney (attrib.), 'Public schools of England', *Edinburgh Review*, 16, August 1810, pp. 326–34
Sutcliffe, John, 'Middle-class and primary education in England: past and present', *Cornhill Magazine*, 4, July 1861, pp. 50–7
Sutherland, James, 'Middle class schools', *Westminster Review*, 90, October 1868, pp. 486–506
'The Maecenas of Liberalism', *World*, 10 February 1867
'The poor and their public schools: The new Minute', *Blackwood's Magazine*, 91, January 1862, pp. 77–102
'The Public Schools' Commission', *Chamber's Journal*, Fourth Series, 42, October 1864, pp. 659–63
Trollope, Anthony, 'Public schools', *Fortnightly Review*, 2, October 1865, pp. 476–87
Wilson, James Maurice (attrib.), 'Natural Science in schools and in general education', *Macmillan's Magazine*, 4, October 1861, pp. 474–80
'Women's education', *Fraser's Magazine*, 79, May 1869, pp. 537–52

F. LATER SECONDARY WORKS

1. Books

Alington, Cyril, *Shrewsbury Fables: Being Addresses given in Shrewsbury Chapel*, London, 1918
Altick, R. D., *The English Common Reader*, Chicago, 1957
  Victorian People and Ideas, London, 1974
Appleman, P., Madden, W. A. & Wolff, M. (eds), *1859: Entering an Age of Crisis*, Indiana, 1959
Aspinall, A., *Politics and the Press c. 1780–1850*, London, 1949

Bamford, T. W., *The Rise of the Public Schools: A Study of Boys' Public Boarding Schools in England and Wales from 1837 to the Present Day*, London, 1967

Beer, Samuel H., *Modern British Politics*, London, 1969

Best, Geoffrey, *Mid-Victorian Britain 1851-1875*, London, 1971

Birch, A. H., *Representative and Responsible Government*, London, 1969

Bishop, T. J. H. & Wilkinson, R., *Winchester and the Public School Elite: A Statistical Analysis*, London, 1967

Blake, Robert, *Disraeli*, London, 1966

Blaug, Mark, *The Economics of Education in English Classical Political Economy. A Re-examination Forthcoming in Essays on Adam Smith*, a bicentenary edition of the works of Adam Smith from the University of Glasgow, Glasgow, 1973-6

Bottomore, T., *Elites and Society*, London, 1964

Bradford, Sarah, *Disraeli*, London, 1982

Brauer, George C., *The Education of a Gentleman: Theories of Gentlemanly Education in England 1660-1775*, New York, 1959

Briggs, Asa, *Victorian People: A Reassessment of Persons and Themes 1851-1867*, London, 1967

Brock, A. Clutton, *Eton*, London, 1900

Brogan, D. W., *The English People: Impressions and Observations*, London, 1945

Burn, W. L., *The Age of Equipoise: A Study of the Mid-Victorian Generation*, London, 1964

Bury, J. P. T. (ed.), *The Zenith of European Power*, X of *The New Cambridge Modern History*, Cambridge, 1960, 14 vols

Cecil, Lord David, *Early Victorian Novelists*, London, 1948
Melbourne, London, 1976

Chandos, John, *Boys Together: English Public Schools 1800-1864*, London, 1984

Clare, James Sabben, *Winchester College after 600 Years 1382-1982*, Southampton, 1981

Clarke, G. Kitson, *The Making of Victorian England*, London, 1970

Cobb, Richard, *A Sense of Place*, London, 1975

Colman, D. S., *Sabrinae Corolla: The Classics at Shrewsbury under Dr. Butler and Dr. Kennedy*, Shrewsbury, 1950

Conacher, J. S., *The Peelites and the Party System 1846-1852*, Newton Abbot, 1972

Connell, W. F., *The Educational Thought and Influence of Matthew Arnold*, London, 1950

Cooper, Duff, *Talleyrand*, London, 1935

Cowburn, Philip, *A Salopian Anthology: Some Impressions of Shrewsbury School during Four Centuries*, London, 1946

Custance, Roger (ed.), *Winchester College: Sixth-Centenary Essays*, Oxford, 1982

Davies, R. W., *Disraeli*, London, 1976

Douglas-Smith, G. F. W., *The City of London School*, Oxford, 1937

E., O. [sic], *Eton under Hornby*, London, 1910

Fitzmaurice, Lord Edmond, *The Life of Granville George Leveson Gower, Second Earl Granville K.G. 1815-1891*, London, 1906, 2 vols

Fox, Archibald, *Harrow*, London, 1911

Fraser, George MacDonald, *et al.*, *The World of the Public School*, London, 1977

Gardiner, A. G., *The Life of Sir William Harcourt*, London, 1923, 2 vols

Gardner, Brian, *The Public Schools: An Historical Survey*, London, 1973

Gathorne-Hardy, J., *The Public School Phenomenon*, London, 1979

Gribble, James (ed.), *Matthew Arnold*, London, 1967

Halsey, A. H., Floud, J. & Anderson, C. A. (eds), *Education, Economy and Society: A Reader in the Sociology of Education*, New York, 1965

Hanson, A. H. & Wiseman, H. V., *Parliament at Work*, London, 1962

Hearder, H., *Europe in the Nineteenth Century 1830-1880*, London, 1966
Italy in the Age of the Risorgimento 1790-1870, 6 of *Longman's History of Italy*, London, 1980-1983, 2 vols to date

Hollis, Christopher, *Eton*, London, 1960

Homans, George C., *The Human Group*, London, 1975

How, F. D., *Six Great Schoolmasters*, London, 1904

Hoyland, G., *The Man who Made a School: Thring of Uppingham*, London, 1946

Hughes, H. Stuart, *Consciousness and Society: The Reorientation of European*

Social Thought 1890–1930, London, 1959

Hurt, John S., *Education in Evolution*, London, 1972

Elementary Schooling and the Working Classes 1860–1918, London, 1979

Johnson, Nancy E. (ed.), *The Diary of Gathorne Hardy, later Lord Cranbrook 1866–1892: Political Selections*, Oxford, 1981

Jones, Donald K., *The Making of the Education System 1851–1881*, London, 1977

Jones, H. F., *Samuel Butler: A Memoire*, London, 1919

Jones, Wilbur Devereux, *Lord Derby and Victorian Conservatism*, Oxford, 1956

Kay-Shuttleworth, James, *Four Periods of Public Education as Reviewed in 1832, 1839, 1846, 1862*, Brighton, 1973

King, Ronald, *The Sociology of School Organization*, London, 1983

Kogan, Maurice, *The Politics of Educational Change*, London, 1978

Krein, David F., *The Last Palmerston Government: Foreign Policy, Domestic Politics and the Genesis of 'Splendid Isolation'*, Iowa, 1978

Lamb, G. F., *The Happiest Days*, London, 1959

Lawrence, E. S., *The Origins and Growth of Modern Education*, London, 1970

Lawson, John & Silver, Harold, *A Social History of Education in England*, London, 1973

Lever, Tresham (ed.), *The Letters of Lady Palmerston*, London, 1957

Longford, Elizabeth, *Victoria R. I.*, London, 1964

Mack, E. C., *Public Schools and British Opinion since 1860*, London, 1938

Magnus, Philip, *Gladstone: A Biography*, London, 1978

Mallet, Charles Edward, *Modern Oxford*, III of *A History of the University of Oxford*, London, 1927, 3 vols

Matthews, H. F., *Methodism and the Education of the People*, London, 1949

Matthias, P. (ed.), *Science and Society 1600–1800*, London, 1972

Maxwell, Rt. Hon. Sir Herbert, *The Life and Letters of George William Frederick, Fourth Earl of Clarendon K.G., G.C.B.*, London, 1913, 2 vols

McCann, Philip (ed.), *Popular Education and Socialization in the Nineteenth Century*, London, 1977

McDonnell, M. F. J., *A History of St. Paul's School*, London, 1909

Merchant Taylors' School Archaeological Society, *Merchant Taylors' School: Its Origin, History and Present Surroundings*, Oxford, 1929

Mitford, Nancy (ed.), *The Stanleys of Alderley: Their Letters between the Years 1851–1865*, London, 1939

Morgan, Iris L. Osborne, *Memoirs of Henry Arthur Morgan*, London, 1927

Morley, J., *The Life of William Ewart Gladstone*, London, 1908, 2 vols

Morris, R. J., *Class and Class Consciousness in the Industrial Revolution*, Economic History Society Studies in Economic and Social History, London, 1979

Musgrave, P. W., *Society and Education in England since 1800*, London, 1968

Namier, Sir Lewis, *Vanished Supremacies: Essays on European History 1812–1918*, London, 1962

Neale, R. S., *Class in English History 1680–1850*, Oxford, 1981

Nevinson, Henry Wood, *Changes and Chances*, London, 1923

Oldham, Basil, *Headmasters of Shrewsbury School 1552–1908*, Shrewsbury, 1937

A History of Shrewsbury School 1552–1952, Oxford, 1952

Ollard, R., *An English Education: A Perspective of Eton*, London, 1982

Parry, Geraint, *Political Elites*, London, 1969

Pendlebury, W. J. & West, J. M., *Shrewsbury School: The Last Fifty Years*, Shrewsbury, 1937

Perkin, H., *The Origins of Modern English Society 1780–1880*, London, 1974

Peterson, A. D. C., *A Hundred Years of Education*, London, 1952

Raistrick, Arthur, *Dynasty of Iron Founders: The Darbys and Coalbrookdale*, Newton Abbot, 1970

Rawnsley, W. F., *Edward Thring: Maker of Uppingham School*, London, 1926

Reader, W. J., *Professional Men*, London, 1966

Rich, E. E., *The Education Act 1870: A Study of Public Opinion*, London, 1970

Ridley, Jasper, *Lord Palmerston*, London, 1970

Robbins, Keith, *John Bright*, London, 1979

Roderick, G. W. & Stephens, M. D., *Education and Industry in the Nineteenth Century*, London, 1978

Roper, H., *Admnistering the Elementary Education Acts 1870–1885*, Educational Administration and History: Monograph 5, Museum of the History of Education, University of Leeds, Leeds, 1976

Runciman, W. G., *Social Science and Political Theory*, Cambridge, 1963

Russell, Bertrand & Patricia (eds), *The Amberley Papers: The Letters and Diaries of Lord and Lady Amberley*, London, 1937, 2 vols

Ryder, Judith & Silver, Harold, *Modern English Society: History and Structure 1850–1970*, London, 1970

Saintsbury, George, *The Earl of Derby*, London, 1906

Sampson, A., *Anatomy of Britain*, London, 1962
    Anatomy of Britain Today, London, 1965

Silver, Harold, *English Education and the Radicals 1780–1850*, London, 1975

Simon, Brian, *Studies in the History of Education 1780–1870*, London, 1960
    The Politics of Educational Reform 1920–1940, Studies in the History of Education, London, 1974
    (ed.), *The Radical Tradition in Education in Britain*, London, 1972
    & Bradley, Ian (eds), *The Victorian Public School: Studies in the Development of an Educational Institution*, Dublin, 1975

Smith, D. M., *Victor Emanuel, Cavour and the Risorgimento*, London, 1971

Southgate, D., *The Most English Minister: The Policies and Politics of Palmerston*, London, 1966

Sprott, W. J. H., *Human Groups*, London, 1958

Stewart, W. A. C. & McCann, W. P., *The Educational Innovators 1750–1880*, London, 1967

Strachey, Lytton, *Eminent Victorians*, London, 1979

Super, R. H. (ed.), *Schools and Universities on the Continent*, IV of *The Complete Prose Works of Matthew Arnold*, Michigan, 1960–1976, 11 vols

Sutherland, Gilliam, *Elementary Education in the Nineteenth Century*, London, 1971
    (ed.), *Matthew Arnold on Education*, London, 1973

Sylvester, D. W., *Robert Lowe and Education*, London, 1974

Thompson, F. M. L., *English Landed Society in the Nineteenth Century*, London, 1963

Thomson, David, *England in the Nineteenth Century 1815–1914*, 8 of *The Pelican History of England*, London, 1955, 8 vols

Trevelyan, G. M., *The Life of John Bright*, London, 1913
    British History of the Nineteenth Century and After: 1782–1919, London, 1965

Trinder, Barrie, *The Industrial Revolution in Shropshire*, London, 1973

Villiers, George John Theodore Hyde, *A Vanished Victorian: Being the Life of George Villiers, 4th Earl of Clarendon 1800–1870*, London, 1938

Vincent, John (ed.), *Disraeli, Derby and the Conservative Party: Journals and Memoirs of Henry Edward, Lord Stanley 1848–1869*, Hassocks, 1978

Wadsworth, A. P., *Newspaper Circulation 1800–1904*, Manchester, 1955

Walling, R. A. J. (ed.), *The Diaries of John Bright*, London, 1930

Wardle, David, *English Popular Education 1780–1970*, London, 1970

Watson, George, *The English Ideology: Studies in the Language of Victorian Politics*, London, 1973

Webb, R. K., *From Dickens to Hardy*, London, 1963

Weinberg, Ian, *The English Public Schools: The Sociology of Elite Education*, New York, 1967

West, E. G., *Education and the Industrial Revolution*, London, 1975

Wilkinson, Rupert, *The Prefects, British Leadership and the Public School Tradition*, London, 1964

Williams, J. Fisher, *Harrow*, London, 1901

Winstanley, D. A., *Early Victorian Cambridge*, London, 1940
    Later Victorian Cambridge, London, 1947

Woodham-Smith, Cecil, *Queen Victoria: Her Life and Times*, London, 1972, 2 vols

Young, G. M., *Victorian England: Portrait of An Age*, London, 1966

2. Articles

Balls, F. E., 'The Endowed Schools Act 1869 and the development of the English grammar schools in the Nineteenth Century', *Durham Research Review*, I and II, 20, April 1968, pp. 207–29

Bamford, T. W., 'Public schools and social class 1801–1850', *British Journal of Sociology*, 12, September 1961, pp. 224–35

'The prosperity of public schools 1801–1850', *Durham Research Review*, III, 12, September 1961, pp. 85–96

Barnett, Correlli, 'Further education and the development of an industrial society', *The Development of F.E.*, VI, Study Conferences 75/39 and 75/39B, Further Education Staff College, Coombe Lodge, 1975

Burn, D. L., 'The genesis of American engineering competition 1850–1870', *Economic History*, II, 1930–1933, pp. 292–311

Coleman, D. C., 'Gentlemen and players', *Economic History Review*, 2nd Series, XXVI, 1, February 1973, pp. 92–116

Gordon, P., 'The endowed schools and the education of the poor 1869–1900', *Durham Research Review*, V, No. 17, September 1966, pp. 47–58

Hurt, John S., 'Education and the working classes: A bibliographical essay', *Bulletin of the Society for the Study of Labour History*, 30 and 31, Spring and Autumn 1975

Jones, D. K., 'The educational legacy of the Anti-Corn Law League', *History of Education*, 3, 1, January 1974, pp. 18–35.

Kiehnbaum, Erhard, 'Samuel Moore', *Beiträge zur Geschichte der Arbeiterbewegung*, Herausgegeben vom Institut fur Marxismus-Leninismus beim Zentralkomitee der Sozialistischen Einheitspartei Deutschlands Redaktion, Berlin, East Germany, 17 January, 1975

Lawson, J. B., '1882 Genesis: Exodus', *Old Salopian Newsletter*, 92, May 1983

Pear, T. H., 'Psychological aspects of English social stratification', *Bulletin of the John Rylands Library*, XXVI, 2, May–June 1942

Turner, Ralph, 'Sponsored and contest mobility and the school system', *American Sociological Review*, XXV, 1960, 5, pp. 855–67

Webb, Michael, 'Past Mayors of Shrewsbury: William James Clement (1862-3, Liberal)', *Shropshire Magazine*, June 1979, p. 16

'Past Mayors of Shrewsbury: John Gregory Brayne (1865-6, Liberal) and James Smith (1863-4 Conservative)', *Shropshire Magazine*, July 1979, p. 25

'Past Mayors of Shrewsbury: Thomas Southam (1865-6, 1871-2, 1884-6, Conservative)', *Shropshire Magazine*, August 1979, p. 25

'Past Mayors of Shrewsbury: James Bratton (1867-8, Liberal) and John Thomas Nightingale (1866-7, Liberal)', *Shropshire Magazine*, October 1979, p. 17

'Past Mayors of Shrewsbury: Thomas Groves (1868-9, Conservative)', *Shropshire Magazine*, November 1979, p. 17

'Past Mayors of Shrewsbury: Harry Fenton (1869-70, Conservative) and Edward Parry (1870-1, Conservative)', *Shropshire Magazine*, December 1979, p. 50

'Past Mayors of Shrewsbury: John Loxdale (1840-1, 1858-9, 1872-3, Conservative)', *Shropshire Magazine*, January 1980, p. 55

Webb, R. K., 'Working class readers in early Victorian England', *English Historical Review*, LXV, July 1950, pp. 333–51

3. Theses

Balls, F. E., 'The origins of the Endowed Schools Act 1869 and its operation in England from 1869 to 1895', PhD thesis, Cambridge University, 1964

Byrne, John, 'The removal of Shrewsbury School 1866-1882', MEd dissertation, Birmingham University, 1983

Ganderton, D. B., 'From "Godliness and Good Learning" to "Muscular Christianity": An examination of the changes in values and curricula of the public schools in the Nineteenth and early Twentieth Centuries', MEd thesis, Birmingham University, 1974

Heritage, Alice, 'Public schools as presented by the Clarendon and Taunton Royal Commissions and by contemporary novelists 1825-1875: A comparative study', PhD thesis, Manchester University, 1977

Shrosbree, C. J., 'The origins and influence of the Clarendon Commission (1861-1864), with special reference to Shrewsbury School', PhD thesis, Birmingham University, 1985

Index